OPENING DAY:
50-FOR-50

ONE FAN. ONE GAME.
A HALF-CENTURY OF BASEBALL STORIES.

MICHAEL ORTMAN

MINDSTIR MEDIA

FANS ARE CHEERING!

"Opening Day is my favorite day of the baseball season. I have covered 42 of them, and all of them were different in their own way. Mike Ortman has beautifully provided 50 years of memories, all of them personal and compelling, from Opening Day. This book just warmed my heart."

Tim Kurkjian
Writer and analyst, ESPN

"During my nearly 40 years in sports and media, baseball changed from a kid's delight to his life's work. I lost the ability to be a fan. Not Mike Ortman. He followed a similar career path, yet managed to keep that youthful exuberance, which comes through in every chapter of his journey. His 50 consecutive Opening Day experiences will make every fan smile with important historical context plus personal stories that stir memories and emotions no matter your decade."

Bryan Burns
Former senior executive with Major League Baseball and ESPN

"This is a *terrific* book! It is very well written and has lots of payoffs for the reader and amazing insights and details. I'm jealous! I wish I had had the foresight to do something like this! Mike humanizes it so well, and yet his recollections and research of baseball themes and personalities are just terrific."

Mike Towle
Sportswriter and author of more than 15 books
including *Pete Rose: Baseball's Charlie Hustle*

"Unwind the yarn inside a baseball and watch how it connects generations: sons become fathers who become grandfathers, and the cycle continues. The Ortman thread is a journey through a half-century of the game's grip on those of us who never let go of that connection. The players may change, and venues come and go, but the game's appeal is everlasting."

Phil Wood
Baseball broadcaster and historian

"As a player and coach over 26 years, Opening Day was always special. After a long winter and spring, we finally got to play! Mike captures that so well, especially for the fans. When I came back to Baltimore in an enemy uniform as a coach for the Red Sox, I got as loud and warm a welcome as Frank (Robinson) and Cal (Ripken)! My Boston players couldn't believe it. That can only happen on Opening Day!"

Al Bumbry
Baltimore Orioles 1973-84, Orioles Hall of Fame 1987

TABLE OF CONTENTS

DEDICATION

To baseball fans everywhere. May we never grow up!

****

"They'll have reserved seats somewhere along one of the baselines where they sat when they were children and cheered their heroes. And they'll watch the game, and it'll be as if they'd dipped themselves in magic waters. The memories will be so thick, they'll have to brush them away from their faces.

"The one constant through all the years, Ray, has been baseball. America has rolled by like an army of steamrollers. It's been erased like a blackboard, rebuilt, and erased again. But baseball has marked the time. This . . . game is a part of our past, Ray. It reminds us of all that is good and could be again."

From Terrence Mann's exhortation to Ray Kinsella
Field of Dreams (1989)

ACKNOWLEDGMENTS

I could not have compiled these detailed stories without . . .

The dedicated people who preserve baseball's rich history: Baseball-Reference.com, the Society for American Baseball Research (SABR.org), the National Baseball Hall of Fame, Baseball-Almanac.com, and so many others.

The hundreds of players, writers, broadcasters, friends, and generations of Ortmans and DeMarcos whose accomplishments, words, and shared experiences enriched these pages.

Victor Guss, who read the earliest drafts of every chapter, made each one better, and made sure his Phillies were treated fairly.

Legendary baseball historian and broadcaster Phil Wood, who kept this honest and accurate, making sure a good story never got in the way of the facts.

My wife, Kate. Without her patience and support, I couldn't have attended the last 37 of these 50 Opening Day games. Without her encouragement, the writing of this book would still be on the bucket list.

And lifelong friends like Steve Ebner, a frequent Opening Day companion in Washington who battled "The Beast" called cancer for way too many years, showing us what it really means to "Stay in the Fight." May his "Bumpy Road Lead to a Beautiful Place."

INTRODUCTION

July 22, 2020, would have been my dad's 105th birthday. The next day was Opening Day of the baseball season, delayed nearly four months by a global pandemic. Never before had these two annual milestones been so close together on the calendar. July 23 marked the end of a streak he and I began more than 50 years earlier. On a cold, rainy April afternoon in 1970, he pulled me out of school early to attend the first game of the season for Ted Williams's Washington Senators. For the next 49 years, I managed to find a way to attend a team's first home game of every baseball season.

The streak traveled from DC to Baltimore to Chicago, back to Baltimore, and ultimately, home to Washington. Three cities. Six stadiums. Five home teams. Fifty Opening Days.

For 19 of those 50 games, Cal Ripken Jr. was in the lineup. I saw Cal and more than 40 other future Hall of Fame players, managers, and coaches on Opening Day. You'll read about some of them in the pages that follow. Ripken's streak of 2,632 consecutive games played will never be broken. Mine ended after five decades.

I did not set out to someday write a book about Major League Baseball home openers. Heck, this streak was barely a thing for the first 20 seasons or so. It was blind luck that it held together during those early years as college, kids, and life happened. Oh yes, and my home team left town when I was only 11 years old. But somehow, year after year, we found a way to celebrate the greatest day of the sports year, every year, somewhere with someone. Like the Energizer Bunny in that old battery commercial, I just "kept going and going and going." At first it was because of my dad. Then it was having fun with college friends. Then it was for work. At that point it had become a ritual which, like a fine wine, improved with age. In 2005 when baseball finally returned to my hometown 35 years into the streak, my fan passion kicked into overdrive, and the sharing of a lifetime of stories became a personal joy.

I didn't take notes or keep a diary—only memories.

In 2020 the baseball season started without me, without anybody. After a three-month shutdown of virtually everything in our lives, professional sports resumed without fans in attendance. COVID-19 had stopped what 50 years of life events could not. The coronavirus pandemic kept me from attending an Opening Day game.

With millions getting sick and dying around the world, baseball seemed trivial. And yet I hoped one day we could emerge from the darkness to embrace a new normal that would include a full house on Opening Day.

What makes Opening Day so special? Answers vary.

"Opening Day is the best day in baseball," proclaimed SI.com's Robin Lundberg in March 2019, just before the last home opener of my streak. "Opening Day is better than the World Series. It's like your good buddy is coming back. He's gonna be there. Some of them are less reliable than other good buddies but it's something you know is going to be there for you, from this point forward through the fall. You know what else it means? The return of warm weather."

This "good buddy" wasn't there for any of us in 2020. In 2021 he was there for only a few: the vaccinated, masked, and socially distant.

Ken Rosenthal has become one of the best-known baseball reporters in America, writing for *The Athletic* and appearing regularly on Fox and elsewhere. In 1998 he was writing for the *Baltimore Sun*. He summed up Opening Day masterfully:

"Opening Day is fathers and sons, mothers and daughters, and grandparents telling you about [their] very first opener...

It is a day to break out your old glove.

To remember the first game you ever attended.

To remember the game that broke your heart.

Opening Day is the dawning of spring, the renewal of life, the beginning of time whatever.

Opening Day is a ballgame.

Play ball."

Tom Boswell, the legendary baseball writer who retired in 2021 after more than 50 years at The *Washington Post*, published a collection of his baseball columns in the 1984 classic *Why Time Begins on Opening Day*. The book title is spot on. In cities and towns all across America, Opening Day is more than an annual baseball game. It's a rite of spring as winter fades away, hope and optimism abound, and all teams are tied for first place.

This book's time began on Opening Day 2015. I took my grandson Johnny and realized he represented the fourth generation to participate at least once in this annual ritual, from my dad to my son's son. I rather whimsically decided to make a list. I'm not sure if I made the list for him or for me. A massive spreadsheet began to take shape—dates, box scores, weather conditions, you name it.

Thanks to the treasure trove of data at Baseball-Reference.com, every relevant baseball detail of every home opener fell into place. For a while it was little more than a tracker, a well-organized collection of game day details any baseball junkie would appreciate.

But questions emerged that weren't in the box scores. Every few weeks something would cross my mind, some factual recollection that would lead to another column in that Excel workbook:

Which President threw out the ceremonial first pitch?

Which labor dispute delayed Opening Day?

What future Hall of Famers were there?

Were there any specific memories of that day?

Who else was there?

Was there anything significant in baseball history linked to any game or its participants worth researching?

It became obvious this streak had the potential to be a book—not just a baseball book, but a collection of stories that others might enjoy about historic moments, icons, family, traditions, people, and relationships. Specific memories came pouring back. In addition to Baseball-Almanac.com and SABR.org, newspaper archives and other online resources added rich details when the memory failed.

This book represents 50 percent memories, 50 percent research, and 100 percent stories.

As the chapters fell into place, certain threads and themes emerged.

The first half of the streak spanned the years of disruptive labor unrest between players and owners (1970–95), including three Opening Days delayed by strikes or lockouts (1972, 1990, and 1995), a season interrupted (1981), and another cut short (1994). Some of those openers also afford the opportunity to share the remarkable stories of pivotal people who stirred the pot and paved the road to modern-day free agency: Curt Flood (Opening Day center fielder for the 1971 Washington Senators), Dave McNally (1973 Opening Day starting pitcher for the Baltimore Orioles), Reggie Jackson (an Opening Day holdout for the Orioles in 1976), and Judge Sonia Sotomayor who some say "saved baseball" with her ruling in March 1995. The 1981 midseason strike allowed for more details about the last great stadium organist in professional sports, Nancy Faust in Chicago, who entertained us during the "re-opener" at Comiskey Park.

I saw five different US Presidents (Ronald Reagan, George H. W. Bush, Bill

Clinton, George W. Bush, and Barack Obama) throw out the season's ceremonial first pitch a total of nine times among them, and I witnessed the christening of two new ballparks (Oriole Park at Camden Yards and Nationals Park). I was there for fan favorite Harry Caray's last opener at Comiskey Park (1981), his first one at Wrigley Field (1982), and the sudden passing of another Hall of Fame broadcaster Harry Kalas on Opening Day at Nationals Park in 2009.

Opening Day 1984 in Baltimore highlighted one of the more conflicted and historic weeks in local sports history as the same fan base mourned the loss of one professional franchise and celebrated the championship of another. Just four days after the Indianapolis-bound Colts snuck out of town in the middle of the night, the Orioles hoisted their 1983 World Series banner in the same stadium they had shared with their NFL housemates for nearly 30 years. That same week a new local cable TV channel, Home Team Sports (for which I worked at the time), launched to only a handful of viewers. But this fledgling venture (now known as NBC Sports Washington) was at the bleeding edge of change for sports television: home games on local TV.

In 2005 Washington welcomed baseball back to RFK Stadium (in the form of the Washington Nationals, previously the Montreal Expos). Three years later the city rejoiced as "Mr. Walk-Off" Ryan Zimmerman electrified a national TV audience on Opening Night with a home run in the ninth inning to beat the Braves in the first game at Nationals Park.

Quite often my most precious memory of Opening Day was of the people with whom I shared it: Dad, kids, grandkids, best friends, and well-known figures we encountered at the ballpark. Memories of certain years are clearer than others. From 1984–2004 I usually attended Opening Day for work-related reasons, while life on the home front intensified. My selfless and generous wife Kate gave birth to our first three children between 1984 and 1988, and we adopted three more between 1994 and 1998. Life in general was a blur, and memories of specific Opening Day games are as well. Online research helped fill in the gaps.

Some years might read like diary entries, while others might read like college history papers. If something spanned many years, like Cal Ripken's career, Baltimore's love affair with John Denver's "Thank God I'm a Country Boy," or the steroids era, I concentrated the story into a single chapter (1993, 1994, and 2003, respectively).

If a chapter sparks an *"I never knew that!"* or *"I remember that!"* moment for you and leaves you hungry for more, Google it! Surely there's a book, blog post, YouTube video, article, or something else that will feed you. We'll help get you started with a companion website with links to box scores and more. Just use the

QR codes scattered throughout these pages.

In August 2020 while players played an abbreviated 60-game schedule in front of empty seats, cardboard cutouts, and recorded crowd noise, I decided the time had come to start writing. I had just turned 60. The memory was still intact, and the streak had ended on a nice, tidy number: 50 games. Although the definition of *my* team had changed over the years, the streak had ended a year earlier with *my* team on top for the first time ever. With strains of "Baby Shark" ringing throughout the nation's capital and after an improbable string of historic comebacks, the Washington Nationals won the 2019 World Series.

A funny thing happened as these stories unfolded, year by year, chapter by chapter. I realized this was not just a collection of baseball stories, but also my story: the journey of a little boy whose favorite thing in the world was taken away. It left such a void. I would spend the next 33 years looking to fill it. I was pretty good at it, but it wasn't quite the same. After I was made whole in 2005, losing seasons followed for the Nationals. Then came winning seasons followed by postseason disappointments.

Throughout all the comings and goings, frustrations and celebrations, losses and wins, sadness and joy, anger and forgiveness, the only constant was the one reliable annual highlight:

Opening Day!

For box scores, play-by-play and more, visit www.OpeningDay5050.com or use this QR code

1970

Roundy

The Game

Who:	Detroit Tigers 5, Washington Senators 0
Where:	Robert F. Kennedy Memorial Stadium, Washington, DC
Attendance:	45,015
When:	Monday, April 6, 1970
Weather:	Miserable! Temperatures in the 40s, 55-minute rain delay

Hall of Famers: Senators 1B coach Nellie Fox and manager Ted Williams and Tigers RF Al Kaline

Game Highlights: Tigers ace Mickey Lolich threw a complete game shutout. He would pitch 16 seasons in the majors, win more than 200 games, and play in three All-Star Games. For the Senators, my childhood hero, slugger Frank "Hondo" Howard, collected three singles. But the game's real highlight came before Lolich faced his third batter and before Hondo's bat made contact with a baseball. His biggest "hit" of the afternoon came when 22-year-old Morganna "The Kissing Bandit" jumped the railing along the third baseline, ran up behind him as he headed to the batter's box, tapped him on the back, and proceeded to hug and kiss the giant twice her size. *Washington Post* reporter Bill Gildea asked the clearly uncomfortable Howard about the incident. "It happened so fast," he said. "It was very embarrassing to me, and I know it was embarrassing to my wife, who was in the stands. Personally, I wish it had never happened." This was one of the first (but certainly not the last) times Morganna would rush up to a pro athlete during a game. Over the next 30 years, she enhanced her career as an exotic dancer by targeting many of sports' most famous players.

The Story

Washington Post columnist Tom Boswell has many fond memories of baseball's Opening Day in the nation's capital. "Once, Opening Day lived here," he wrote of his hometown. "It was Washington's World Series, the capital city's bonus Christmas."

"The Presidential [opener]," Boswell continued, "was the dawn of the year's better half—a cherry blossom declaration of independence from winter, a springtime bill of rites." Since 1910 the President of the United States was almost always on hand to throw out the ceremonial first pitch from the front row of the stands.

A week before Opening Day 1970, more than 4,000 fans spent a very chilly night in line outside Robert F. Kennedy Memorial Stadium to buy up the 20,000 remaining tickets to watch their Washington Senators, a team which the year before under rookie manager Ted Williams had posted a winning record for only the second time since 1945. The most powerful city in the world was well known for being "First in war, first in peace, and last in the American League."

In the early research for this book, I searched YouTube for "Washington Senators" and found a treasure. Local radio personality Ernie Kyger had preserved most of the radio broadcast of Opening Day 1970. The memorable, long-ago voices of Shelby Whitfield and Ron Menchine on WWDC 1260 AM triggered something powerful. Memories came pouring back of a little boy with his small transistor radio tucked under his pillow, *way* past his bedtime those summer nights. While some kids might have had a stuffed animal, I had a small, black plastic battery-powered device that connected me in real time to heroes. It was maybe three inches by three inches and had two knobs, one for volume (always turned to low) and the other for tuning to the station.

The biggest hero of all was Frank "Hondo" Howard, a gigantic outfielder who was one of the sport's most prolific home run hitters of the time. My parents took me and a few friends to one of my first Senators games for my ninth birthday on August 9, 1969. Washington was playing the Seattle Pilots (who would later become the Milwaukee Brewers). It was also Autograph Day, but the line to meet Hondo was way too long. He made it up to all of us about an hour later when he crushed a second-inning pitch from Jim Bouton farther than this little boy could have imagined possible.

I was hooked for life.

Kyger's uploaded audio file of Opening Day 1970 included Whitfield describing a "cool gray day here in Washington." I remembered sitting way above the third baseline, enduring a cold, miserable rain delay, then peering down as nine men in white uniforms and red caps ran out to "play ball!" on the green and brown diamond that, through the mist, seemed a mile away.

To this day, I can rattle off most of the lineups from Williams's years as manager in Washington (1969–71). Shelby, Ron, and some newspaper headline writers occasionally would refer to the Senators as the Nats. At first, I thought they were comparing them to some sort of pesky insect, the underdog that might, from time to time, beat the perennial powerhouse and American League East rival Baltimore Orioles. I later learned the official team name of the original iteration of DC's American League team was changed from Senators to Nationals ("Nats" for short) in 1905 to appease fans of the city's nineteenth-century National League team of the same name. But in the decades that followed, sportswriters and fans just couldn't shake it and used the two names almost interchangeably.

The preserved radio broadcast was an emotional gold mine. At one point, Nats center fielder Del Unser struck out. Another familiar voice in the background could be heard: Opening Day stadium announcer and legendary DC sports publicist Charlie Brotman. He'd been the team's promotions director and stadium announcer before the team moved to RFK in 1962 and reclaimed the microphone every Opening Day thereafter. He introduced the next hitter with a memorable intonation made famous by his friend and fellow stadium voice Phil Hochberg: "Paul Cas-a-NOOOH-vuh!" In addition to his Senators duties over the years, Charlie served as Master of Ceremonies for every Presidential Inaugural Parade from Eisenhower through Obama, plus a cameo during Biden's virtual inaugural Parade Across America. I would intern and later work for Charlie from 1980–83. More on him in Chapter 1983.

With the Tigers up 3–0 in the seventh inning, Shelby let listeners know "President Nixon, who arrived in the fifth inning (is) watching the second half of this ball game, along with the First Lady, their two daughters, son-in-law . . . Bowie Kuhn, the commissioner, is here, along with American League President Joe Cronin . . . Mayor and Mrs. Walter Washington also in the Presidential box . . ."

Clearly, this day was something special.

It was special to skip part of a school day to spend time with Dad. It was special because we thought the President and other important people would be there.

Spending time with my father was always special but sometimes awkward as well. We spent Opening Day together from 1970–78 and again in 1983. But if you're expecting a sappy story about a father passing along his love of the game to his son, you'll be disappointed.

Dad had absolutely no interest in baseball. He started this streak and made sure it continued, but he probably could not have named more than three players from those games. He was more about big events than he was about baseball. That's an understatement!

He often shared the self-deprecating story of his bizarre behavior while attending a historic World Series game years before I was born. It was 1956, Game Five. New York Yankees pitcher Don Larsen would throw the only perfect game in World Series history. I have no idea why this then-41-year-old DC lawyer would have been at Yankee Stadium that October afternoon, but we heard the story repeated so often, it must have been reasonably true. It illustrates how absolutely clueless he was about the game of baseball. He certainly had no rooting interest in the game. Maybe Mom did? She'd relocated from her native New York to Washington in 1942 to marry Dad.

As the story went, Larsen took the mound in the top of the ninth inning with the bottom of the Dodgers order due up, including pitcher Sal Maglie (who had no-hit the Philadelphia Phillies just two weeks prior). Larsen had retired all 24 Dodgers he'd faced. Perfect! So far. If there's one baseball superstition every fan knows: *Don't talk about no-hitters while they are in progress, lest you jinx the outcome.* But with two outs in the ninth and pinch hitter Dale Mitchell batting for Maglie, Frank Ortman, surrounded by more than 60,000 Yankee fans, reportedly stood up and yelled, *"We want a hit!"*

Ugh! Had to be the beer talking!

Imagine the reaction of those around him had the batter broken up the perfect game. Frank would have been pummeled! But Mitchell struck out, an exuberant catcher Yogi Berra leaped into his pitcher's arms, Larsen's place in baseball history was sealed, and Dad escaped unscathed from "The House That Ruth Built."

As devoid as he was of baseball decorum, he was even more lacking in baseball skill. There was a reason he never tried to help coach my Catholic Youth Organization baseball team. We once tried to play catch in the alley behind our row house. It wasn't exactly a *"Wanna have a catch?"* moment like that one from *Field of Dreams.* I used my baseball glove, of course. He used a kitchen trash can in hopes of keeping my tosses from getting by.

One could only hope the neighbors weren't watching.

I was very young when my parents took a few of us siblings to suburban Maryland for the Montgomery County Fair. There was the classic clown sitting over a water tank, taunting patrons who'd paid for the privilege of throwing a baseball in hopes of dunking the heckler. Not surprisingly, Dad missed the target. Noting my father's rotund physique, the clown blasted into his microphone for all to hear, "Look at old Roundy! He couldn't hit the broad side of a barn!"

The nickname stuck. For the rest of his life, my father would be known to his kids as Roundy.

Considering what he lacked in baseball knowledge and skill, I thought for the longest time that Roundy's commitment to Opening Day had something to do with our significant age gap. As best he could, he'd show his love by sharing something I loved—baseball. That was part of it, but it also had to do with the magnitude of Opening Day. It was special. It was memorable. It was a big event. Dad had a remarkable grasp of historic moments. He wanted to be a part of them and share some of them with his kids, including his youngest son.

In 1963 as the nation mourned the assassination of President John F. Kennedy, Dad burned this historic moment into my memory, even though I was only three years old. The Law Offices of Raysor, Ortman, Barbour, Welch, and Bell occupied part of a floor in a building on the corner of 17th and L Streets, NW, just blocks from St. Matthew's Cathedral where President Kennedy's funeral took place. On that cold November day, we stood on the corner outside his office to see the President's flag-draped, horse-drawn caisson roll by on its way to Arlington National Cemetery.

In 1968 after the assassination of the President's brother, Senator Robert Kennedy, Roundy made sure we were there to pay our respects. On the day of the funeral, we stood outside Washington's Union Station to again watch a Kennedy casket en route to Arlington. Dr. Martin Luther King Jr. had been gunned down just weeks earlier, and racial tensions were high. Protests, riots, and curfews ruled the city. Some might have thought it dangerous to be out on the streets, and yet there we were in the shadow of the Capitol. I will forever remember the image of thousands of black men and women, young and old, covering every inch of the two-tiered fountain and surrounding area in front of the train station prayerfully singing "We Shall Overcome."

By 1969 Dad's office had moved four blocks south to the corner of 17th and Pennsylvania Avenue, just a block from the White House. That January, Roundy made sure we were on the roof of his office building (decades before trained snipers would occupy these perches), looking down as an open-air limousine transported just-inaugurated President Nixon and his wife, Pat, to their new home.

Roundy was a native Washingtonian, growing up just blocks from Griffith Stadium, then home to the Washington Senators. He went straight from St. John's College High School to the Columbus School of Law and later served in the Army during World War II. Of his time in the service, he'd often say, "I went in a single private and came out a married major with two children. It was a hell of a war!"

I was the youngest of six children. Dad was 45 when I was born. His only athletic accomplishments were played out on the golf course. A four-year high school letterman, he scored his only hole in one the day he graduated in June 1933. Coincidentally, four months later, Washington would make its last trip to the World Series until the Nationals won it all in 2019.

That first iteration of the Senators left to become the Minnesota Twins after the 1960 season but was quickly replaced with another equally dreadful expansion team of the same name. It did not matter that the Senators were consistently bad. Opening Day in Washington was a national, major event, Roundy's kind of thing.

For box scores, play-by-play and more, visit www.OpeningDay5050.com or use this QR code

1971

Curt Flood: Dred Scott in Spikes

The Game

Who:	Washington Senators 8, Oakland Athletics 0
Where:	Robert F. Kennedy Memorial Stadium, Washington, DC
Attendance:	45,061
When:	Monday, April 5, 1971
Weather:	Spectacular!

Hall of Famers: Senators 1B coach Nellie Fox and manager Ted Williams, Athletics RF Reggie Jackson and manager Dick Williams

Game Highlights: Pitcher Vida Blue's breakout season got off to a rather inauspicious start. The 21-year-old lefty lasted only until the second inning against the lowly Senators. But after this Opening Day disappointment, Blue was a different pitcher the rest of the season. He started the 1971 All-Star Game for the American League (the first of six ASG appearances over his 17-year career) and won the Cy Young Award with an astounding 24–8 record and microscopic 1.82 ERA. On the opposite side this day, Senators ace Dick Bosman tossed a six-hit complete game shutout.

The Story

Hopeful but skeptical Washington Senators fans filled RFK Stadium on a picture-perfect Monday afternoon. Without support from his third-year manager Ted Williams, unlikable owner Bob Short had revamped the roster around his two returning stars, pitcher Dick Bosman and the home run hero of my youth, Frank Howard. Fans were hoping for wins. Short was hoping for ticket sales.

The owner was losing money and threatened to move his team out of the nation's capital if business did not improve. Short gambled on a pair of big-name superstars who, in the late 1960s, had been the absolute best in the game at their respective positions. Yet, in 1970, each played little or no baseball. The first was Denny McLain who was acquired in an eight-player trade with the Detroit Tigers. He had won the American League Cy Young Award during the Tigers 1968 World Series championship season and again in 1969, starting 82 games over that span, pitching an arm-numbing 661 innings. But McLain's off-the-field troubles resulted in multiple suspensions in 1970, just 14 starts, and only 91 innings on the mound.

Short's other marquee acquisition started in center field on Opening Day 1971. Curt Flood played the final, forgettable 13 games of his otherwise remarkable major-league career for perhaps the only team that would have him, the Washington Senators. He was arguably the best center fielder in the game by the end of the 1960s, earning seven straight Gold Gloves (1963–69) playing for the powerhouse St. Louis Cardinals. Flood was a bona fide star, playing on a team that included future Hall of Famers Bob Gibson and Lou Brock and won three National League pennants and two World Series. Yet it was his unwillingness to play in 1970 that earned Flood an extraordinary place in sports history as he selflessly challenged baseball's "reserve clause" all the way to the Supreme Court.

Flood had played 12 years with the Cardinals, loved St. Louis, and was popular with the fans. But things started to unravel for him after the 1968 season. He was unfairly blamed for his team's World Series loss to the Tigers after misplaying a ball in center field late in Game Seven. Two runs scored, Detroit won the game, 4–1, and the Series. During the offseason, Flood strained his relationship with ownership and fans, publicly demanding a 24 percent raise to $90,000 for 1969. The Cardinals ultimately gave in to his demands, but the damage was done. In those days, players routinely accepted what management offered, but not Flood.

In October 1969, Flood's career as a Cardinal came to an end when he and catcher Tim McCarver were traded to the Philadelphia Phillies. Flood refused to go and explored his options. The path he pursued with unwavering conviction was a lonely journey that cost him the rest of his career and lit a fuse that changed the game for future players, most of whom don't even know his name.

Flood had spent 31 years preparing for martyrdom. As a young minor-league player in the 1950s, Flood experienced the same racist indignities of the Deep South more closely associated with the Negro Leagues or Jackie Robinson, 19 years Flood's senior. In his review of the 2011 HBO documentary *The Curious Case of Curt Flood*, Allen Barra explained that Curt's righteous activism had been seeded, nurtured, and stoked for decades. "Born in Houston in 1938, Flood was raised in the relatively tolerant Oakland, California. His mother, who had fled the intense racial bigotry of the pre–World War II South, never let him forget what things had been like where she grew up, and in 1962, having little idea of what he was about to encounter, the 24-year-old Flood went to Mississippi to join his idols Dr. Martin Luther King and Jackie Robinson to support the non-violent protests organized by the NAACP."

Less than two years later, Flood battled racial prejudice closer to home when he rented a house for his pregnant wife and four small children in the Oakland suburb of Alamo. In a public and tense confrontation, they were denied access by an owner who didn't know they were black when he signed the lease. He blocked the entrance with a loaded shotgun. Flood knew injustice, sued the owner in court, and won. Five years later, this same search for justice drove Flood to take on the baseball establishment.

Flood felt strongly that, at some point, players should be free to choose where they played. To Flood, baseball's unique reserve system amounted to legalized slavery. The reserve clause—Paragraph 10(a) of the Uniform Player's Contract—in effect, bound a player in perpetuity to his original team or any team to which he might be traded or sold.

Flood did not want to go to the Phillies. In his 1971 autobiography *The Way It Is*, he called Philadelphia the "... northern-most southern city in America." He audaciously decided instead to pursue an antitrust lawsuit against Major League Baseball. He reached out to Marvin Miller, head of the nascent Major League Baseball Players Association (MLBPA). At the time, Miller's greatest challenge was convincing well-paid players to stop accepting paternalism and understand their true value.

Just as Brooklyn Dodgers owner Branch Rickey needed to find a Jackie Robinson a generation earlier to finally break down baseball's racial barrier, so, too, did Miller need someone courageous enough to take on the fight if they were to eventually break down the game's feudal structure. In Curt Flood, he found a willing pawn, poised to make the first move, knowing it was unlikely he would still be in the game when the king was toppled.

"Not many players in those early years wanted to talk about the legalities of the reserve clause," Miller told HBO in 2011. During a four-hour lunch in December 1969, Miller warned Flood of the price he'd likely pay to pursue this. "I told him that given the court's history of bias towards the owners and their monopoly, he didn't have a chance in hell of winning. More important than that, I told him even if he won, he'd never get anything out of it—he'd never get a job in baseball again.

"It almost didn't matter what I said," Miller concluded. "I realized this is really a man of principle."

A determined Flood asked if moving forward would benefit other players. "I told him yes," Miller said, "and those to come."

"That's good enough for me," Flood responded.

Still trying to fathom the complex character sitting across the table, Miller simply said, "You're a union leader's dream."

Flood accompanied Miller to a meeting later that month with the MLBPA player representatives, one from each major-league team. They voted unanimously to cover the costs of the lawsuit, but it was clear to Flood that this would be the only measurable support he would get from his contemporaries. Teammate McCarver said, "Sadly, what came out of that meeting was that even though the association was going to cover the expenses, Curt was isolated, and he felt that isolation."

His best friend in baseball, teammate Bob Gibson asked the rhetorical question followed by an answer that could have come from almost any active major leaguer: "Was I behind Curt? Absolutely! About 10 steps back in case there's fallout."

Miller added to the legal team a former colleague from the United Steelworkers, Arthur Goldberg. Goldberg had the right résumé for the job: labor secretary under President John Kennedy and associate justice on the US Supreme Court (1962–65). Together with Flood and MLBPA General Counsel Dick Moss, the four men carefully crafted a masterpiece. The December 24, 1969, letter from Flood to Commissioner Bowie Kuhn has been analyzed, critiqued, and applauded for generations for its pointed simplicity.

Writing in 2019 on the document's 50th anniversary, Marc Carig of *The Athletic* wrote, "The letter consists of just five sentences. It is written in the first person, signed by a sole author, and addressed to just one man. It uses no similes, no metaphors, no literary flourishes. There is no mention of 'free agency,' or the 'reserve clause,' or 'slavery,' though each of those ideas is embedded within its 128 words. From its austerity flows an authority that endures."

More than 20 years after signing it, Flood shared his retrospective as part of Ken Burns's 1994 documentary, *Baseball*.

"I guess you really have to understand who 'that' Curt Flood was," Flood recalled. "I was a child of the sixties . . . a man of the sixties. During that period of time, this country was coming apart at the seams. We were in southeast Asia. Good men were dying for America and the Constitution. In the southern part of the United States, they were marching for civil rights, and Dr. King had been assassinated, and we had lost the Kennedys, and to think that merely because I was a professional baseball player, I could ignore what was going on outside the walls of Busch Stadium was truly a hypocrisy. And now I find that all of those rights that all of these great Americans were dying for, I didn't have in my own profession.

"By God, this is America. I'm a human being. I'm not a piece of property. I'm not a consignment of goods."

He then read the letter aloud.

Dear Mr. Kuhn:

After twelve years in the Major Leagues, I do not feel that I am a piece of property to be bought and sold irrespective of my wishes. I believe that any system which produces that result violates my basic rights as a citizen and is inconsistent with the laws of the United States and of the several States.

It is my desire to play baseball in 1970, and I am capable of playing. I have received a contract offer from the Philadelphia Club, but I believe I have the right to consider offers from other clubs before making any decisions. I therefore request that you make known to all the Major League Clubs my feelings in this matter, and advise them of my availability for the 1970 season.

Sincerely yours,

Curt Flood

Six days later, Kuhn acknowledged Flood was not a piece of property, but that he could not see "its applicability in this situation," and went on to write, "I cannot comply with the request in the second paragraph of your letter."

While Flood sat out the 1970 season, his case against the commissioner played out in US District Court. Of the 24 player representatives who just five months earlier had voted unanimously to support Flood's case financially, not one, nor any other active player, expressed public support or visited during the three-week trial—not even his St. Louis teammates who were in town for a series against the Mets.

A few former players appeared to testify. One even approached Curt and whispered words of encouragement, "Keep your head up. You're doing the right thing."

Flood's eyes filled with tears. The former player was Jackie Robinson.

In August, the court ruled in favor of the owners. "Since baseball remains exempt from the antitrust laws unless and until the Supreme Court or Congress holds to the contrary," wrote Judge Irving Ben Cooper, "we have no basis for proceeding to the underlying question of whether baseball's reserve system would or would not be deemed reasonable if it were in fact subject to antitrust regulation."

Flood's legal team began the appeal process, but his life was falling apart. He was deeply in debt. He had stopped paying child support to his ex-wife two years earlier, his non-baseball business interests were failing, and he had little income. After the trial, he fled the country to avoid the stress and harassment that accompanied the high-profile fight that bore his name.

In November 1970, Flood got the call from the Senators. Short had acquired Curt's rights in a trade with the Phillies and offered him $110,000 to play for Washington in 1971, reportedly half in advance, an eye-popping amount under the circumstances. While Flood was desperate, he didn't want to do anything that might undermine his legal appeal. With assurances from Miller and others, he accepted Short's offer and reported to the team's winter training facility out of shape. By his own admission, Flood had spent most of his year away from the game "bedding and boozing."

While most players silently supported Flood, fans did not, fueled by owners and sportswriters. Brad Snyder, author of *A Well-Paid Slave*, a Flood biography published in 2006, said, "Most of the sportswriters were in the pockets of the owners. This was not a liberal baseball press." Some of the game's biggest stars were speaking out against Flood, including Carl Yastrzemski of the Boston Red Sox and Harmon Killebrew of the Minnesota Twins. Even Ted Williams and Frank Howard had been critical, although they said all the right things once Flood put on a Senators uniform.

Flood's fan mail became hate mail. Instead of sprinting across an outfield chasing down deep threats, he was getting death threats: five a day according to Gibson.

Flood reached base three times on Opening Day 1971 but clearly was not the player he had once been. Two days later, a three-judge panel of the United States Court of Appeals for the Second Circuit ruled unanimously against Flood. Any attempt to concentrate on playing baseball was futile. By the end of the week, he had been benched by Williams, and by the end of the month, he had fled the country once again, this time, for good. He apologized to Short in a cryptic telegram: "A year and a half is too much. Very serious personal problems mounting every day."

Flood did not appear with his attorneys when the final appeal was argued in March 1972 before the Supreme Court. In June, the court ruled 5-3 in favor of the owners (Justice Lewis Powell recused himself, citing the fact he owned stock in Anheuser-Busch, owner of Flood's former team in St. Louis). The majority opinion deflected to Congress to ultimately take up the question of eliminating baseball's antitrust exemption.

As Miller had predicted, the suit did not end well for Curt Flood, but it put pressure on the owners and emboldened the players. In the years that followed, Miller seized on opportunities to win two legal proceedings resulting in free agency for three specific players: Jim "Catfish" Hunter, Andy Messersmith, and Dave McNally. By 1976 the floodgates were open. Flood had clearly started something. Between 1972 and 1995, the players either went out on strike, or the owners locked out the players eight times. The regular-season schedule was impacted four times, including three Opening Days.

As Miller also predicted, Flood never saw a dime of the game's new riches for players. The downward spiral of his life continued for more than 15 years until he was rescued from alcoholism by friends, family, and a familiar characteristic: his own determination. By 1989 time had healed some wounds within the baseball establishment. Flood returned to the game he loved as commissioner of the short-lived Senior Professional Baseball Association, a Florida-based league of retired players.

In 1993 Flood finally accepted his seventh Gold Glove, earned a generation before in St. Louis but never collected. Under the headline, "Dred Scott in Spikes," conservative columnist and baseball junkie George Will wrote on the occasion, "Curt Flood, a 165-pound whippet of a center fielder, could outrun most fly balls, but it took him twenty-four years to catch up to his 1969 Gold Glove Award.

"There was poetry and portent," Will continued, "in the fact that Curt Flood's career blossomed in St. Louis, the city where Dred Scott had taken his case to court. In 1966 the Cardinals moved into a new stadium that is located just a long fungo from the courthouse where Scott, a slave, argued that he lived on free soil and therefore should be free.

"Talk about lighting a long fuse. That one led to four years of Civil War. Scott's case went all the way to the United States Supreme Court which ruled against him and thereby against the strong-running tide of history. It was not the last time the Supreme Court would blunder when asked whether a man can be treated like someone's property."

Of even greater personal significance than leading a league of old-timers or placing another trophy on his mantle was an invitation in 1994 from the MLB-PA to speak to a gathering of active players, to inspire solidarity, remind them of the freedoms they now enjoyed, and, most important to Flood, accept their gratitude.

On January 20, 1997, Flood died of throat cancer. Among the eulogists at his funeral were conservative columnist Will and liberal icon Reverend Jesse Jackson. "Baseball didn't change Curt Flood. Curt Flood changed baseball," Jackson said. "Curt lost a case and won the race. Curt opened the floodgates. He freed black, white, and brown."

"Curt Flood must go in the Hall of Fame," Jackson added. "Curt is the winner. People are better. America is better."

Not a single then-current major-league player attended the service.

The day after Flood died, Senate Bill 53 was introduced in the 105th Congress, taking up what the Supreme Court had suggested 25 years earlier in *Flood v. Kuhn*. The bill was signed into law on October 27, 1998, formally giving Major League Baseball players the same rights under antitrust laws as other professional athletes. It was officially, and appropriately, the "Curt Flood Act of 1998."

In 1999 *TIME* magazine included Flood on their list of the 10 Most Influential Athletes of the 20th Century, joining, among others, Muhammad Ali, Pelé, Babe Ruth, and, of course, Jackie Robinson.

By the early decades of the twenty-first century, Flood had faded from the forefront of baseball history, perhaps cherished only by Cardinals fans of the 1960s and those players who had taken the time to learn about the sacrifice and, eventually, solidarity that contributed to their current freedom. But two events in December 2019 brought Flood back into the headlines: the 50th anniversary of his famous letter to the commissioner and Marvin Miller's unlikely enshrinement in the Baseball Hall of Fame, an honor some see as incomplete without Flood there to join him.

On December 18, 2019, the New York Yankees introduced their newest free agent acquisition, 29-year-old right-handed pitcher Gerrit Cole. He'd just signed the most lucrative contract in baseball history: reportedly $324 million with an average annual value of $36 million. At the press conference, Cole mastered the obligatory list of those to thank: God, family, his agent, coaches, and teammates. But before thanking the Steinbrenner family and Yankees management, he did something no newly minted multi-millionaire in baseball had done before.

He publicly thanked Marvin Miller *and* Curt Flood.

Just 10 days before Cole's unveiling at Yankee Stadium, Miller had finally been elected to the Hall after three different iterations of special committees failed seven times over a 17-year period to enshrine the executive acknowledged by most as the one who changed the business of professional sports for the better by orchestrating a system that allowed players to eventually choose where they wanted to play.

"I would be remiss if I didn't mention ... Marvin Miller, specifically," Cole said. "We've seen competitiveness blossom and free agency blossom, and he played a major role in that. Curt Flood as well. Challenging the reserve clause was essential to the blossoming sport we have today."

"He lost the 1970 season and lost in the Supreme Court," Will wrote of Flood's significance, "but he had lit a fuse.

"The national pastime is clearly better because of that. But more important, so is the nation, because it has learned one more lesson about the foolishness of fearing freedom."

For box scores, play-by-play and more, visit www.OpeningDay5050.com or use this QR code

1972

Charting a New Course, Strike One!

The Game

Who:	Baltimore Orioles 3, New York Yankees 1 (7 innings)
Where:	Memorial Stadium, Baltimore, MD
Attendance:	13,153
When:	Sunday, April 16, 1972
Weather:	Miserable! Cold and rainy

Hall of Famers: Orioles manager Earl Weaver, P Jim Palmer, and 3B Brooks Robinson

Game Highlights: This was, by far, the most sparsely attended Opening Day of the streak. A player strike had wiped out the season's first week, and rain postponed Saturday's rescheduled season opener into what was to be a rare Sunday afternoon Opening Day doubleheader. But the foul weather continued through the weekend. They managed to squeeze in only one rain-shortened, seven-inning game. Fans across the country were angry at the players, and many stayed home. In Baltimore they expressed their displeasure in a way that seems unimaginable in retrospect. They heckled Brooks Robinson! One of the city's most cherished sports figures of all time was also the Orioles' union representative. The few who braved the elements booed Brooks when he came to the plate for the first time since the work stoppage. The future Hall of Famer later insisted with a smile it was remnant cheers for Boog Powell who batted just ahead of him. Robinson was quickly forgiven as he drove in two runs. Doyle Alexander came on after a long rain delay to relieve starting pitcher Pat Dobson. The 21-year-old Alexander had been acquired during the offseason from Los Angeles in a six-player deal that sent future Hall of Famer Frank Robinson to the Dodgers. Robinson remains the only man to win the Most Valuable Player Award in both the American and National Leagues (NL MVP in 1961 while playing with the Cincinnati Reds and AL MVP in 1966 with the Orioles).

A personal highlight might have been a meaningless fifth-inning single by Yankees second baseman, Bernie Allen who had played for the Washington Senators the past five seasons.

The Story

By all rights, my Opening-Day streak should have ended after just two years. Major League Baseball had taken away my team. Dad and I were there on September 30, 1971, the night of the franchise's last game as the Washington Senators. Bob Short had followed through on his threat to move the team to Texas, and American League owners had approved. It was an angry night at RFK. Fans brought banners to display their disdain for the owner. I remember sitting along the first-base line staring out at center field as one fan unfurled from the upper deck a long vertical white scroll with black letters that read SHORT. A minute later, a second scroll completed the message: STINKS. The Senators rallied from a 5–1 deficit against the visiting New York Yankees to take a 7–5 lead into the ninth inning. My idol Frank Howard had homered in the sixth to tie the game, his 237th and last as a Washington ballplayer. It was a DC baseball record that would stand for 47 years until Ryan Zimmerman broke it in 2017!

The crowd was delirious, but the end was near—the end of the game and the end of the Washington Senators. The team needed just one more out for a win that would have allowed them to close out the season just 37 1/2 games behind the first-place Baltimore Orioles. More than needing the win, the fans needed souvenirs. Without waiting for the final out, they poured onto the field in droves, grabbing anything they could: the bases, sod, banners, seats, you name it. The Yankees won by forfeit.

I cried myself to sleep that night.

Opening Day 1972 should have been a nonevent for me. My team was gone, and I would be rooting for the Texas Rangers from afar. Fans in Washington weren't the only ones who were angry. Emboldened by Curt Flood's unsuccessful legal challenge, the players had gone on strike just before the 1972 season, a first in baseball history, but certainly not the last. Players were seeking improvements to their pension fund and, more importantly, binding arbitration in salary disputes, a critical steppingstone on the path to free agency. Ultimately, the players prevailed that spring, although the owners claimed victory, refusing to reschedule or pay players for games missed in early April. The strike delayed the start of the season by nearly two weeks.

I don't remember the details, but I suspect after Mass that Sunday morning, the conversation went something like this:

Roundy: *"Let's go to the game!"*

Me: *"What game?"*

Roundy: *"Opening Day!"*

Me: *"Where?"*

Roundy: *"Baltimore."*

Me: *"Huh?"*

Then out would have come a paper map about the size of a brochure, crisply folded more than 100 times. Once unfolded for use, it would never again be restored to its precise, original condition. We would chart the 50-mile adventure from our house in northwest Washington, DC, to Memorial Stadium, a previously unknown journey into enemy territory.

The Orioles at the time were the best in baseball but rivals to my beloved Senators. The Birds had won more than 100 games and the American League pennant each of the previous three seasons. They were a big deal, and in Roundy's mind, worth the trip. They returned a starting rotation which the year before had accomplished something that had not happened since 1920: four starting pitchers each won at least 20 games in a single season (Jim Palmer, Mike Cuellar, Dave McNally, and Pat Dobson).

I doubt we were still in the stadium when the game ended. I suspect when Dobson exited, so did we, if not earlier. A whiny, cold 11-year-old probably wanted to go home.

But the streak continued.

 For box scores, play-by-play and more, visit www.OpeningDay5050.com or use this QR code

1973

Curt Flood II: Dave McNally

The Game

Who:	Baltimore Orioles 10, Milwaukee Brewers 0
Where:	Memorial Stadium, Baltimore, MD
Attendance:	26,543
When:	Friday, April 6, 1973
Weather:	Sunny and 60s

Hall of Famers: Orioles manager Earl Weaver, P Jim Palmer, and 3B Brooks Robinson

Game Highlights: As a result of the Senators move to Texas, the American League executed a one-for-one swap of two of baseball's perennial cellar dwellers with the Senators-Rangers franchise moving from the AL East Division to the AL West, while the Milwaukee Brewers joined the powerhouse Baltimore Orioles in the AL East. Beginning only their fifth season since being part of baseball's 1969 expansion, the "Brew Crew" was humiliated on Opening Day 1973. Baltimore's Don Baylor, who had taken over the outfield spot vacated a year earlier by Frank Robinson, went 4-for-4, drove in four runs, scored twice, and homered. Dave McNally went the distance and gave up only three hits for Baltimore.

The Story

For the first time, fans found letters they'd never seen before in the box score: DH. It stood for designated hitter, players who would bat for the notoriously weak-hitting pitchers. The rule change adopted by the American League after decades of discussion and debate added more offense to the game and took away the bat from the Orioles 1973 Opening Day starter Dave McNally, one of only two pitchers with two career World Series home runs (Bob Gibson was the other). McNally sat on the bench throughout Baltimore's at bats watching Terry Crowley go 2-for-4 in his spot.

If Curt Flood had been Marvin Miller's willing pawn in the MLBPA's first move toward free agency, then McNally was one of the two all-important bishops. Over his 13-year career in Baltimore, he'd earned the reputation as one of the American League's most consistent and dominant pitchers. But it was his performance off the field in late 1975 that earned him a spot on the Mount Rushmore of baseball free agency, right there with Flood, Miller, and his fellow chess piece, Andy Messersmith.

McNally had posted an 87–31 record from 1968 to 1971 and was rewarded with a $105,000 contract for 1972, making him the first AL pitcher ever in the $100,000 club, a magic number in those pre-free-agency days. "He's worth every cent," Orioles pitching coach George Bamberger told Phil Jackman, writer for *The Sporting News* and *Baltimore Evening Sun*. "Nobody in baseball has worked as hard as he has. He never pouts or moans, no matter how he's hurting."

McNally accumulated his strong work ethic and moral compass growing up in Billings, Montana. His father was killed serving in World War II when Dave was only two years old. His mother raised four children on her own, and everyone had to pitch in. McNally was only 17 when he signed with Baltimore for $80,000 in 1960. A year later he married Jean Hoffer, his sweetheart from Billings Central Catholic High School. They settled in Baltimore where they raised their five children.

As popular as McNally may have been with fans, coaches, and teammates, he was strongly disliked by management. Not only was he the team player rep with the union, but he was one of the first players to hire an agent to negotiate his contract, considered an affront by ownership. In John Eisenberg's 2002 book on the Orioles history, *From 33rd Street to Camden Yards*, Orioles general manager Frank Cashen described McNally as "a tough son of a bitch. 'Intractable' is a good word for him."

After the 1974 season, the winningest pitcher in Orioles history asked to be traded. "I haven't been pitching the way I'm capable," McNally told Doug Brown of *The Sporting News*, "and maybe a trade would wake me up." Some speculated his contentious contract talks in recent years or rumored difficulties with Weaver also played a part in his decision. In December his wish was granted. Along with outfielder Rich Coggins, he was traded to the Montreal Expos for outfielder Ken Singleton and pitcher Mike Torrez. McNally never agreed to terms with his new team, so the Expos invoked the reserve clause and gave McNally notice they had renewed his 1974 contract.

As a union leader, McNally knew what Miller needed to mount a legal challenge to the reserve clause. Paragraph 10(a) of the Uniform Player's Contract said, in part, that if the player and his team had not reached a new agreement by March 1 each year, then the team ". . . shall have the right by written notice to the Player... to renew this contract for the period of one year on the same terms..." With binding arbitration now in hand from the April 1972 strike settlement, Miller and MLBPA General Counsel Dick Moss needed at least one player to play one year without signing a contract. The union would offer the arbitrator an alternative interpretation of the reserve clause—that a team's right to automatically renew a player's contract was not in perpetuity, but rather lasted *only* "one year." In McNally and Messersmith, Miller had found his bishops, two players who played the 1975 season under the owner-invoked renewed terms of their 1974 contracts.

On the field, McNally's 1975 season with the Expos was disappointing and brief. After 14 seasons in the major leagues, he announced his retirement just two months into the season. "It got to the point where I was stealing money," McNally told Ian McDonald of *The Gazette* in Montreal, echoing the same sentiments he had expressed just a few months earlier in Baltimore. "I was trying to tell myself it would come around. If I had arm trouble or any kind of arm injury, then I could say I had an excuse. There is absolutely nothing wrong with my arm."

His playing days were over, but he never signed the formal retirement papers. In the months that followed, this would prove to be important. In June he walked away from the remainder of his $115,000 salary and began planning to move his family from Baltimore back to Billings.

The owners weren't done with their maneuvering, trying to outflank Miller and Moss. If they could somehow get the two players off the grievance for the arbitration hearing, they could at least buy themselves another year of controlling the players. They hoped the Los Angeles Dodgers could work out a deal before the late November hearing with their star pitcher Messersmith, just as the San Diego Padres had done a year earlier with outfielder Bobby Tolan. But what to do about McNally?

In November 2000 ESPN.com's Darren Rovell wrote a retrospective on the infamous 1975 arbitration process:

"Twenty-five years ago, on a cold night in early November, Montreal Expos President John McHale called Dave McNally to tell the former Orioles great that he just happened to be in Billings, Montana. McHale invited McNally, who lived just minutes away, to stop by and have some lunch.

"'Yeah, passing through Billings, Montana, in November,' laughed Dick Moss."

Rovell continued:

"McHale had an offer to make for his apparently useless pitcher . . . He offered McNally a $25,000 signing bonus and $125,000 if he made the team in 1976. The four-time 20-game winner had never seen a paycheck that big before.

"And that wasn't all.

"'The Expos were going to pay his family's expenses in Florida in the winter time and no matter how spring training turned out, he would get to keep the $25,000,' said Miller."

Like Flood, McNally had a selfless streak. He understood the greater good for future players. He declined McHale's attempted bribe and the hearing proceeded later that month. On December 23, 1975, arbitrator Peter Seitz ruled in favor of the two pitchers, effectively ending the reserve clause for labor matters and changing the business of professional sports forever.

And like Flood, McNally never saw a dime of the game's newfound riches.

For box scores, play-by-play and more, visit www.OpeningDay5050.com or use this QR code

1974

Booooooog!

The Game

Who:	Baltimore Orioles 3, Detroit Tigers 2
Where:	Memorial Stadium, Baltimore, MD
Attendance:	23,918
When:	Friday, April 5, 1974
Weather:	Rain delay, 60s

Hall of Famers: Orioles manager Earl Weaver, P Jim Palmer, and 3B Brooks Robinson, Tigers RF Al Kaline

---

Game Highlights: Rain once again had postponed Opening Day to Friday, and early afternoon showers delayed the start by nearly an hour. But once things got started, time flew by as pitchers Jim Palmer for Baltimore and Mickey Lolich for Detroit breezed through their opponents in just over two hours! Palmer, who had won the first of his three Cy Young Awards in 1973 and would finish in the Top 5 on five other occasions during his brilliant 19-year Hall of Fame career with the Orioles, needed relief help in the ninth from Grant Jackson to close out the win. Orioles outfielder and 1973 American League Rookie of the Year Al Bumbry scored the winning run in the eighth inning.

The Story

I must have felt an odd sense of déjà vu on Opening Day 1974. Just like Opening Day 1970, Detroit was the visiting team, Mickey Lolich was pitching for the Tigers, and it was raining at game time. A twinge of nostalgia must have tugged at my heart. There they were: former Senators Eddie Brinkman and Aurelio Rodriguez playing shortstop and third base, respectively, for the Tigers, both part of that disastrous trade that brought Denny McLain to Washington following the 1970 season. When Brinkman led off the game with a walk followed by a Rodriguez single, I probably stood up and cheered!

For Roundy and me, this was our third road trip to Baltimore for Opening Day, but I don't think he'd quite yet figured out the best way back to DC. Baltimore's one-way streets made it difficult to simply retrace the route for the journey home. We must have lingered a bit after the game, because I remember the close-by parking spaces outside the third base side of Memorial Stadium being generally empty. As we walked toward 33rd Street, we spotted a monster of a man getting into a vehicle large enough to accommodate his immense size. It was Orioles first baseman Boog Powell. We had no camera, and I don't remember asking for an autograph. I do remember my dad doing a most un-Roundy-like thing: he asked for directions.

Boog could not have been more gracious. He explained something about St. Paul Street this way and Greene Street that way. In an instant, the wall of dislike between me and the northern enemy of my Senators had been penetrated. As I pondered this awakening on the long drive home, I must have recrafted my fan logic. The Texas Rangers, I surmised, could be my favorite team in the American League West and Boog Powell's Orioles could be my favorite team in the AL East.

Settled.

John Wesley "Boog" Powell was one of the biggest stars in the game at the time, both literally and figuratively. He was listed as being six feet, four inches, 230 pounds. He seemed significantly larger to a 13-year-old boy. Between 1966 and 1974, one reason that allowed five different Oriole infielders to accumulate 19 Gold Gloves over nine seasons—Brooks Robinson (9), Mark Belanger (4), Davey Johnson (3), Bobby Grich (2), and Luis Aparicio (1)—was the sheer size of the first base target at which they were throwing. My memory of Powell is of a first baseman gracefully extending his left leg in an extreme stretch, lunging toward his infielder teammate: a cross between a gymnast on the balance beam and a powerlifter! He was even more intimidating with a bat, hitting more than

300 home runs during his career in Baltimore. He was named the American League MVP following the 1970 season and played in four straight All-Star Games (1968–71).

It was that same affable personality Roundy and I experienced in the parking lot that afforded Powell a second and third career once his playing days were over in 1977. He starred in a series of famous Miller Lite beer commercials in the 1980s. And when the Orioles moved from Memorial Stadium to Oriole Park at Camden Yards in 1992, Powell's career as a restaurateur was launched. Boog's BBQ extended the big guy's baseball career more than 25 years, well into the 21st century, feeding another generation of fans a bit of nostalgia with their pulled pork and ribs. The wildly successful business spawned an additional location in Maryland and another in Boog's native Florida.

In August 2017 a home run ball landed in the right-field flag court and was on a path straight to Boog's place. It was the first major-league home run for 24-year-old Boog Powell—Herschel Mack "Boog" Powell IV (no relation) of the Oakland A's. Young Boog played only 59 games in the majors in his short career and hit only three home runs. What are the odds one would land so close to the man who inspired his dad (an Angels fan) to assign such a nickname to his son?

The two met the next day for a made-for-TV meet and greet. While visiting the right-field eatery, Boog the elder fed his young guest well as the two gushed with mutual admiration. When they were done, if Boog the younger needed help getting back to the clubhouse, he just needed to ask for directions. Surely the ever-gracious elder would have shown him the way back home.

For box scores, play-by-play and more, visit www.OpeningDay5050.com or use this QR code

1975

Yaz, Hank Stram, and Notre Dame

The Game

Who:	Boston Red Sox 6, Baltimore Orioles 5 (12 innings)
Where:	Memorial Stadium, Baltimore, MD
Attendance:	38,655
When:	Friday, April 11, 1975
Weather:	Cloudy, 50s

Hall of Famers: Orioles manager Earl Weaver and 3B Brooks Robinson, Red Sox 1B Carl Yastrzemski and LF Jim Rice

Game Highlights: Fans back in New England listening to this game on radio were gleeful—no, tearful—as two of their most iconic Red Sox, Tony Conigliaro and Carl Yastrzemski, both homered. Yastrzemski's came in the 12th inning off pitcher Doyle Alexander, then in his sixth inning of relief work. But it was Tony C's blast off starter Mike Cuellar in the fifth that truly stirred the heart of Red Sox Nation. Conigliaro had been the brightest star of his generation in 1967 when he was hit in the face by a pitch at Fenway Park. The gruesome injury to his left cheek and retina was so severe, it was generally assumed the career of the youngest American League player ever to hit 100 homers was over. After missing the entire 1968 season, Conigliaro mounted an improbable comeback in 1969, belting 60 more homers before retiring after the 1971 season, saying his eyesight had deteriorated. In early 1975 when 30-year-old Conigliaro and the Red Sox announced he was going to give it one more try, hearts swelled. His Opening Day homer in Baltimore was special beyond words. His second comeback was brief, but inspiring. After just 21 games, Conigliaro was sent down to Pawtucket, his major-league career over.

The Story

Football fans of a certain age will remember Hall of Fame coach Hank Stram, who guided the Kansas City Chiefs through their first glory years in the 1960s and '70s before working in the CBS broadcast booth well into the 1990s. And baseball fans certainly know of the legendary stature of Boston Red Sox Hall of Famer Carl Yastrzemski, or perhaps more recently of his grandson Mike of the San Francisco Giants. What may surprise both fan groups is their brief overlap for a year in South Bend, Indiana, and their reunion more than 25 years later.

Let's start with Yaz.

We generally don't think of Major League Baseball players of the 1950s or '60s as having attended college. Before the amateur draft was instituted in 1966, acquiring young talent was a free-for-all among major-league scouts, scouring the country in search of "can't miss" talent. Teams would dangle huge sums of money in front of teenage standouts and their parents in hopes of securing them for life. Remember, at that time, thanks to the reserve clause, once a player signed with a team, he was theirs forever. Carl's eyes were on baseball. His dad had other ideas.

Young Carl's "kitchen cabinet" consisted of two men: his father, Carl Sr. and Father Joe Ratkowski, their pastor at St. Jerome's Church. "As a 17-year-old senior at Bridgehampton High in the spring of 1957, I would have signed for any amount I was offered if it had been up to me," recalled Yastrzemski in his 1968 autobiography *Yaz*.

"But it wasn't up to me. As a minor, I couldn't sign anything. Dad was the boss, and behind him was Father Joe. He was more than just a baseball fan. An outstanding athlete in his youth, he could have been a professional baseball player if he hadn't chosen the priesthood.

"My parents had decided not to accept any big-league baseball offers at that time unless somebody came up with those magic six figures Father Joe had been talking about [$100,000]. Nor would my family consider college scholarship offers from anywhere except Notre Dame."

At a time before the National Collegiate Athletic Association frowned upon such things, Yastrzemski had plenty of impressive college scholarship offers, including most New York-area schools, Duke, and Miami. Major-league teams made offers, too, including the Yankees, but at less than half the figure Dad demanded. Among the college offers, Notre Dame was not young Carl's first choice.

"Other colleges came up with some fantastic packages that included, besides the conventional board, room, tuition, books, and laundry, spending money up to a hundred dollars a month, a complete new wardrobe, an apartment of my own, and a car. I had never owned even a jalopy, never had more than one suit, never slept in a room by myself, and although Dad let me keep what I earned in the fields, had never had anywhere near a hundred dollars a month to spend.

"Not being as fussy about Notre Dame as Mom and Dad, I wanted to grab one of those fancy scholarships. 'What difference will it make if I don't go to Notre Dame?' I asked Dad. 'A college education is a college education. Why can't I go to the place that offers the most?'"

"Because Notre Dame is the best Catholic college in the country," he said.

"I don't even see why I have to go to a Catholic college."

"Well I do," he said. "So does your mother. And if Father Joe can arrange it, it will be Notre Dame."

In the fall of 1957, Yastrzemski enrolled at Notre Dame.

In the summer of 1980, Bill Marquard, a sportswriter for Notre Dame's student newspaper *The Observer*, sat down with Yaz, then in the twilight of his 23-year big-league career. He reflected on his time in South Bend. "The things I remember most about Notre Dame are the high academic standards and the strict discipline. The work I did in high school was nothing like the studies I did at Notre Dame."

Now onto Stram.

Notre Dame's football team, meanwhile, was a perennial Top 20 team in the late 1950s. They had hired Southern Methodist University assistant Hank Stram to coach the backfield. He would spend two years with the Fighting Irish and one more season as a college assistant before being hired by Lamar Hunt as the first coach of his Dallas Texans of the new American Football League (which would later merge with the National Football League). Hunt's Texans moved to Kansas City in 1963. In 15 seasons Stram led the franchise to three AFL titles, won Super Bowl IV and, in 2003, was inducted into the Pro Football Hall of Fame.

Before his year at SMU, Stram had coached eight seasons at his alma mater Purdue, the last five of which (1951–55) he doubled as head baseball coach. It was during his final season coaching the Boilermakers that a certain high school ballplayer in New England likely caught his attention. As a fellow Polish American, Stram was quite fond of young Yaz, and the two wound up on the same

Indiana campus for the 1957–58 school year.

"Being a freshman, Yastrzemski was ineligible for the varsity squad when he arrived in South Bend," Marquard explained in his April 1981 Opening Day article for *The Observer*. "He thus came under the watchful eye of Jim Gibbons, then the freshman baseball coach."

"'I must admit that it was pretty easy to look at Carl as a freshman and realize he was a cut above everyone else,' remembers Gibbons. 'He did everything so effortlessly.'"

The freshman team's primary role was to scrimmage against the varsity. Even there, Yastrzemski made his mark. In one intrasquad game, he reportedly hit a ball more than 500 feet onto the adjacent football practice field where it rolled to the feet of the Fighting Irish backfield coach.

"Yastrzemski hit that, didn't he?" Stram asked.

Marquard summarized the final chapters of Carl's time in South Bend. "Yastrzemski inked a Sox contract midway through his sophomore year at Notre Dame. With baseball occupying much of the spring and summer, Yastrzemski began attending Notre Dame for the first term of each school year in order to graduate. Even after marrying the former Carol Casper, Yastrzemski returned to campus for the fall semesters of 1960 and 1961. But it just became too much of a burden to move all the time, what with spring training, then the regular season, then Notre Dame. 'I finished the equivalent of my junior year at Notre Dame before I finally called it quits.'" Yastrzemski completed his degree in business administration in 1966 at Merrimack College in Massachusetts.

More than a quarter century later, Stram and Yastrzemski were reunited. Stram was inducted into the National Polish-American Sports Hall of Fame in 1985. Yastrzemski joined him in the following year.

For box scores, play-by-play and more, visit www.OpeningDay5050.com or use this QR code

1976

Where's Reggie?

The Game

Who:	Baltimore Orioles 1, Boston Red Sox 0
Where:	Memorial Stadium, Baltimore, MD
Attendance:	46,425
When:	Friday, April 9, 1976
Weather:	Sunny and cool

Hall of Famers: Orioles manager Earl Weaver, P Jim Palmer, and 3B Brooks Robinson, Red Sox 1B Carl Yastrzemski, P Ferguson Jenkins, C Carlton Fisk, and LF Jim Rice

Game Highlights: The largest Opening Day crowd since the St. Louis Browns became the Baltimore Orioles 22 years earlier watched Jim Palmer and Ferguson Jenkins lock horns without giving up an earned run all afternoon. They were so efficient that fans were heading home just two hours after the game started. Jenkins went the distance while Palmer got relief help in the ninth from Dyar Miller. Baltimore pushed across the game's only run thanks to two Boston errors in the fourth. Shortstop Rick Burleson's errant throw allowed Lee May to reach base and he later scored on a single by Bobby Grich when 1975 AL MVP and Rookie of the Year Fred Lynn's throw from center field to third skipped off shortstop Rico Petrocelli, allowing May to score.

The Story

The stage featured one of the most star-studded Hall of Fame cast of any Opening Day during the streak, with seven in uniform. On Boston's side of the box score were catcher Carlton Fisk, outfielder Jim Rice, and Carl Yastrzemski (playing first base this day), plus the afternoon's starting pitcher, Ferguson Jenkins—all four destined for Cooperstown. For the 20th consecutive year, 39-year-old Brooks Robinson appeared in Baltimore's Opening Day starting lineup, and for the third straight time, manager Earl Weaver gave the ball to pitcher Jim Palmer to begin the season.

But it was the future Hall of Famer *not* yet wearing an Orioles uniform who was drawing the most media attention: Reggie Jackson.

Jackson was the biggest name in baseball in the early '70s. I remember one time in 1969 when his Oakland Athletics visited Washington to play the Senators. My dad's law office was above Rinaldi's Cleaners near the White House. After every Senators game the locker room staff sent the uniforms over for a quick cleaning. One Saturday Mr. Rinaldi let me try on one jersey from each team: Frank Howard and Reggie Jackson. Both shirts were bigger than I was. The A's visiting grays were vests, so at least my arms showed in the once-cherished-now-lost black-and-white photos.

If you were to ask baseball fans from the 1970s and '80s to list the teams for which Reggie Jackson played during his 22 major-league seasons, most would quickly recall his early years in Oakland (1967–75) who he would represent in six All-Star Games and where he was named the AL MVP in 1973. And they'd remember his more lucrative glory days as "Mr. October" playing for the New York Yankees (1977–81). Both teams later retired his jersey: Oakland No. 9 and the Yankees No. 44.

Fans might even remember Jackson's most lucrative twilight years with the California Angels (1982–86) before a final season back in Oakland (1987). His seasons as an Angel might have been galvanized in the memories of many by his cameo appearance in the 1988 comedy classic *The Naked Gun: From the Files of Police Squad!* with Leslie Nielsen in which he played himself as a robot programmed to kill Queen Elizabeth II.

But ask any fan outside of Baltimore if they remember his time as an Oriole, and the response will likely be, "Huh?"

A week before Opening Day 1976, new Orioles general manager Hank Peters completed a blockbuster trade with the A's to acquire the game's biggest star and the left-handed power his team needed. But it was Oakland's maneuvering in 1976 that garnered far more attention than Baltimore's.

In the early '70s, the Athletics were as dominant a team as the game had ever seen, with five straight American League West Division titles (1971–75) and three straight World Series crowns (1972–74). Owner Charlie Finley had amassed an all-star roster that would be expensive to maintain. Arbitrator Peter Seitz's landmark ruling in December 1975 meant that, by 1977, dozens of players would likely become free agents for the first time. Finley had plenty of these potentially pricey players. Expecting baseball's first bidding war to begin at season's end (the terms of free agency weren't finalized until the new collective bargaining agreement was reached in July), Finley tried to get what he could in return for his biggest stars, determined not to pay top dollar for top talent (a characteristic some suggest lingered with the franchise long after Finley sold the team in 1980). In addition to the Jackson trade, Finley tried to sell stars Joe Rudi, Rollie Fingers, and Vida Blue for cash in June, but the deals were nixed by Commissioner Bowie Kuhn.

Oakland's big names in the deal with the Orioles were Jackson and Ken Holzman. Heading west from Baltimore were pitcher Mike Torrez and outfielder Don Baylor (who would later become 1979 AL MVP for the California Angels). Holzman was already in Baltimore on Opening Day, set to start the season's second game, but Jackson was a no-show. "As of late yesterday, he was still nowhere to be seen," reported Ken Nigro in that morning's *Baltimore Sun*, "preferring to remain in Arizona where he has numerous business interests."

"The thought that Reggie might be here any day is encouraging," Weaver told Nigro, "but I have got to worry about the guys who are here. After Jackson or anybody else gets in, then I'll tell him what to do. But I can't do anything about it now. I can't offer him money. My job is to take what's on the club and win with it."

Palmer was less diplomatic. "Reggie not being here is psychologically destructive to this ball club," he said. "We gave up quality players to get him. If we start the season without him, the first inclination is to ask, why did we make the trade? I would sure like to have Don Baylor playing than no Reggie Jackson. Now we have neither."

Jackson's holdout lasted a month. Conventional wisdom suggested it was about money. In part, it was. Jackson had been paid $140,000 in 1975 and was demanding $200,000 for 1976. Finley would have none of that.

Reggie's reputation was to stir the pot. In his 1991 book, *A Whole Different Ballgame*, Marvin Miller revealed a little-known detail about Reggie related to baseball's first-ever players' strike in April 1972. After the owners rejected their proposal for binding arbitration, Miller and MLBPA General Counsel Dick Moss acknowledged privately the time was not right for a strike. They realized a group of ball players with no strike fund who had been without paychecks since the end of the previous season was in no position to stop working. "The last thing I expected in 1972 was a strike," Miller admitted.

But on the flight to Dallas for the executive board meeting, Reggie told the union boss the players he represented did not want to back down. At the meeting Reggie led the charge. In his 1994 book, *Lords of the Realm*, John Helyar quotes Reggie's exhortation to his fellow player reps: "Goddammit, there are just times when you've got to stand up for your rights."

The players voted to strike and won the right to arbitration.

Reggie picked fights with Finley in Oakland and later made headlines in New York for his dust-ups with manager Billy Martin and owner George Steinbrenner. And while Baltimore's Weaver had a fiery temper, in Peters and Hoffberger, Jackson could not find a suitable sparring partner.

To his credit, Peters coddled the over-sized ego for a month and landed the prize in Baltimore for most of one season. According to baseball broadcaster and historian Phil Wood, years later Peters admitted "the biggest mistake he made in Baltimore was not giving Reggie Jackson what he wanted in a long-term deal: $1.25 million for five years. It would have been the biggest bargain in baseball."

When he arrived in town, Jackson said all the right things. "I was never informative and probably was a real pain in the butt to talk with," Jackson admitted. "I never met anybody quite like Hank Peters or Jerry Hoffberger. It was the consistency of their interest, their humaneness, sensitivity, and fairness in continually leaving the door open that made me come here without a signed contract."

So what took four weeks?

"Probably it took me that long to realize it. They won me over as nice guys."

No wonder Reggie lasted only five months in Charm City.

For box scores, play-by-play and more, visit www.OpeningDay5050.com or use this QR code

1977

My Banner Day: Go Senators!

The Game

Who:	Texas Rangers 2, Baltimore Orioles 1 (10 innings)
Where:	Memorial Stadium, Baltimore, MD
Attendance:	31,307
When:	Thursday, April 7, 1977
Weather:	Sunny, windy, and cool

Hall of Famers: Orioles manager Earl Weaver, P Jim Palmer, DH Eddie Murray, and 3B Brooks Robinson, Texas Rangers P Bert Blyleven

Game Highlights: Imagine this in the 21st century: Two future Hall of Fame pitchers square off on Opening Day, and both throw 10-inning complete games in just two hours and 34 minutes. Unheard of! Although Major League Baseball did not start keeping pitch counts as an official statistic until 11 years later, chances are that on Opening Day 1977 both Baltimore's Jim Palmer and Bert Blyleven of Texas well exceeded the 100-pitch checkpoint the game would embrace decades later as arms became less durable and more expensive. During his 19-year career, Palmer was Baltimore's Opening Day starter a team-record six times, and this was the only one he lost. Rangers rookie Bump Wills singled home Juan Beníquez in the top of the 10th inning. Beníquez had reached on a double when Orioles rookie center fielder Larry Harlow misjudged a fly ball. For the Orioles, this game would mark the major-league debut of 21-year-old rookie Eddie Murray and the first Opening Day in a generation without Brooks Robinson in the starting lineup.

The Story

By the spring of 1977, our treks to Baltimore entered a new phase. I had a driver's license. Roundy handed me the keys for the cruise up Interstate 95 in "our" 1974 Pontiac Grandville convertible. It was too cold to put the top down, but that didn't seem to matter.

My loyalty to the Texas Rangers (née Washington Senators) remained unwavering. I couldn't wait to get my hands on each week's issue of *The Sporting News*, a weekly tabloid with heavy emphasis on baseball, so I could clip every Rangers box score and tape them into a special binder. This was my way of keeping track of a team I could neither watch on TV nor listen to on the radio. Roundy and I had visited Memorial Stadium more than once over the past few summers to see *my* Texas Rangers. This year the Rangers were the opponent on Opening Day. I needed something special to mark the occasion.

The dictionary says a "banner day" is a term used to "describe the kind of excellent day or occurrence that deserves a banner hung in a prominent place . . . as if to mark a celebratory occasion." In the 1970s it was common to see large homemade banners in the ballpark before they were banned for aesthetic reasons. During that infamous Senators finale at RFK Stadium in September 1971, banners were everywhere. Some bid fond farewells to the team, while others eviscerated owner Bob Short for stealing our team.

When Roundy and I made the trip to Super Bowl VII in January 1973, I felt I had to make a banner, a bold statement as our team prepared to face the undefeated Miami Dolphins in Los Angeles. After all, how many other 12-year-olds had saved up enough money from their newspaper routes to make such a cross-country trip?

I remember laying out an old bed sheet on the basement floor, cutting it in half down the middle so I could sew together a single white scroll roughly 3' x 12'. I would carefully lay out newspapers so the black paint wouldn't stain the black-and-white-checkerboard tile flooring. We arrived early to the Coliseum on Super Bowl Sunday so I could carefully affix my clever, all caps banner to a fence near our seats in the corner of the end zone for all to see:

"REDSKINS EAT FISH ON SUNDAYS!"

It was unlikely many saw it, other than the few hundred fans in our section. Those who did nodded politely, grasping the word play perhaps familiar to Catholics who ate fish on Fridays.

I tried again three years later, this time at the 1976 Major League Baseball

All-Star Game in Philadelphia. To get picked up on television, there were two requirements: hang it in a more prominent place and give a shout out to the network televising the game.

With an usher's permission, I hung it high above center field. After climbing to my single seat, high above first base, I could clearly see in the distance my tribute to the only former Washington Senator in the game, Texas Rangers shortstop Toby Harrah. It read:

"WASHINGTON SENATORS FAN CLUB – GO TOBY! HI WARNER" (a reference to DC sportscasting legend Warner Wolf, now with ABC).

By the third inning, all dozen or so banners in center field had been removed. I stormed over and confronted the usher who earlier had given the approval. He explained "the boss" wanted them all down, that management didn't want the stadium looking cluttered on national television. Outraged, I wrote a letter to *Sports Illustrated*. They did not publish it.

This banner crusade deserved one more try, perhaps without the glare of national television cameras.

Opening Day 1977 provided the opportunity. The message needed to be concise and more mature. After all, I was now 16. More direct. A bold statement to encourage *my* team.

Just as we had done more than four years earlier in Los Angeles, we arrived early on this sunny, windy afternoon, armed with appropriate supplies to affix the banner for all to see. This time we weren't stuck away in some obscure corner. Roundy got us tickets on the mezzanine level above first base in the front row!

Upon arrival I carefully climbed over the railing onto the photo deck directly in front. As I'm writing this, I'm wondering how similar actions would have been handled decades later. How quickly would stadium security escort me from the building? But not in 1977.

The Rangers roster still included a few holdovers from that final Senators season six years earlier: Tom Grieve, Toby Harrah, and Bill Fahey. I was sure each would appreciate the banner's message when they saw it:

"GO SENATORS!"

I can't say for certain if any of the three former Senators took notice. But I know others saw it, a whole lot of others. Imagine my shock the next afternoon when I opened DC's evening newspaper, the *Washington Star*. Right there on the front page of the sports section, directly below superstar columnist David Israel's piece on Jim Palmer and the Orioles but still above the fold, was a larger-than-life photograph of *my banner*.

"Not everybody at yesterday's Baltimore-Texas baseball opener at Memorial Stadium was an Orioles fan," the photo caption read. "There was some visible support for the Rangers, formerly the Washington Senators, before their move to Arlington, Tex., following the end of the 1971 season. The Rangers won, 2–1, beating Orioles ace Jim Palmer in the process."

I was famous!

For box scores, play-by-play and more, visit www.OpeningDay5050.com
or use this QR code

1978

Al Who?

The Game

Who:	Baltimore Orioles 6, Milwaukee Brewers 5
Where:	Memorial Stadium, Baltimore, MD
Attendance:	36,086
When:	Friday, April 14, 1978
Weather:	Sunny, breezy, 60s

Hall of Famers: Orioles manager Earl Weaver, P Jim Palmer, and DH Eddie Murray and Brewers SS Paul Molitor

Game Highlights: The surroundings were familiar for the Brewers highly regarded rookie manager George Bamberger. After more than a decade as the Orioles pitching coach, Bambi made the jump to the head job in Milwaukee in 1978, leading a franchise which had never had a winning season since its arrival in the 1969 expansion. The team's turnaround was off to an impressive start, winning its first five games, while the Orioles lost their first five of 1978 on the road. Baltimore's home opener brought both streaks to an end. A five-run rally in the third gave the Birds the runs they needed to give 24-year-old starter Dennis Martinez the win. Martinez would go on to enjoy a 23-year big-league career, primarily with the Orioles and Montreal Expos.

The Story

Roundy's knowledge of the game had improved a little over these past eight years, but not much. I'm sure that did not stop him from needling me while the Orioles were batting in the third inning. Baltimore left fielder Al Bumbry singled to drive in one run and later came around to score, capping the decisive five-run uprising.

My dad likely poked his elbow into my ribs and said something snarky like, "Who is that Al Bumbry guy? Pretty good player. Ever heard of him?"

The Al Bumbry jokes had been circling around our family for five years. My dad couldn't let it go. As a 12-year-old baseball "know-it-all" in the spring of 1973, I had embarrassed myself and my parents in front of Al's mother, and Roundy wouldn't let me forget it.

That spring, my parents and I drove down to Dahlgren, Virginia, to visit Lucille Keys, a loveable woman trusted by my parents to care for us kids overnight, when needed, especially my brother Louis. Six years my elder, "Love Bug" (as my oldest sister, Genny, called him) was born with a heart condition and Down syndrome, so Mom and Dad wouldn't leave him with just anyone. My siblings remember Lucille fondly. She always wore a white uniform and fed them very well. She was there the day Mom brought me home from the hospital in 1960.

I suspect the purpose of my parents' trip to Dahlgren was to reconnect with the aging Lucille, and perhaps reintroduce her to their youngest son, now almost a teenager. During the visit the conversation drifted to baseball, and dear Lucille insisted I meet her neighbor Helen. Her son, Lucille claimed, was a Major League Baseball player. I perked up with excitement.

Minutes later I met the likable Helen Newman. The adults in the room let her know I was quite a fan of the game. She asked if I knew of her son.

"What's his name?" I asked.

"Alonza Bumbry," she said, gushing with pride.

And with all the social graces you'd expect of an underinformed 12-year-old, I blurted out, "Never heard of him."

My mother was mortified.

During the long car ride home, I vaguely remember insisting this Bumbry guy must be a nobody. After all, if I hadn't yet heard of him, he couldn't be that big a deal.

Brother, was I wrong.

In the weeks that followed, I checked the box scores for his name. Sure enough, he was there most days, getting hits, stealing bases, and scoring runs. Bumbry collected so many hits, steals, and runs in 1973 he was named American League Rookie of the Year, kicking off a marvelous 14-year career and was inducted into the Orioles Hall of Fame in 1987.

Within weeks of that failed encounter with his mother, I was well versed in Al's accomplishments. In June, Roundy took me to a Texas Rangers game at Memorial Stadium. We got there early enough to get Bumbry's attention during pregame warm-ups. He took a break from his drills to meet us at the railing and reminisce about growing up in Dahlgren. We shared with him our mutual connection to "Mrs. Keys" and the fact we'd met his mother. Unlike our encounter a few years earlier with Boog Powell, this time Roundy had a camera. Since I asked for an autograph and picture, it felt like my childish blunder a few weeks earlier was washed away.

Bumbry's journey to the major leagues was anything but conventional. He attended Virginia State College on a basketball scholarship, graduating in 1968. He served a year in combat in Vietnam where Second Lieutenant Bumbry led a platoon in an Armored Cavalry Division. Kent Baker of the *Baltimore Sun* wrote an in-depth piece on him in April 1982. "Bumbry left active service in May of 1971 with a bronze star, some agonizing memories, and a commitment to become a major league–baseball player," Kent wrote. "Within 16 months, he was in Baltimore to stay."

Now in his 70s, Bumbry still lives in the Baltimore area and fondly remembers Mrs. Keys from his childhood in Dahlgren. "I remember she had a garden, and we might go to her house sometimes to get something to eat. She was a really good cook!"

My siblings would agree.

For box scores, play-by-play and more, visit www.OpeningDay5050.com or use this QR code

1979

Comiskey Park

The Game

Who:	Toronto Blue Jays 10, Chicago White Sox 2
Where:	Comiskey Park, Chicago, IL
Attendance:	41,043
When:	Tuesday, April 10, 1979
Weather:	Cold, really cold

Hall of Famers: None

Game Highlights: Outside Comiskey Park, more than two dozen major-league umpires were walking a picket line, seeking higher pay and better benefits (which they eventually got). But inside the ballpark, the game's outcome could not be blamed on replacement umps. The 1979 Toronto Blue Jays, only three years into existence since joining with the Seattle Mariners in the 1977 expansion, were a really bad baseball team. The Chicago White Sox were too. Game highlights? There were none. The White Sox were dreadful. Five Chicago pitchers walked 12 and gave up 9 hits and 10 runs. Only 4 were earned thanks to two White Sox errors. The team played so badly, owner Bill Veeck apologized to the fans and begged them to come back the next day for free. "We stunk the joint out," Veeck admitted. "We certainly couldn't play as bad as this two days in a row. Give us another chance, please."

The Story

For the second time in less than a decade, the baseball gods boldly decided this Opening Day streak should continue. If losing my home team Senators didn't end it, why let college get in the way?

A 10th straight Opening Day was the furthest thing from my mind when I arrived in the fall of 1978 at the University of Notre Dame in South Bend, Indiana, nearly 100 miles from the closest Major League Baseball team. I was quickly immersed in a sports media subculture, working as a student assistant in the sports information department, a sportswriter for the student newspaper *The Observer*, and a sports voice on the ragtag student radio station WSND. My brother Hugh had been the sports information director at Villanova (the "Notre Dame of the East") during the Wildcats first basketball glory days in the early 1970s and helped get my foot in the door at ND. A cast of characters and friends would emerge from these "work" experiences to shape much of my personal and professional life for decades.

Not surprisingly, I skipped my first college class on Monday, October 2, 1978. Options included staying in a dorm room glued to a small, portable black-and-white TV set watching the win-or-go-home, one-game playoff at Fenway Park between the New York Yankees and Boston Red Sox or attending Professor Meredith Scoval's Economics 101 class. It was no contest. The game won. Econ 101 lost. Yankees won, too, as the Red Sox wrote another chapter in their storied curse.

Among my coworkers in the sports information department, at *The Observer*, and WSND was sophomore Craig Chval of Clarendon Hills, Illinois. His writing talent was immense, his sarcasm and humor sharp, and his passion for baseball comparable to mine. He was a fan of the Chicago White Sox, who, like the Senators, had very little experience in postseason play. In fact, his White Sox had been to the World Series only once since 1920. The Senators, twice (1924 and 1933). Craig was often quick to point out he had been to the Sox's last World Series in 1959. His mother, Arlene, was pregnant with him when she attended a Series game at Comiskey Park.

As the gray South Bend winter melted into spring, talk of baseball began. Craig would tell me stories about the White Sox irreverent broadcast team of Harry Caray and Jimmy Piersall. He gushed with pride describing Harry's antics on game day at Comiskey. His imitation of Harry was spot on! Craig had the three things that mattered most at the time: a passion for a team, a desire to have a good time, and a car. In the spring of 1979, we made it to Comiskey Park for

Opening Day.

The atmosphere around Comiskey was unlike anything I had experienced in Washington or Baltimore. RFK Stadium was situated on the banks of the Anacostia River, surrounded by parking lots and residential neighborhoods. Similarly, Memorial Stadium was surrounded by blacktop, then homes, then Lake Montebello about four blocks away. Comiskey was different. It was a ballpark, not a stadium, at least 50 years older than any baseball venue I'd visited. It sat along the Dan Ryan Expressway and was surrounded by small businesses and watering holes, each with their own unique Opening Day rituals, like throwing out the season's first Cubs fan! There was a special decadence and charm that reeked of tradition.

I didn't realize it at the time, but 1979 marked the 60th anniversary of the infamous Black Sox scandal that played out, in part, here at Comiskey Park. Eight members of the 1919 White Sox were brought down for their part in a scheme to fix World Series games. Included in the controversial outcome was perhaps the greatest hitter of the era, Shoeless Joe Jackson, the motivating figure in the 1989 movie classic *Field of Dreams*.

Like the Presidential Openers in Washington, a sellout crowd was expected and that added to the excitement, regardless of the opponent, outlook, outcome, or weather. In Baltimore in the 1970s, even though the team was winning, the electricity associated with sellout crowds was rare.

The atmosphere inside Comiskey was magical. Canned music had not yet arrived. Organist Nancy Faust, an enduring fan favorite from 1970–2010, would improvise and entertain. In the era before players picked their piped-in walk-up music, Nancy might decide for them, and she could be relentless, especially when taunting visiting players. Detroit Tigers outfielder Gates Brown had been incarcerated as a teenager. When he came to the plate in Chicago, she once played Elvis Presley's 1957 hit "Jailhouse Rock." When my gigantic hero Frank Howard would come to bat, she'd channel her inner Carole King with "I Feel the Earth Move." Her rendition of the 1969 pop hit "Na Na Hey Hey Kiss Him Goodbye" brought waving fans to their feet, taunting opposing pitchers as they exited the game. It became a baseball staple for decades in Chicago and elsewhere.

On this day, the White Sox pitchers were so bad, she might have been tempted to play the Na song during one of the two pitching changes in the *top* of the seventh inning when the Blue Jays scored three times. But she refrained, I suspect, because minutes later, the fans would rise for another Faust-supported ritual during the seventh-inning stretch.

Because of the cold and the lack of a rooting interest, I probably would have wanted to leave early, especially once the Blue Jays went up 5–1 in the top of the seventh. But then something magical happened that caused me to pledge allegiance to the White Sox. This slightly slurred, booming voice rolled through the ballpark.

"All right! Let's do it better this year! Let me hear you! All right, Nancy . . ."

After she played an all-too-familiar introduction, future Hall of Fame broadcaster Harry Caray, with a microphone in one hand and perhaps a cold beer in the other, led more than 40,000 fans in a stirring rendition of "Take Me Out to the Ballgame." Many were not in complete grasp of their faculties, but all were in complete control of the ritual.

I was hooked.

For box scores, play-by-play and more, visit www.OpeningDay5050.com or use this QR code

1980

Busted! Sitting Out in the Cold!

The Game

Who:	Baltimore Orioles 5, Chicago White Sox 3
Where:	Comiskey Park, Chicago, IL
Attendance:	35,539
When:	Thursday, April 10, 1980
Weather:	Cold, really cold, 40s and windy

Hall of Famers: Orioles manager Earl Weaver, P Jim Palmer, 1B Eddie Murray, White Sox manager Tony La Russa and OF Harold Baines

Game Highlights: This would be 34-year-old Tony La Russa's first full season managing the White Sox. The youngest skipper in baseball at the time was called up from Chicago's top minor-league club in August 1979 in hopes of turning the team around. While La Russa's Hall of Fame managerial career would eventually blossom in Chicago (and Oakland and St. Louis), his team's performance today would not contribute to that legacy. Fans' first impression of the 1980 White Sox was as bad as it had been a year earlier as the first four Orioles batters reached base and came around to score, thanks, in part, to a hit batter, a balk, and a fielding error. Harry Caray and organist Nancy Faust's seventh-inning stretch must have been especially inspiring, as the Sox would rally for three runs in the seventh and eighth but not enough to overcome the game-opening debacle.

The Story

On the morning after this Opening Day, a photo on the front page of the *Chicago Tribune* sports section said a lot. It was of a mom holding her son, waving a pair of American flags, wrapped in a heavy blanket, and dressed as if they were at a football playoff game in January—not what was supposed to be a rite of spring. The flags might have been motivated by the lingering infusion of nationalistic pride sparked by the United States' stunning hockey victory over the heavily favored Soviet Union at the Winter Olympic Games just a few weeks earlier. Regardless of their patriotic motives, the wardrobe had become something of an Opening Day necessity in Chicago.

In the decades that followed, baseball's weather-resistant options for season openers became more numerous. Expansion had recently brought domed stadiums into the American League in Seattle and Toronto. Future expansion would welcome three new teams in states better known for spring training than the regular season: Florida and Arizona. They had just broken ground for a new domed stadium in Minneapolis for the Minnesota Twins and another retractable dome would be coming to Milwaukee. But in April 1980, teams in places like Boston, New York, Detroit, Cleveland, and Chicago had to live with the harsh whims of nature.

While we endured some pretty miserable weather on Opening Days over 50 years, including this one in 1980, no experience was more memorable than a modified Opening Day two years later when two college kids learned an unexpected lesson about the power of television, both of whom would eventually earn their living in the television industry.

From that Notre Dame crew of sports media friends came Skip Desjardin. We worked together at *The Observer* and WSND, and after college we enjoyed a couple of coincidental, concurrent professional experiences in TV production and distribution in the '80s and '90s. Born and bred in New England, Skip was determined to see his Boston Red Sox play whenever he could, even while in college.

In 1982 the Red Sox were to have opened the season against the White Sox, but Mother Nature had a different plan. A spring snowstorm rocked everything from Chicago to Boston, forcing the season's first two games at Comiskey to be rescheduled as a twi-night doubleheader on an open date on both Sox schedules just three weeks later. By April 26, each team had managed to play more than a dozen games, but to Skip this was Opening Day. The atmosphere at Comiskey suggested otherwise.

The snow might have melted, but the game time temperature was near freezing and the wind was blowing, of course. These were the days before the so-called day-night doubleheader, so instead of playing one game in the afternoon, clearing the ballpark, then reloading for the nightcap, the teams would play two games, back-to-back, starting at 5:00 p.m. Tickets were readily available: box seats for $7, general admission tickets for $3. On a college budget, we opted for the latter. Two games for $3. Couldn't beat it.

Comiskey was so empty and quiet, you could practically hear Joe McConnell's play-by-play from the press box without a radio. Announced attendance was 5,798. In those days, teams announced tickets used, not tickets sold. The evolution of revenue sharing among the teams sparked a policy change in the 1990s.

As the wind continued to whip through the ballpark and the temperature dropped, so did the number of fans in attendance. After Chicago lost Game One, there seemed to be only a few hundred spectators left to experience Game Two. Skip and I decided to attempt an upgrade. We had no trouble moving to the type of seats Bob Uecker once tried to claim, except in our case the ushers had fled the freezing cold. No one checked our tickets. There we were in the *front row*, right next to the on-deck circle, and no one except the umpire and a few players within 100 feet of us! We stayed until Skip's Red Sox completed the sweep just after 10:30 p.m.

A couple of days later, Skip was having the weekly phone call with his parents back home in Auburn, Maine. After the routine exchange of pleasantries, the conversation turned toward academics and preparation for impending final exams.

"These are going to be really tough," Skip told his father. "I'm putting in a lot of hours studying. Studying a lot!"

"Now that you're a senior, tougher than before?"

"Absolutely, Dad," Skip responded. "Surprisingly tough."

"Glad to know you're working hard, Son."

"Really am, Dad."

"All the time?" his father asked intently.

Skip started to squirm. "Just about," he responded honestly. "I mean, I need to break to eat and sleep, but yeah, pretty much all the time."

"Even Monday night?"

Deep breath. Skip knew a lot was riding on the integrity of his next answer as he pondered how much his dad knew and how he knew it.

"Well, now that you mention it, Dad, I did take a break Monday to see the Sox."

"Was that Ortman with you?"

"Sure was," Skip replied, now realizing that thanks to our ill-advised seat upgrade, we'd been caught on camera more than once in the game telecast back home on Channel 38 (WSBK-TV).

We'd always heard parents had eyes in the back of their heads. This time, we made it way too easy for them.

For box scores, play-by-play and more, visit www.OpeningDay5050.com or use this QR code

1981

Our Olympic Moment:
"Throw a Strike, You Bum!"

The Game

Who:	Chicago White Sox 9, Milwaukee Brewers 3
Where:	Comiskey Park, Chicago, IL
Attendance:	51,560
When:	Tuesday, April 14, 1981
Weather:	Sunny and 50s

Hall of Famers: Brewers CF Paul Molitor, SS Robin Yount, P Rollie Fingers, and C Ted Simmons and White Sox manager Tony La Russa, C Carlton Fisk, and OF Harold Baines

Game Highlights: The excitement in and around Comiskey Park was the highest it had been in recent memory. Earlier that afternoon every fan in every bar within walking distance of Comiskey was glued to the TV, anxiously watching the historic conclusion of the first space shuttle mission, *Columbia*. They then filed into the ballpark to celebrate their new team. In just three months since taking over, owners Jerry Reinsdorf and Eddie Einhorn had quickly overhauled the roster, adding some big names with big bats and big paychecks. Designated hitter Greg "Bull" Luzinski and catcher Carlton "Pudge" Fisk headlined the list of offseason acquisitions. The two had made a combined 11 All-Star Game appearances between 1972–80 for Philadelphia and Boston, respectively, and did not disappoint this Opening Day against the vaunted Brew Crew. The Bull's two-run single in the third and Pudge's grand slam in the fourth signaled to fans a new day had arrived. "Some people collect diamonds, and some people collect sports cars," wrote Robert Markus in the next day's *Chicago Tribune*. "Carlton Fisk collects cities. The All-Star catcher, who owned Boston for nine years, took possession of Chicago Tuesday with a grand slam homer in the fourth inning that turned the White Sox home opener into a 9–3 romp." The crowd cheered so long, Fisk was forced to take a curtain call, something that never happened in all those seasons in Boston.

The Story

The most memorable thing about Opening Day 1981 was not who was on the *field* in front of us, but rather who was in the *row* in front of us: David Israel.

You won't find David Israel's name on most top 10 lists of great sportswriters. That might be because he walked away from the craft when he was only 30. In the minds of two 20-year-old Notre Dame sportswriters—Craig Chval and me—Israel might have been the best in the business in 1981. I got a healthy dose of Israel's writing style during his time in the late 1970s at the *Washington Star*. In fact, when the *Star* shared the photo of my GO SENATORS! banner after Opening Day 1977, it appeared just below Israel's insightful column about Jim Palmer and the Orioles. Craig, who introduced me to Harry Caray and his hometown White Sox two years earlier, had feasted on Israel's work earlier at the *Chicago Daily News* (1973–75) and, more recently, the *Chicago Tribune* since 1978. In an era before sportswriters were able to double as TV personalities on cable channels or host their own podcasts, being a syndicated columnist was as good as it got. That meant for every piece he wrote for the *Tribune*, Israel would also get paid a little something from each of the many other papers around the country that would print the same article.

His direct, unapologetic, colorful writing earned him stature. By early 1980 it also had earned him and the *Tribune* a privileged seat near the front of the makeshift press box in the tiny hockey arena in Lake Placid, New York, covering the US Olympic hockey team's stunning progress to and through the medal round. He was only 28 years old.

More than 40 years later, his social media profile picture is a relic of the "Miracle on Ice" win over the Soviet Union: CCCP No. 20 sweater of Russian netminder Vladislav Tretiak. Considered the greatest goalie in the world, Tretiak was pulled from the "Miracle" game after just one period by coach Viktor Tikhonov, a move he later admitted was the biggest mistake of his coaching career. Israel's Twitter profile lists his two current roles in Hollywood (writer and producer) plus only five pieces of his past: "Chair CA Horse Racing Board, LA Coliseum prez, LA Olympic exec, newspaper columnist DC, Chicago, LA, Lake Placid Witness." Fellow members of the news media remember him as more than merely a "witness."

Like Israel, Hubert Mizell was a giant in his craft during this golden era of sports writing. Before retiring in 2005, like so many of his contemporaries, he ranked the "Miracle" game as the greatest event he ever covered. While reflecting on that historic event a quarter century later, he singled out a certain sportswriter from Chicago. "The media had a section in the stands," Mr. Mizell told his *Tampa Bay Times* colleague Dave Scheiber. "We're all schooled to be neutral observers. But David Israel . . . stood up in his seat, put his back to the rink, faced us all in press row and said, 'Gentlemen, there will be cheering in the press box.' And there was. It was just amazing."

Clearly, Israel's unabashed approach to writing was sometimes evident in his approach to life. On this Opening Day, we would witness it firsthand. Thanks to the prominent photo that accompanied his work in the *Tribune*, Israel had an unmistakable look that included a ginormous crop of dark hair. Imagine our shock when he and some friends filed into the row directly in front of ours along the third-base line.

Following a patriotic pregame ceremony and national anthem, the flag-waving fans took their seats while White Sox starter Ross Baumgarten took the mound. Brewers leadoff hitter and future Hall of Famer Paul Molitor took the first pitch for a ball. Without a moment of hesitation, Israel rose from his seat, faced the pitcher's mound, and yelled,

"Throw a strike, you bum!"

Love this guy! This was *our* "Olympic moment." While it paled by comparison to the historic events in Lake Placid, or the global significance of the next Olympics chapter of David's life, it was memorable for us, even decades later.

For the record, Molitor singled but Milwaukee did not score until the fifth. The "bum" Baumgarten threw plenty of strikes the rest of the afternoon, pitching into the ninth to earn the win.

Nearly 40 years later I reconnected with Israel, thanks to the wonders of social media. David shared what details he could remember of this Opening Day (Craig and I were not among them!), his friendship with Baumgarten, and the next "Olympic moment" of *his* life that would play out in 1984.

Opening Day 1981, it turns out, was Israel's farewell to Chicago. He would soon leave for Los Angeles where he would write a cityside column for the *Los Angeles Herald Examiner* while beginning a career in Hollywood. Accompanying him to those seats at Comiskey Park that day was, among others, *Chicago Tribune* Sports Editor George Langford. "Neither Langford nor I were used to sitting in the stands," he recalled, "so it was kind of a novel experience."

The heckling of Baumgarten was more good-natured than it appeared. "Ross, actually, was a friend," he shared in an email. "And later his brother Craig was involved in my career in Hollywood."

"I remember nothing about the game," Israel admitted. "It led to a long night at The Palm afterwards." This might have been influenced by enthusiastic beer vendors at Comiskey or attentive bartenders at the high-end Chicago restaurant. That "long night" was hosted by his good friend Bill Veeck, who less than three months earlier had sold the White Sox to Einhorn and Reinsdorf for $20 million.

David's memory of his next "Olympic moment," however, is crystal clear. It came in 1984 when he was serving as chief of staff to Peter Ueberroth, President of the Los Angeles Olympic Organizing Committee and future commissioner of Major League Baseball. Israel described it as ". . . the only thing remotely resembling a real job I have ever had in my life."

Months after the US humiliated the Soviets in Lake Placid, President Jimmy Carter elected to boycott the 1980 Summer Olympics in Moscow in response to the Soviet invasion of Afghanistan. Four years later there were rumors the Russians would retaliate and influence other communist nations to do the same by boycotting the 1984 Summer Olympics in Los Angeles. On the morning of May 8, Israel and Ueberroth were at the United Nations in New York for the beginning of the cross-country Olympic torch relay when they learned the Russians weren't coming.

"Peter Ueberroth immediately did two things," Israel recalled. "He contacted the White House and he called the office to have them book a private jet to fly us from LaGuardia to National Airport in DC as soon as possible.

"That afternoon Peter met with President Reagan, and I met with Mike Deaver and Bill Sittmann, deputy chief of staff and assistant chief of staff to the President, respectively.

"Thus was hatched a plan to keep as many of the Soviet satellites in the games as possible. Soon thereafter, Ueberroth and I went to Cuba to meet with (President Fidel) Castro and his principal deputies to no avail. But other trips were more successful. Romania and Yugoslavia both participated. So did China. Communist countries that were energy independent and did not rely on the Soviet Union for financial assistance participated.

"It worked out for them. Romania won 53 medals, China 32, and Yugoslavia 18. In total they won 42 golds."

It worked out for the USA, as well. The Americans racked up a total 174 medals, 83 of them gold. The general reaction of the American people to the Soviets?

"Go ahead and strike, you bums!"

 For box scores, play-by-play and more, visit www.OpeningDay5050.com or use this QR code

1981-R

Swing and a Miss, Strike 2!

The Game

Who:	Chicago White Sox 3, New York Yankees 1 (8 innings)
Where:	Comiskey Park, Chicago, IL
Attendance:	30,787
When:	Wednesday, August 26, 1981
Weather:	Rain, lots of rain

Hall of Famers: White Sox manager Tony La Russa and C Carlton Fisk, Yankees OFs Dave Winfield and Reggie Jackson and coach Yogi Berra

Special Recognition: Comiskey Park organist Nancy Faust, not yet enshrined in baseball's Hall of Fame but in 2018 inducted into the Shrine of the Eternals, Baseball Reliquary's "alternate Hall of Fame" which honors special individuals who have altered the baseball world in ways that supersede statistics. Her "play" this night was epic!

Game Highlights: It had many of the traditional trappings of Opening Day. Comiskey Park hadn't seen a real Major League Baseball game in months, the weather was shaky, and a large crowd of well-lubricated, baseball-starved fans was on hand for the first home game of the season (actually, the first home game of the second half of the strike-interrupted season). Organist Nancy Faust kept fans engaged and entertained through two rain delays (47 minutes before the game started and another 20 after the seventh inning) as beer vendors did a robust business. She only scratched the surface of her vast repertoire of polkas, sixties classics and more, including fan favorite "Runaround Sue." Each time the grounds crew covered or uncovered the infield, fans were dancing in the aisles to "Roll Out the Barrel." After Greg Luzinski's decisive three-run homer in the bottom of the eighth, Yankee manager Gene Michael replaced pitcher Ron Davis. Nancy led the farewell serenade for the 27-year-old reliever with her signature "Na Na Hey Hey Kiss Him Goodbye," the taunting walk-off music Faust made famous. Two batters later the heavens opened again and the game was called. Sox win!

The Story

The pandemic-shortened 2020 season was not the first time baseball had to get creative with its playoff format to deal with a significantly truncated season. In 1981, for the second time in less than a decade, baseball players went out on strike. From their brief 1972 strike, the players won the right to arbitration, a right they later parlayed into free agency. This time there were no winners. The midsummer work stoppage cost each team more than 50 regular-season games, resulted in split season champions for each division, and left no one happy, especially the fans. The 51-day midseason strike in 1981 wiped out more than 700 games and accomplished nothing material for either side.

From the time Curt Flood cast the first stone in late 1969, Players Association Executive Director Marvin Miller had masterfully played the owners, step by step. In Flood, he had someone to light the fuse, but Flood was all alone. In Ken Burns's 1995 PBS documentary *Baseball*, Flood reflected on his lonely journey. "My colleagues didn't stand up with me. If the superstars had stood up and said, 'We're with Curt Flood,' I think that the owners would have gotten the message very clearly."

In 1972, perhaps inspired by Flood, the game's biggest superstar, Reggie Jackson, implored his fellow players to take a stand. As a result of the brief strike that delayed the start of the 1972 season, Miller secured the first of two things he needed to overturn the reserve clause with respect to labor matters: binding arbitration. Three years later he got the second: a test case with McNally and Messersmith (see Chapter 1973). Arbitrator Peter Seitz warned the owners to come up with a more equitable approach. When they refused, he ruled in late 1975 in favor of the players, effectively ending the reserve system. Seitz later opined, "The owners were too stubborn and stupid. They were like the French barons of the 12th century. They had accumulated so much power, they wouldn't share it with anybody."

Their stubbornness and stupidity reached new levels in the summer of 1981, still failing to grasp the power shift that was happening within baseball. They continued to underestimate the players' resolve. The central issue was the compensation a team would receive if they lost a free agent to another team. The owners wanted the right to pick whomever they wanted from the invading team. The unified players favored a system that would instead create a pool of players from all the clubs from which the invaded team could pick a player to restock their roster with another major leaguer.

On July 31, they settled their differences by agreeing to a proposal quite similar to what the players had put forth in early June. So contentious were the talks that the parties declined the customary handshake photo when it was over. The owners' attempt to break the union had failed. Play resumed August 10 with some teams not playing their first home game until the end of the month.

The timing of the settlement was not coincidental. From the outset it was clear to many that the owners were trying to break the players' union by "starving them out" for a couple of months without pay while the owners enjoyed well-planned financial protections. On the day the strike began, 24-year-old sportswriter Tim Kurkjian of the *Washington Star* foretold the owners' union-busting strategy. "The owners feel they're better prepared for a strike this time," Kurkjian reported. "They will reach into an $11 million 'financial assistance fund' that should bring them through the first two weeks of a strike and then begin to collect from a $50 million strike insurance fund that will begin paying off each club $100,000 a day for each game missed effective June 24."

Later interviewed for MLB Productions's 1981 episode of the series, *Baseball's Seasons*, pitcher and player rep Jim Kaat explained he tried to warn Commissioner Bowie Kuhn, with whom he had a close relationship at the time. "I told him, 'Bowie, the players are not going to give in. You might as well appeal to the owners, and let's get this thing settled for the good of the fans.' Of course, that fell on deaf ears."

Kaat, who spent more than 20 years as a major-league player, and many subsequent years as a broadcaster, added sarcastically, "Ironically, the owners had 51 days of strike insurance and that's when the strike ends. It was something that never should have happened."

For box scores, play-by-play and more, visit www.OpeningDay5050.com or use this QR code

1982

Harry's Wrigley Debut

The Game

Who: Chicago Cubs 5, New York Mets 0
Where: Wrigley Field, Chicago, IL
Attendance: 26,712
When: Friday, April 9, 1982
Weather: Brutal! Cold and rainy

Hall of Famers: Cubs P Ferguson Jenkins, P Lee Smith, 3B Ryne Sandberg, and coach Billy Williams

---

Game Highlights: An April snowstorm had barreled through Chicago earlier in the week, canceling the southside White Sox's first two games of the season on Tuesday and Thursday. With plenty of snow (ripe for snowballs!) in the stands, but the field clear to play (except when littered with said snowballs), the northside Cubs opted to tough it out on Friday, despite the incredible cold (34 degrees at game time) and drizzle. Many stayed home and others enjoyed the atmosphere for about an inning before heading home. The hardiest among them saw two future Hall of Fame pitchers, Fergie Jenkins and Lee Smith, shut out the hapless Mets. Those who stayed might not have done so for the baseball, but rather the Wrigley Field debut of someone Cubs fans would cherish for 16 seasons: Harry Caray and his rendition of "Take Me Out to the Ballgame" during the seventh-inning stretch.

The Story

By senior year of college, the Chicago White Sox were firmly entrenched as my favorite team. A few one-time Washington Senators were still active around the majors, but I had moved on (although seeing my idol Frank Howard coaching third this day for the Mets did warm my heart!). That connection three years earlier on Opening Day 1979 to Harry Caray was more about having a good time at the ballpark. Since the White Sox 1982 season-opening series earlier in the week was wiped out by snow, and classes at Notre Dame were canceled for the Easter weekend, the possibility of following Harry uptown presented itself. I asked Craig if he wanted to go see Harry at Wrigley. The answer was a resounding, "Hell no!" Craig's loyalty to the White Sox was much more mature than mine. I did not fully appreciate the need to choose sides in the Windy City's civil war—north or south.

Breaking local protocol to follow Harry, I recruited David Dziedzic, another Chicago native and coworker at *The Observer* and WSND, for a trip to Wrigley Field. Just as loyal as Craig was to his White Sox, David was to his Cubbies. And yet I brought to the ballpark that day a new treat for David: Harry Caray. David had the courage to pursue a post-college career in baseball. He was instrumental in developing the earliest MLB All-Star Fanfest in the early '90s and spent time working for the Texas Rangers during George W. Bush's time as managing general partner.

Thanks in large measure to Harry's unprecedented exposure on national cable superstation WGN, a younger generation of baseball fans across the country, even some in Chicago, perceived incorrectly that the heavens opened one spring day in 1982 and Harry Caray descended on a cloud with a microphone and a clever idea to start a new ballpark tradition by singing "Take Me Out to the Ballgame" during the seventh-inning stretch. The true story is better.

By the time Harry completed his 11th and final season with the White Sox in 1981, the 68-year-old already had been broadcasting baseball for more than 35 years, including 23 with the St. Louis Cardinals. In the 1950s he could be heard calling Cardinals games well beyond St. Louis on powerful KMOX radio. For decades, in everyday conversations, fans throughout the Midwest might fall into Harry impersonations, intoning his signature line of "Holy Cow!" or reciting his home run call of "It might be . . . It could be . . . It is!"

The iconic song that helped embellish his brand dates back to the earliest part of the 20th century and has been sung at baseball games for decades. But not like this.

The idea of singing with the fans was not Harry's, and initially he was not pleased when it happened for the first time without his knowledge. Bill Veeck took ownership of the White Sox in 1975 and continued his decades-long search for the right person to lead fans in this game day ritual. One night he noticed Harry singing the song. The next night Veeck secretly installed a stadium microphone in the radio booth so all could hear, much to Harry's surprise. In April 1996 Harry opened up to Nancy Gay of the *San Francisco Chronicle* about that night.

"When the game was over, I walked up to Veeck and said, 'What the hell was that all about?' He said, 'Harry, I've been looking for 45 years for the right man to do this, sing this song.' I began to puff up with flattery. 'Yes,' he said, 'everybody, no matter where they were sitting, as soon as they heard you, they knew they could sing better than you, so they'd join in.'"

Countless books and articles have been written over the years about the career and antics of Harry Caray as well as his broadcaster son and grandson, Skip and Chip. He empowered generations of baseball fans to stand up at the "old ball game" and "root, root, root" for their home team, knowing that if they didn't win, they'd sing again tomorrow, just as off-key as Harry.

For box scores, play-by-play and more, visit www.OpeningDay5050.com or use this QR code

1983

The Voice of Opening Days and Presidents, Charlie Brotman

The Game

Who:	Kansas City Royals 7, Baltimore Orioles 2
Where:	Memorial Stadium, Baltimore, MD
Attendance:	51,889
When:	Monday, April 4, 1983
Weather:	Sunny and 60s

Hall of Famers: Orioles 1B Eddie Murray, SS Cal Ripken Jr., Royals 3B George Brett

Game Highlights: Baltimore fans warmly welcomed new manager Joe Altobelli, but his team fell flat in front of the second largest baseball crowd ever at Memorial Stadium. While his predecessor Earl Weaver played golf that morning in Florida, Joe began his Opening Day with Bryant Gumbel on NBC's *Today Show* and ended it promising more wins in the future. He was right. The 1983 Orioles would go on to win the AL East, beat the AL West champion Chicago White Sox in the ALCS, and beat the Philadelphia Phillies in the World Series. The 1982 AL Rookie of the Year Cal Ripken Jr. started his 141st consecutive game on Opening Day 1983 and notched the first of 102 runs he would drive in over the course of this MVP season. For Kansas City, future Hall of Fame third baseman George Brett homered and scored three times for the winning Royals.

The Story

For most 22-year-old men in their first job out of college, taking off work for Opening Day 1983 might seem unlikely. But I had the privilege of being an overworked, underpaid disciple of legendary DC sports and entertainment publicist, Charlie Brotman.

Three years earlier I was offered an unpaid summer internship at Charles J. Brotman & Associates. I pounced! The opportunity to learn from a master like Charlie was like no other, and I loved every minute of the work in his cozy little sweatshop in the summer of 1980. Among other things, I got to work the press room at major events like the PGA TOUR's stop at Congressional Country Club (Kemper Open) and the Volvo Grand Prix men's tennis event at the Rock Creek Tennis Stadium (Washington Star International). I returned for a few weeks in June 1981 to work at the Kemper, but this time I told Charlie I'd need to make a few dollars (very few, as Charlie was notoriously frugal), and he agreed. When I graduated from Notre Dame in May 1982, a job was waiting for me.

Charlie had been the public address announcer and promotions director for the first iteration of the Washington Senators (1956–60). When the team moved to Minnesota, they asked him to come along but he declined, opting instead to open his own small public relations firm. He continued to handle the public address announcing on Opening Day for the new Washington Senators, first at old Griffith Stadium in 1961, and then at the new DC Stadium (renamed Robert F. Kennedy Stadium in 1969). He would play a similar role for the Nationals when Major League Baseball returned to Washington in 2005.

Charlie's first Opening Day at the mic led to another unexpected announcing job, one that would last more than seven decades. On April 17, 1956, President Dwight D. Eisenhower was at the Presidential Opener to throw out the season's ceremonial first pitch. It was also Brotman's first game at the Griffith Stadium microphone, so it fell to him to introduce the President to the friendly, capacity crowd of nearly 28,000. The 28-year-old must have made quite an impression. After Eisenhower won re-election in November, a White House staffer called. Charlie recounted the conversation decades later.

"The President has been looking for you. He'd like you to introduce him again." Humbled, I said, "Well just tell me when and where." The lady said, "January 20, 1957."

Brotman knew the significance of the date. For the second time, the diminutive DC native would be handling the announcing duties for the Presidential inaugural. Eight years earlier he was selected by Harry Truman's 1949 inaugural organizers as a student from the National Academy of Broadcasting to broadcast the first-ever-televised inaugural ceremony.

The 1956 Opening Day encounter with Ike set in motion a string of consecutive quadrennial assignments for the bipartisan Brotman that would span 72 years and 12 US Presidents, from Truman through Biden.

Charlie never met a microphone he didn't like. As public address announcer for the Senators, he earned an uncredited cameo in the 1958 baseball movie *Damn Yankees*. In addition to baseball and inaugurals, Brotman also could be heard over the stadium sound systems at various tennis venues, from Madison Square Garden in New York to DC's Rock Creek Tennis Stadium.

In the early '80s, the professional tennis complex in Rock Creek Park was little more than a collection of portable bleachers, trailers, tents, a muddy parking field, and a rickety scaffolding that supported the press box, the perch from which Charlie would introduce the players and make other public service announcements.

Now a seasoned announcer, Charlie would spread his wings on occasion. Over the course of a summer afternoon, he'd make a dozen or more requests for tennis fans to move their cars. "Your attention please. Would the owner of a blue Volvo with Virginia license plate B2R 6G2 please move your vehicle. Your car is blocking the driveway." They became routine. Then late in the day Charlie would check to see if fans were still paying attention.

"Your attention please. Would the owner of a green Honda Civic with Maryland license plate V7R 6W3 Y9L 5R2 R7M 1P3 J9D please move your vehicle. Your *license plate* is blocking the driveway."

A few would chuckle. By the third or fourth day of the tournament, the regulars would eagerly await the day's expected "dad joke" while the first-time attendees would groan.

During the January Volvo Grand Prix Masters at Madison Square Garden, well-heeled tennis fans sitting in front row seats above the baselines routinely draped their winter coats over the railing. It was distracting for players at the opposite end of the court. Charlie had a unique way of solving the problem.

"Your attention please. Would the spectators sitting in the front row please remove your clothes ..."

[Long pause. Very long pause.]

"... from the railing."

And then the signature close that caught Eisenhower's attention and was so familiar to Senators fans at old Griffith Stadium: "THANK youuuuu."

By Opening Day 1983 Charlie had no current business relationship with the Orioles but was well connected. Like me, he longed for the day baseball would return to the nation's capital. Baltimore partially filled the void while we waited. Orioles public relations director Bob Brown tapped Charlie to help out on Opening Day due to the influx of national media. Things were reasonably quiet at CJB & Associates. Our best-known client at the time, boxer Sugar Ray Leonard, had retired, or so we thought, at a star-studded charity event we staged in Baltimore five months earlier. The Washington Federals of the short-lived United States Football League (the original USFL lasted three seasons) were five games into their inaugural campaign, and the Kemper Open was still seven weeks away. Since Charlie would be at Memorial Stadium, I had no problem getting the afternoon off from work. Due to my four-year Opening Day detour through ballparks in Chicago, it had been a while since Roundy and I had been to Memorial Stadium. We were still able to figure out how to get there.

As the game dragged on, there was only one thing keeping us at Memorial Stadium. After the Royals went up 6–2 in the seventh, I suspect Roundy was ready to go. I probably urged him to stay a few more minutes. "We can go after 'Country Boy.'" Instead, the Orioles unveiled a new stretch song ("That Magic Feeling") that went over like a lead balloon. After a cascade of boos, they brought back "Country Boy" an inning later. It was too late. We were already in the car. (More on "Country Boy" in Chapter 1994.)

Six months later I was sitting in my office late one Tuesday when Charlie called from Game One of the World Series.

"How quickly can you get to Memorial Stadium?" he asked.

"With traffic, probably an hour and a half, boss. Why?"

"They need an extra sound system for the postgame press conference," he explained calmly. "I need you to get the P.A. system out of my closet and get up here fast. There will be a parking and press pass waiting for you."

I don't remember the drive, and didn't see the game, but I distinctly remember meeting an Oriole legend that night, Charlie's pal and Memorial Stadium public address announcer Rex Barney. Rex had pitched for the Brooklyn Dodgers in the late 1940s, including four seasons with Jackie Robinson. I would later work with Rex at Home Team Sports. But tonight I was awed to meet Mr. Barney, the man whose voice and two signature lines were well known. Ever since he began as the Orioles public address announcer in 1974, whenever any spectator caught a foul ball, he would instruct the ushers to "Give that fan a contract!"

His other signature line? I think Rex might have borrowed it from his friend Charlie.

"THANK youuuu!"

For box scores, play-by-play and more, visit www.OpeningDay5050.com or use this QR code

1984

The "Mourning" After, a Banner Day on TV

The Game

Who:	Chicago White Sox 5, Baltimore Orioles 2
Where:	Memorial Stadium, Baltimore, MD
Attendance:	51,333
When:	Monday, April 2, 1984
Weather:	Sunny and 60s

Hall of Famers: Orioles 1B Eddie Murray, SS Cal Ripken Jr., White Sox C Carlton Fisk, P Tom Seaver, and OF Harold Baines

Game Highlights: In an Opening Day rematch of the previous year's American League Championship Series, the Chicago White Sox grabbed a small bit of revenge, routing the Orioles on a day that was otherwise picture perfect for the 1983 World Series champions. Cal Ripken Jr. homered in the first and Eddie Murray drove in another in the eighth, but that's all the scoring the Birds could muster against 1983 Cy Young Award winner LaMarr Hoyt and reliever Britt Burns. After a substantial career as a starting pitcher, Burns moved to the bullpen to start the 1984 campaign to make room in the starting rotation for Tom Seaver. Seaver had joined the team when the White Sox plucked the future Hall of Famer from MLB's free agent player compensation pool. He had been left unprotected by the New York Mets. Chicago had lost journeyman pitcher Dennis Lamp in free agency to the Toronto Blue Jays, and Seaver was a "make good." Clearly, the system was still broken.

The Story

The list of historically significant events all packed into one week—both to local sports fans and to me personally—make this year's Opening Day story draining, exhilarating, nostalgic, and exhausting. Consider that on April 2, 1984:

+ Baltimore sports fans were angry, mourning the loss of their football team. The Colts had bolted to Indianapolis just a few days earlier.

+ At the opposite end of the emotional spectrum, jubilant baseball fans would officially celebrate the Orioles's 1983 World Series championship with the raising of their third championship banner at Memorial Stadium in just 18 years with the President of the United States throwing out the ceremonial first pitch.

+ Today's game would be televised live on local, over-the-air television (WMAR Channel 2) for the first time in team history.

+ Two days later, a new cable TV channel—Home Team Sports, The Channel You Cheer For—would usher in a new era in televised sports. Fans would be able to watch most of their team's home games on TV. Similar cable channels were launching in other markets around the country.

+ Oh yes, and during the offseason, I got married, changed jobs, and changed my allegiance from the Chicago White Sox to the (unthinkable) Baltimore Orioles. I now worked for Home Team Sports (HTS).

It was a helluva year! Let's take them one at a time.

On Friday, March 30, 1984, I was sitting in my little cubicle in the HTS offices in downtown Washington, DC. Jody Shapiro, Director of Programming came over from his office with a somber look.

"This Baltimore Colts thing . . . it's a problem for us," he reported. "A big problem. You need to fix it."

Our little cable channel wasn't even on the air yet. A group of about 20 of us had been working around the clock for months, planning our debut set for next Wednesday afternoon. We'd be televising the second game of the Orioles season plus that night's Washington Capitals hockey playoff game. Having lost a team of my own 13 years earlier, my heart went out to Baltimore football fans. We'd read about the 14 Mayflower moving trucks that arrived less than 48 hours earlier on Wednesday night and early Thursday morning at the Colts training complex in Owings Mills. They packed up quickly, then scattered on their way to Indianapolis. But I didn't immediately grasp why this was a problem for HTS.

"We need a new photo for the set, and we need it right away," Jody fretted.

I was the public relations manager, the guy with the pictures. For tasks like this, in those days, we needed a color slide and had only a precious few. Jody was worried about the larger-than-life backlit letters H T S: the centerpiece of the humble set that would appear on live TV in just five days. The three-letter photo collage hung on the back wall between two comfy chairs. At the top of the letter "T" was a game photo capturing the intensity of offensive line play: the Colts's offensive line. Jody couldn't allow us to sign on the air with an image that might be perceived as taunting angry Baltimore fans. We scrambled, purchased a replacement slide, and fixed it.

Like the Senators, the Colts had a universally disliked owner, Bob Irsay, who'd rudely challenged fans, media, and elected officials to support his failing franchise *or else!* Attendance had dwindled, averaging a little more than 38,000 in 1983. Only 20,418 showed up for what turned out to be their final game at Memorial Stadium, a win over the Houston Oilers. Ironically, the Oilers fled Houston for Tennessee 14 years later. Like Short, Irsay dangled his franchise in front of multiple cities, looking for a better deal, infuriating loyal locals.

At least I had a chance to say goodbye to my team that raucous night in 1971. Colts fans never had the opportunity. Once Maryland Governor Harry Hughes signed legislation giving the government the right to seize the franchise through eminent domain, Irsay took swift action. Within hours, the Colts had packed their bags and left town.

The city licked its wounds over the weekend. When the sun rose Monday morning, the city enjoyed a day-long celebration of their latest championship. More than twice as many fans packed Memorial Stadium as had been there less than four months earlier for the Colts's finale. The Opening Day crowd looked skyward, not for a plane buzzing the upper deck (as had happened only a few years earlier following a Colts game), but for the Oriole Bird, parachuting onto the field with a special delivery. The mascot handed the game ball to President Ronald Reagan who then threw a strike to 1983 World Series MVP Rick Dempsey. Accompanied by Orioles legend Brooks Robinson and manager Joe Altobelli, Dempsey proudly marched to center field where the trio hoisted the World Series Champion banner. Commissioner Bowie Kuhn then handed out the championship rings.

For a time, it seemed no one was thinking about the Colts.

Perhaps it was fitting that a movie-star-turned-politician, running for re-election, would grab the pregame spotlight prior to a home game on live local TV, something that had never happened before. At the time, team owners feared that home games on TV would hurt gate receipts. Conventional wisdom suggested that if home games were on TV, no one would buy tickets. That was about to change.

This Opening Day was available to all on free TV, and as Bill Carter reported in that morning's *Baltimore Sun*, HTS would televise another 56 home games as part of its 90-game package. Few homes had cable TV at the time (including exactly no one in Baltimore City). Those who had cable had to pay an additional $15 or so per month for the HTS channel, so the theoretical impact on ticket sales in 1984 was minimal.

It was a whirlwind week of change. The change for Colts fans was heartbreaking. Orioles fans would enjoy their team in a whole new way on TV. Things were changing for me as well. Just six months earlier I was excited to experience playoff baseball for the first time. It was a memorable October night in Baltimore with my then-fiancée Kate DeMarco. After *my* heavily favored White Sox took Game One (their only win of the 1983 ALCS), Kate and I returned to my car, safely parked in a residential neighborhood nearby. My Chevy Chevette had been vandalized: the back window smashed with a rock.

It was an omen. Perhaps the baseball gods had shattered the lens through which I had seen Baltimore all those years. The best view of Baltimore, or so I thought, was through the rearview mirror. That was about to change *radically*. Unbeknownst to me in October, a seismic shift in my loyalty was coming, akin to Babe Ruth moving from the Red Sox to the Yankees. A month later while on our honeymoon, I accepted the job at Home Team Sports (HTS is now NBC Sports Washington). I remember telling my parents I was leaving Charlie Brotman to go work for HTS, a startup cable TV channel. They thought I was crazy. For years when friends asked where Michael was working, their response was something like, "That cable thing!"

By Opening Day, this Orioles-hating Senators fan who followed his team to Texas only to fall in love with the Chicago White Sox was now a fan of the Baltimore Orioles.

It's funny how a team's contribution to a newlywed's livelihood can shift that allegiance overnight.

For box scores, play-by-play and more, visit www.OpeningDay5050.com or use this QR code

1985

Fatherhood

The Game

Who:	Baltimore Orioles 4, Texas Rangers 2
Where:	Memorial Stadium, Baltimore, MD
Attendance:	50,402
When:	Monday, April 8, 1985
Weather:	40s, windy and snowing at game time (this was Baltimore, not Chicago!)

Hall of Famers: Orioles 1B Eddie Murray and SS Cal Ripken Jr.

Game Highlights: Eight years earlier when these same two teams met on Opening Day, I proudly hung my Go Senators! banner. On this day when one of the last still-active Washington Senators, 36-year-old Toby Harrah, led off for the Rangers, I barely noticed. I needed these Orioles to win so HTS could thrive.

Baltimore scored four runs on only two hits, including a decisive two-run homer in the eighth by Eddie Murray. The Birds were aided by 10 walks, eight off Rangers starter Charlie Hough. The 37-year-old knuckleball specialist would start on Opening Day again in 1993, the first game ever for the expansion Florida (now Miami) Marlins. He completed a 25-year career and retired following the 1994 season, just shy of his 47th birthday, having given up 1,665 walks to rank eighth all time. He also holds the distinction of being one of only two players (Goose Gossage is the other) whose career spanned all eight work stoppages. He was in his third year with the LA Dodgers during the first strike in 1972 and started 21 games for the 1994 Florida Marlins before yet another labor dispute interrupted play for the eighth time. He never returned.

This would be Joe Altobelli's third, and final, Opening Day as Baltimore manager, less than two years after winning the 1983 World Series. The Orioles fired him in June. Ironically, Altobelli was fired by the San Francisco Giants late in the 1979 season, just a year after being named National League Manager of the Year. "Hey Joe, what have you done for us lately?"

The Story

On Easter Sunday afternoon, I was sitting in a hospital room holding my three-day-old, firstborn son, Bradley. On the TV was a game between the Houston Gamblers (star quarterback was Jim Kelly) and Donald Trump's New Jersey Generals (star quarterback Doug Flutie and running back Herschel Walker) of the short-lived United States Football League. It may sound like a stereotypical father-son football moment, but at the time, it was anything but that. Kate had been rolled back into surgery due to complications from Thursday morning's emergency C-section. All the worst thoughts of post-op problems were racing through my head. Once the doctor said the worst was over and she'd be fine, I invited her parents to come join us. They lived in Arlington, Virginia, only a few minutes away.

The furthest thing from my mind was tomorrow's Opening Day game in Baltimore and my 15-year Opening Day streak.

Let's go back three days. This was long before we used the term "paternity leave." Only recently had we emerged from the dark ages of the "father's waiting room" where anxious dads-to-be would first learn the gender of the child and the condition of the mother. The fact I was able to be in the delivery room during Thursday morning's delivery was a pretty big deal. However, Friday I was back at work while Kate's mom doted over her new grandson and daughter. Early April was the busiest time of year for HTS. Part of my job was to make sure the TV listings in the newspapers were accurate. The schedules for the next several days were uniquely complex with the Orioles, NHL Washington Capitals, and NBA Washington Bullets all playing during the same week. We had only one channel, so the games we didn't televise would be on free TV.

I was working in our downtown office at the shared word processor when the phone rang. It was Kate.

"What's wrong?" I asked.

"It's the nurses," she explained. "They're trying to get me! You need to come back."

As I quickly saved my work on a floppy disk, she continued.

"I think they're under the bed!"

I asked if her mom was there. Patricia DeMarco took the phone.

"She's fine," Pat said calmly. "I think it's her medication. For pain they gave her something called Percocet."

I was relieved to know they hadn't started filming a scene for a horror movie in my wife's hospital room.

While the effects of the Percocet subsided over the weekend, her discomfort did not, necessitating the successful follow-up procedure Sunday afternoon. Spending the weekend with my wife and newborn son was an anxiety-filled joy. Changing my first diaper with my mother-in-law looking over my shoulder? Not so much. Sunday night Pat insisted she had everything under control and that I should plan to go home, get some rest, and go to the office Monday morning. She'd heard me and Kate express concerns in recent weeks about the future of HTS. Other similar startups around the country were shutting down, and we feared we might be next. Pat thought it best for me to be at work. Pat also had a special place in her heart for baseball, having spent her entire life rooting for her Boston Red Sox.

Following my mother-in-law's orders, Monday morning, I went to work. Monday afternoon, I was at Opening Day.

For box scores, play-by-play and more, visit www.OpeningDay5050.com or use this QR code

1986

The Presidential Opener

The Game

Who:	Cleveland Indians 6, Baltimore Orioles 4
Where:	Memorial Stadium, Baltimore, MD
Attendance:	52,292
When:	Monday, April 7, 1986
Weather:	Perfect! Sunny and 70s

Hall of Famers: Orioles manager Earl Weaver, 1B Eddie Murray, and SS Cal Ripken Jr., Indians P Phil Niekro

Game Highlights: "Earl Weaver Tour of Duty II" left the Hall of Fame manager yearning to return to the golf course in Florida. The Earl of Baltimore took over for Joe Altobelli 58 games into the 1985 season, but the Orioles still finished 16 games behind the Toronto Blue Jays. The 1986 season got off to a bad start, and things went downhill from there. The Orioles would finish dead last in the American League East, and Earl would retire for good. On Opening Day, the lowly Indians roughed up 1979 Cy Young Award winner Mike Flanagan for five runs in just two innings before Weaver pulled him in the third.

The Story

President Ronald Reagan threw out the ceremonial first pitch on Opening Day 1986 in Baltimore, his second time in three years, seeming to resurrect a tradition started decades earlier by one of his predecessors, William Howard Taft. Reagan's pitch at Memorial Stadium generated more excitement than any thrown that afternoon by a major leaguer.

The Presidential Opener was once an annual tradition in Washington. Between 1910 and 1969, every President participated, throwing out the first pitch at the Senators Opening Day game 44 times over 60 years. When they didn't, they usually had a good excuse, like the sinking of the *Titanic*, World War II, or the passing of the President (Franklin Roosevelt died five days before the 1945 opener). I was introduced to Opening Day, in large part, because it was a monumental big deal, my dad's kind of event. The reason Roundy pulled me out of fourth grade lunch one day in April 1970 was because he expected President Nixon to be at the game. He'd thrown out the first pitch in 1969 and would do so later in 1970 at the All-Star Game in Cincinnati but was stuck at the office during both of my DC Openers (1970–71).

With no baseball in Washington after 1971, Presidents Reagan, George H. W. Bush, and Bill Clinton made the trek up I-95 to Baltimore for the first pitch ceremony twice each between 1984 and 1996. While their predecessors made ceremonial little tosses from the stands, Reagan was the first to do it from the field. Bush and Clinton went even further, throwing from the mound, as did their successors, George W. Bush and Barack Obama.

Here's a critique of each of the 18 pitching Presidents (13 righties, three lefties, and two ambidextrous (this describes the arm(s) with which they threw, not their political leaning)). I ranked those I saw in person, and opine about those we can all see on YouTube.

Ones I saw in person:

No. 1 – George W. Bush (RHP). I saw "W" do it twice. Opening Day 2005 at RFK Stadium was the first-ever home game of the Washington Nationals, and the second term right-hander was in excellent form. A one-time managing general partner of the Texas Rangers (1989–98), Bush made a perfect toss from the mound to catcher Brian Schneider who was crouched behind the plate. He returned to the mound in Washington three years later to christen Nationals Park. Once again, respectfully clad in a home team Nationals jacket, he delivered a high strike to manager Manny Acta.

While these two were impressive, no ceremonial first pitch was as memorable as the one this President threw at Yankee Stadium to open the 2001 World Series, just seven weeks after the September 11 terrorist attacks. Writer Steve Wulf summarized its significance in his 2017 piece on Presidential first pitches for ESPN.com:

"It was by far the most nervous moment of my presidency," Bush said years later.

Wearing an FDNY jacket, he waved to the crowd as he strode to the mound. Once there, he gave a thumbs up, quickly went into his delivery and threw a perfect strike, with pace, to Yankees catcher Todd Greene.

"I wasn't supposed to be the catcher," Greene said. "It was Jorge Posada, but Roger Clemens took too long warming up in the bullpen, so they told me to grab my glove. I guess I have Rocket to thank. I caught the most important pitch a president has ever had to make."

As W walked off the mound, Greene and Bush exchanged compliments and public address announcer Bob Sheppard said in that godlike voice of his: "Thank you, Mr. President." And the crowd began to chant, "U-S-A, U-S-A."

Thank you, indeed.

"I still get tingly watching it," Greene said. "Any American old enough to understand the significance of that pitch has to feel the same way."

No. 2 – George H. W. Bush (LHP). Bush 43 got the nod over his dad, but Bush 41's love of the game was unrivaled. He captained the Yale baseball team in 1948 and kept his first baseman's mitt in his desk drawer in the Oval Office, oiled and ready for play each Opening Day of his presidency. I saw him throw to Mickey Tettleton at Memorial Stadium in 1989 and to Chris Hoiles at Oriole Park in 1992. In between, he pitched at Opening Days in Toronto (1990) and Texas (1991).

No. 3 – Bill Clinton (LHP). It took a lot of guts to go out there in front of more than 40,000 people at Oriole Park on Opening Day 1993 and 1996 with little baseball skill. The left-hander threw from the mound to Chris Hoiles crouched behind the plate. Clinton was the first President to respectfully wear the home team garb over his bulletproof vest. Although a bit awkward, the lefty got the ball to the catcher each time.

No. 4 – Ronald Reagan (RHP). The tradition of the Presidential Opener began in 1910, just a few months before the 40th President was born! At 73 years young, Reagan was the oldest first time Opening Day pitching President ever (by more than a decade) when he took the ball in 1984 from the Oriole Bird mascot, who had parachuted into center field in a scripted pregame ceremony befitting Reagan's Hollywood roots. Two years later, Reagan's arrival at Memorial Stadium after the national anthem was such a surprise that there was virtually no extra security on the field to control the paparazzi media mayhem. Reagan tried not to upstage the afternoon's scheduled first pitch star, 11-year-old cystic fibrosis patient Brian Gray. The President escorted young Brian from the dugout, nudging photographers out of the way while asking the young man how far away he wanted his battery mate, Orioles catcher Rick Dempsey. Brian threw a perfect strike. Mr. Reagan wasn't as sharp. The Commander in Chief directed Dempsey to move back, then threw the ball well over his catcher's head. The do-over was on target. While Reagan was the first President to venture from the seats to the field on Opening Day, his tosses to Dempsey were on the infield. In the final year of his presidency in one of the final games of the Chicago Cubs 1988 season, Reagan would launch an impressive toss from the mound at Wrigley Field to Cubs catcher Damon Berryhill, cheating to within about 40 feet of his 77-year-old pitcher.

No. 5 – **Barack Obama (LHP).** It was great to see the President celebrate the 100th anniversary of the first Presidential Opener by joining the festivities on Opening Day 2010 at Nationals Park. The lefty trotted onto the field appropriately clad in a home team Nationals jacket. When he arrived on the mound, however, he reached under his jacket and promptly placed a White Sox cap on his head, reconnecting his personal passion with Chicago's South Side. He was cascaded with boos from offended Nationals fans. Making matters worse, his toss sailed wildly high. Ryan Zimmerman's lunging stop saved the President any further embarrassment. A year earlier, Mr. Obama delivered a much more impressive pitch at the All-Star Game in St. Louis where his White Sox jacket blended in better at this annual fan melting pot.

No. 6 – **Gerald Ford (Ambidextrous).** I never saw Gerald Ford throw out a first pitch on Opening Day, but I did see his bilateral throws at the 1976 All-Star Game at Veterans Stadium in Philadelphia—one right-handed to National League catcher Johnny Bench and one left-handed to American League catcher Thurman Munson—a pair of little five-foot tosses from the first-base railing. Since it was an election year, the 38th President was working both sides of the aisle. Three months earlier, Ford made Opening Day in Arlington, Texas, a Presidential Opener. His pitch at the Rangers's first game of the season wasn't enough to sway the voters. Texas went with Jimmy Carter in November.

Ones we can all see on YouTube:

Jimmy Carter (RHP). Without a doubt, the best arm of the pitching Presidents! Nearly 15 years after leaving the White House, the 71-year-old former

President and former Georgia governor took the mound at Atlanta's Turner Field before Game Six of the 1995 World Series. He threw some serious heat to little-used utility player Mike Mordecai, causing NBC's Bob Costas to exclaim, "You know, if the ump wants to give him the high strike, that's right in there, and with some *hop* on it!" Carter never did the honors on Opening Day but took a lighthearted jab from Orioles catcher Rick Dempsey after the 39th President threw a perfect pitch prior to the final game of the 1979 World Series. "Next time," Dempsey said to the country's most famous Sunday school teacher, "get your ass here before Game Seven!" The Orioles lost the game and the Series to the Pirates.

Presidents Taft through Ford (1910–76) need to be judged differently. Their assignment was simply to stand at their seat and toss the ball. No pressure. Many videos from Senators home openers from the 1930s through the early 1960s show a scrum of players converging on the ball like a soccer team of five-year-olds. It resembled a newlywed tossing a bouquet or garter to an anxious horde of singles.

The other 11 fall into two groups: those who appear to have thrown a ball before and those who have not (or, at least, had not in a very long time). The *haves* and the *have nots*.

Haves – **Lyndon Johnson, John Kennedy, Dwight Eisenhower, Harry Truman,** and **Woodrow Wilson.**

Have Nots (embarrassing) – **Richard Nixon, Herbert Hoover, Calvin Coolidge, Warren Harding,** and **William Taft.**

Special call out – **Franklin Roosevelt** spent the entire 12-plus years of his presidency paralyzed from the waist down. While his condition was well known, those close to him, including the news media, protected his brand, rarely showing him in public in his wheelchair. He handled first pitch ceremonies eight times at Washington's Griffith Stadium. Aides would assist him to his feet, and he would stand at the railing and toss the ball to the adoring ballplayers below.

Epilogue

The Washington Nationals original "Racing Presidents" foursome has no connection to the Presidential Opener. All four larger-than-life Presidents (a.k.a. "The Rushmores") who participate during each game in this fan favorite "competition"—George, Tom, Abe, and Teddy (George Washington, Thomas Jefferson, Abraham Lincoln, and Theodore Roosevelt)—occupied the nation's highest office before the first Presidential Opener in 1910. Attempts by the Nationals to expand the cast included Presidential Opener notables Bill, Cal, and Herb (William Taft, Calvin Coolidge, and Herbert Hoover), but none caught on with crowds at Nationals Park and the trio has since retired to Florida where they can be seen at spring training games in West Palm Beach.

More on the Racing Presidents, especially Teddy, in Chapter 2012.

For box scores, play-by-play and more, visit www.OpeningDay5050.com or use this QR code

1987

Remembering Jackie Robinson, Kind Of...

The Game

Who:	Baltimore Orioles 2, Texas Rangers 1
Where:	Memorial Stadium, Baltimore, MD
Attendance:	51,650
When:	Monday, April 6, 1987
Weather:	Cloudy and 40s

Hall of Famers: Orioles 1B Eddie Murray and SS Cal Ripken Jr.

Game Highlights: It was a very unfamiliar feeling for Orioles fans: Opening Day after a losing season. It hadn't happened in almost 20 years, but after the previous year's last-place finish, there was only one way to go. In Cal Ripken Sr.'s managerial debut, his seemingly improved Birds sent the faithful home jubilant with a bottom-of-the-ninth, walk-off sacrifice fly by Larry Sheets, putting the Orioles in the win column. There wouldn't be enough of those wins the rest of the way, as the Orioles would finish six games worse than the year before. Texas scored their only run in the first, a home run off the bat of Rangers outfielder Oddibe McDowell. Or as ESPN's Chris Berman might have called it that night on *Sports Center*, "Oddibe 'Young Again' McDowell facing Orioles ace Mike Boddicker ... Back, back, back, back ... Gone!"

The Story

As part of Opening Day 1987 pregame activities at Memorial Stadium, four men walked out to second base for a special ceremony to honor Jackie Robinson on the 40th anniversary of his historic debut with the Brooklyn Dodgers in April 1947: Orioles first baseman Eddie Murray, Baltimore Mayor Clarence "Du" Burns (the first black mayor in the city's history), Memorial Stadium public address announcer Rex Barney (a teammate of Jackie's 1947–50), and Sam Lacy, sports editor of the *Baltimore Afro-American* newspaper since 1944. Mayor Burns planted a special commemorative second base bag inscribed with a large blue number "42," the number worn by Robinson throughout his 10-year career with the Dodgers.

Similar ceremonies were playing out across Major League Baseball this Opening Day. In Los Angeles, where Robinson's Dodgers never played, but where the storied franchise moved in 1958, his widow, Rachel, and daughter, Sharon, headlined the ceremony as one of his grandsons anchored the base.

In Baltimore, the gesture received little attention. There was no mention of the pregame activity in the next day's *Baltimore Sun.* In the newspaper's game day issue, a box of "Opening Day Facts and Figures" appeared next to Tim Kurkjian's season preview, including a single paragraph detailing the tribute. Dedicating second base to Robinson made sense. It was the position he played more than any other. It was also a base he stole more than 100 times during his too-brief career.

More than a decade later, Major League Baseball realized this kind of tribute wasn't enough. It was a nice start but was lost in the hoopla of Opening Day. It was clear the game, and the country, still had a long way to go, as painfully illustrated on national television that night by Los Angeles Dodgers executive, Al Campanis.

Several days earlier George Will had reached out to his ABC News colleague Ted Koppel with a suggestion. Will was a devoted baseball man and a respected contributor on the network's *This Week with David Brinkley* Sunday morning talking heads news program. After an unsuccessful attempt to convince the team at *This Week* to do a story on the Robinson anniversary, Will pitched the idea to Koppel for his award-winning *Nightline* program.

In a 2005 archived interview for the Television Academy Foundation, Koppel recalled the conversation. "George Will had called me up and said I can't get those people over at *This Week* to commemorate the occasion. Someone ought to and it's a good story. Why don't you do it? As my colleagues here know, I know nothing about baseball, but I was perfectly happy to do it. I saw it as an interesting story.

"We invited Al Campanis on because he and Jackie Robinson had, at one time in the 1940s, been roommates," Koppel continued. "Our assumption was that here was this white ballplayer who had been roommates with the first black ballplayer in the major leagues. They must have been pretty good friends, and that Al Campanis must be a pretty extraordinary guy also, because that took some guts back in those years when Jackie Robinson was routinely taunted and people were throwing trash at him, and his life was being routinely threatened. So to be his roommate took some courage."

It certainly had the potential to be interesting as Koppel had hoped. Surely the 70-year-old Dodgers executive would have some eye-opening stories about the racist attacks Robinson endured during those early years. Instead, it became one of the most talked about, cringeworthy segments in Koppel's 25 years hosting *Nightline*.

Campanis shared the split screen that night with noted sportswriter and author Roger Kahn. Koppel challenged both men with questions. After Kahn acknowledged that Robinson, who died in 1972, would be disappointed to know that in 1987 there were no black managers or general managers in Major League Baseball, Koppel turned to Campanis and asked, "Why?"

The courteous Campanis struggled with his answer. "Well, Mr. Koppel, there have been some black managers (author's note: there had been exactly two at that point, Frank Robinson and Larry Doby), but I really can't answer that question directly. The only thing I can say is you have to pay your dues when you become a manager. Generally, you have to go to the minor leagues. There's not very much pay involved. And some of the better-known black players have been able to get into other fields and make a pretty good living in that way."

At that point the interview started to go sideways for Campanis. Koppel pressed on, asking if prejudice was involved. "I don't think it's prejudice," Campanis responded. "I truly believe they may not have some of the necessities to be a field manager or perhaps a general manager."

Necessities?

After Koppel pointed out that the comment sounded like garbage, Campanis persisted.

"How many quarterbacks do you have? How many pitchers do you have that are black? Why are black people not good swimmers? Because they don't have the buoyancy."

Koppel snapped back, "It may just be that they don't have access to all the country clubs and the pools."

The Dodgers fired Campanis the next day.

"I later met Al Campanis and found him to be a decent man," Koppel recalled in 2005. "I think he was as much a victim of his own generation as anything else. Back in the 1940s or '50s for someone to have said something like that would not have been the subject of any criticism in any white audience. To say it in the mid-1980s was another thing altogether. He was just an old man who didn't realize that certain times had come, and certain times had gone, and that was not an appropriate thing for a vice president of the L.A. Dodgers to be saying."

Ignorance was not confined to older executives and fans. In his 1987 biography, *Jackie Robinson: A Life Remembered*, author Maury Allen quotes St. Louis Cardinals 25-year-old star outfielder and 1985 National League Rookie of the Year Vince Coleman as saying, "I don't know nothing about no Jackie Robinson."

Coleman was not alone. In 1989, *Sport* magazine interviewed several then-current black ballplayers. To some, Robinson was a heroic figure, just as he had been to Curt Flood some 20 years earlier. Too many weren't sure who Jackie was. Clearly, the game, and the country, had work to do. Eventually, the movement to honor Robinson got more traction. At first, certain players, then certain teams, and eventually all of baseball would honor him and reflect on the journey each April 15, Jackie Robinson Day. Every player would wear No. 42 on that day, and no one would wear it on any other day. As one player put it in the years leading up to the jersey retirement, "No one is really worthy to wear that number."

Vince Coleman would steal 752 bases during his 13-year major-league career, a league-leading 109 of them in 1987, most of which found him standing on second base. Putting Jackie's number 42 on that base in 1987 must not have made enough of an impression. Today, putting it on the back of every player in baseball one day a year has not brought down the curtain on racial prejudice, but it certainly has helped further enlighten a generation.

For box scores, play-by-play and more, visit www.OpeningDay5050.com
or use this QR code

1988

0–21

The Game

Who: Milwaukee Brewers 12, Baltimore Orioles 0
Where: Memorial Stadium, Baltimore, MD
Attendance: 52,395
When: Monday, April 4, 1988
Weather: Spectacular! Sunny and 70s

Hall of Famers: Orioles 1B Eddie Murray and SS Cal Ripken Jr., Brewers DH Paul Molitor and CF Robin Yount

---

Game Highlights: Just four years since they raised a World Series championship flag, the once-mighty Orioles continued their years-long slide this Opening Day in a game more indicative of what was to come than anyone realized. The team which had been to the World Series six times in 18 years was now coming off back-to-back losing seasons for the first time since 1960. Baltimore's offense could produce nothing against Brewers ace Teddy Higuera. When the Birds were in the field, they resembled the Bad News Bears. The defense committed two errors, and four Orioles pitchers gave up 16 hits, walked five batters, and hit two others, while the Brewers stole four bases off All-Star catcher Terry Kennedy.

The Story

For all but two of my 60-plus years, I have lived in the greater Washington-Baltimore area. In late 1986 I decided to accept a job at Vince McMahon's World Wrestling Federation (now World Wrestling Entertainment) in Stamford, Connecticut (perhaps the topic of another book someday, but I digress). Kate and I packed up our two little boys and moved north. While the job was relatively lucrative and the work entertaining, the pangs of home pulled on us throughout our 24 months in exile. It was painful to watch the Orioles slide, knowing the negative effects a losing team had on a fragile young business like Home Team Sports. I know what a strain it had to be on my former coworkers and friends as they tried to hold things together.

We became a two-car family in 1988, and frequently one or all four of us would drive up and down the East Coast for work, play, family or, yes, Opening Day. I hadn't burned any bridges when I left HTS after its first three years and was welcome at a variety of game day social events in 1987–88, a source of continuity that would lead to my return in 1989.

Opening Day 1988 was spectacular, perfect for a family outing. Kate and I unloaded the boys and our collapsible double stroller from the back of our 1986 Colt Vista wagon and made our way to Memorial Stadium's picnic area under the scoreboard in left-center field. We were HTS guests at an upbeat pregame bullpen party.

Baltimore Sun writer M. Dion Thompson described an experience that could have been any year, anywhere: "A festive atmosphere swirled outside the stadium: brass bands played show tunes; fans milled about in search of spare tickets; . . . Opening Day. The day of hope. The day when every team is equal. The day that, perhaps more than any other, signals that winter is finally gone and spring is finally here with all its sense of renewal and possibility."

The triviality of a couple of Orioles losing seasons, a front office shake-up, and a roster overhaul seemed so unimportant.

Then they played the game.

We didn't stay long. We couldn't let the kids watch this train wreck.

In the *Sun* the next day, columnist John Eisenberg concluded a sarcastic rant with a simple statement: "No, the Orioles are not as pitiful as they played yesterday."

He was wrong. This band of Birds was every bit as pitiful as they played on Opening Day. This was a team that was about to make history. The Orioles would not win a single game for more than three weeks. They lost their first 21 games, the longest season-opening losing streak in the history of the game. The previous record was 0–13 shared by the 1904 Washington Senators and the 1920 Detroit Tigers. For all the wrong reasons, interest in the 1988 Baltimore Orioles grew daily, first locally, then nationally. There would be time later to talk about the "Bash Brothers" in Oakland—Jose Canseco and Mark McGwire—and about National League MVP Kirk Gibson of the Los Angeles Dodgers, en route to his heroic walk-off home run in Game One of the World Series. But during April, there was only one story in Major League Baseball: the Baltimore Orioles.

After the first week (0–6), they fired manager Cal Ripken Sr., an emotional jolt for a team whose middle infield was anchored by his sons: Cal Jr. at shortstop and Bill at second base.

Over a five-and-a-half-year period, the Orioles managerial carousel saw the reins pass from Weaver to Altobelli back to Weaver to Ripken Sr. and now to Frank Robinson, a Hall of Fame player over 21 seasons including six in Baltimore, where he helped lead the Orioles to the World Series four times. In Robinson, owner Edward Bennett Williams and general manager Roland Hemond had an experienced, successful big-league manager (Cleveland 1975–77 and San Francisco 1981–84), so they moved him from the front office to the dugout to help stop the bleeding.

The losing continued. The media frenzy grew with every loss. On April 19 (0–12) local disc jockey Bob Rivers vowed to stay awake and on the air until the Orioles won a game. Rivers became a national media magnet, napping only while tunes were playing. His one-man Bird-a-thon lasted *11 days!!!*

The Orioles could not escape a single national network newscast or late-night comedy show. Robinson figured, "If you can't beat 'em, join 'em" during his April 21 (0–14) appearance on *CBS This Morning.* "The fans are really rooting for us. They're behind us. They're trying to get us out of this thing. They're doing everything that they can do. I just wish they could hit, pitch, and field, but they can't!"

On April 25 (0–18), President Ronald Reagan called Robinson to express his support. "He told me, 'I've been accused of being a jinx by coming on Opening Day, but you can't blame me for this one,'" Robinson said then. "He told me to win one for the Gipper."

Tim Kurkjian, the Orioles beat reporter at *The Sun* in 1988, tweeted in 2018, "This date 1988, the Orioles fall to 0–18. Next day, manager Frank Robinson confirms he received a call of support from President Reagan. 'Frank,' he said, 'I know what you're going through.' Frank respectfully responds, 'Mr. President, you have no idea what I'm going through.'"

Just 14 months after showcasing on a March 1987 cover, baseball's happy and proud first family—Cal Sr., Cal Jr., and Bill—*Sports Illustrated* brought a beleaguered Bill to the forefront once again. This time it was with eyes closed, elbows on knees, and the barrel of his bat pressed to his forehead. The headline: "0–18. The Agony of the Orioles."

Just after 11:00 p.m. eastern time on Friday, April 29, and after 258 sleepless hours, Rivers was able to go home and sleep. The streak was over. The Orioles ended it in grand fashion with homers by Eddie Murray and Cal Ripken. They clobbered 22-year-old starter Jack McDowell en route to a 9–0 victory. Baltimore's win at Chicago "improved" the Orioles's record to 1–21. Baseball's all-time record for consecutive losses (23 by the 1961 Philadelphia Phillies) remained intact.

There's always next year.

For box scores, play-by-play and more, visit www.OpeningDay5050.com or use this QR code

1989

What a Difference a Year Makes!

The Game

Who:	Baltimore Orioles 5, Boston Red Sox 4 (11 innings)
Where:	Memorial Stadium, Baltimore, MD
Attendance:	52,161
When:	Monday, April 3, 1989
Weather:	Great! Sunny and 60s

Hall of Famers: Orioles manager Frank Robinson and SS Cal Ripken Jr., Red Sox P Lee Smith, 3B Wade Boggs, and OF Jim Rice

Game Highlights: In spite of the fact the Orioles finished the 1988 season with the worst record in baseball, more than 52,000 showed up for Opening Day 1989. A year after the most humiliating, season-opening losing streak in baseball history, the Baltimore Orioles rewarded their loyal fans with a walk-off win over the defending AL East champions. The Orioles got to the game's best pitcher, Boston's Roger Clemens, for four runs in seven innings. Cal Ripken Jr.'s three-run homer in the sixth delivered most of Baltimore's runs, and rookie Craig Worthington delivered the walk-off single in the 11th. Reliever Brian Holton pitched four and a third innings to earn the win.

The Story

This was one of those "pinch myself" kind of days. In late 1988 I accepted a job back at the company I loved, Home Team Sports, in a more senior role than the one I'd left just two years earlier. As a member of the management team, I hoped to spend the next several years helping to grow the business. Here I was on Opening Day at 28 years of age, working for a cable network that televised Major League Baseball games, wearing a press pass I didn't deserve (I was not a member of the working press) that allowed me to roam just about anywhere I wanted to entertain VIP clients. I was in heaven!

There were only six sky boxes in Memorial Stadium, three on each side of the high home plate press box. Included in our parent company's multimillion-dollar deal with the team was the use of one of these boxes above the first-base dugout. You certainly wouldn't call it a suite or luxury box. It included three rows of four chairs and a small, well-stocked refrigerator just like the one I had in my college dorm room. The fridge in our box even had a baseball-sized dent in the door from a Lee Lacy foul ball in 1985.

I had roamed Memorial Stadium during my first tour of duty at HTS (1984–86), but today felt different. In 1984 I was too new an Orioles fan to appreciate the pregame World Series flag raising. After all, I had attended the 1983 ALCS, rooting for the other team! That Colts cloud hung over everything in '84, and we were scrambling to put a cable network on the air later that week. Even President Reagan made an early exit that day (as he did in '86) after his pregame appearance. By 1989 I was in a new job and had three kids. We had a new President who planned to stay for a while, and the Orioles had only one way to go in the standings—up!

Despite my powerful press pass, today there was only one thing keeping me from visiting the boxes on the third-base side and the seats beyond: the US Secret Service. I was awestruck, staring across the mezzanine level at Baseball Commissioner Bart Giamatti, his "guest" President George H. W. Bush, and the President's "wing men": Secretary of State Jim Baker, Defense Secretary Dick Cheney, and baseball legend Ted Williams. Williams had played 19 seasons for the Red Sox, managed the Washington Senators (1969–71), and was good friends with the President. Bush had thrown out the first pitch earlier to Orioles catcher Mickey Tettleton, believed to have been the first time a President had ever made such a ceremonial toss from the pitcher's mound.

President Jimmy Carter threw out the first pitch before the Orioles lost Game Seven of the 1979 World Series. And they lost both times when President

Reagan did the honors on Opening Day. Superstitious fans were anxious, knowing that when the Commander in Chief was in the house, their team was 0–3.

The congestion on the mezzanine level cleared out in the fifth inning as the President and his entourage left the building, leaving fans to focus on baseball for the rest of the afternoon. They were studying their new team that bore little resemblance to the one that had lost 107 games the year before. Minutes after the President departed, the crowd erupted as their superstar delivered. Cal Ripken Jr.'s three-run blast to right-center field put the Orioles ahead. The Red Sox quickly tied the score in the seventh, before the Orioles won in extra innings. After Tettleton touched home plate with the winning run, his teammates rushed the field and the fans celebrated. For the first time in 22 months, the Baltimore Orioles had a winning record. They were 1–0.

The win kicked off an improbable season that would have the Birds in playoff contention all the way until the season's second-to-last game. They finished 87–75, marking the fourth biggest one-year turnaround in baseball history.

They also had snapped the Presidential winless streak, causing some fans to wonder, "Could Bush maybe come back tomorrow?"

For box scores, play-by-play and more, visit www.OpeningDay5050.com or use this QR code

1990

Locked Out

The Game

Who:	Baltimore Orioles 4, Detroit Tigers 2
Where:	Memorial Stadium, Baltimore, MD
Attendance:	49,288
When:	Thursday, April 19, 1990
Weather:	Perfect! Sunny and 60s

Hall of Famers: Orioles manager Frank Robinson and SS Cal Ripken Jr., Tigers manager Sparky Anderson and SS Alan Trammell

Game Highlights: After playing their first eight games of the season on the road, the Orioles came home to a very warm welcome, especially for the starting pitcher. Maryland native Dave Johnson started this home opener and earned the win. On the opposite side of the box score, Tiger starter Kevin Ritz didn't make it out of the first inning. After just 34 pitches and a pair of bases-loaded walks, Detroit skipper Sparky Anderson had seen enough of this once-promising young right-hander. Over the course of the afternoon, the Orioles scored four runs on just seven hits (six of them singles) by taking advantage of four Detroit errors and eight walks.

The Story

As much as things were changing in Major League Baseball, one thing seemed to remain the same: labor unrest. For the seventh time in 19 years, baseball came to a halt in 1990, and for the second time, Opening Day was impacted. The collective bargaining agreement between the players and owners expired at the end of 1989. With spring training set to start on February 15, the owners locked the players out of camp until a new agreement was reached. The central issue was answering the question of when a player would be eligible for salary arbitration: after two years or three. After 32 days of name-calling and finger-pointing, they settled in the middle. The owners also agreed to raise the annual pension fund contribution to $55 million and increase the major league–minimum annual salary from $68,000 to $100,000. The work stoppage wiped out most of spring training and delayed Opening Day by a week. Games missed in April were made up later in the season.

As bad as baseball had become at avoiding shutdowns, by 1990, leadership was getting better at figuring out how to return to play. Games lost during the two-day midseason strike in 1985 were easily rescheduled, but the back-to-work plans in 1972 and 1981 were seriously flawed.

The 14-day strike at the start of the 1972 season resulted in an unbalanced schedule with teams playing between 153 and 156 games, rather than the regular 162. Since the owners refused to pay the players for games missed in April due to the strike, those games weren't made up. In Boston, fans were fuming in October as the Red Sox finished a half game behind the American League East champion Tigers because Detroit had played one less game.

The split season settlement in 1981 was even worse. Following the 51-day midseason strike, the owners decided on a format calling for division champions for each half season to play each other in October for the right to advance to the League Championship Series. When the postseason arrived, fans in Texas were crying foul. The Rangers finished the first half a game and a half behind the Oakland A's in the American League West but played four fewer games and weren't invited to the postseason party. In the National League, both the St. Louis Cardinals and Cincinnati Reds posted the best *overall* records in their divisions but were excluded from postseason play because they finished second in each half season. Fans were seething!

By 1990 the owners and players seemed to have figured out a better plan.

An abbreviated, three-week spring training plus a one-week delay in Opening Day was a workable solution. The six games missed in early April would be made up by tacking three games onto the end of the regular season (delaying the post-season a bit) and slotting the other three games into mutually agreed upon open dates on the teams' schedules.

The schedule shuffle disrupted one Opening Day tradition and threatened another. The game's traditional first game host, the Cincinnati Reds, opened the season on the road for only the third time in 114 years. On the north side of Chicago, the Cubs would have been forced to host their first-ever Opening *Night* on Monday, April 9 (lights were finally installed at Wrigley Field in 1988). However, rain forced the game to be rescheduled to a more traditional Tuesday afternoon setting.

On Chicago's South Side, the White Sox began their final season at Comiskey Park before moving to their new stadium next door in 1991.

The first pitch ceremony was newsworthy in multiple cities. In Boston, Toni Giamatti honored her late husband, a lifelong Red Sox fan, at Fenway Park. Bart Giamatti served as commissioner of baseball for only five months in 1989. Just days after officially taking charge of the sport, Giamatti was with President Bush when he threw out the first pitch on Opening Day at Memorial Stadium just a year earlier. The 51-year-old Giamatti died suddenly in September 1989 of a heart attack. At Shea Stadium in New York, Giamatti's friend and successor Fay Vincent handled the first pitch duties, one of four 1990 Opening Day games the new commissioner attended, part of his effort to heal the game following the work stoppage. After the Mets lost to Pittsburgh, Vincent flew to Toronto where he joined Canadian Prime Minister Brian Mulroney and President Bush for yet another first pitch ceremony. The President's son, 43-year-old George W. Bush was the managing general partner and part owner of the Texas Rangers, the Blue Jays's opponent that day. Rumors were circulating that young George might someday run for higher office, like governor of Texas. Hmmm?

By Opening Day, Commissioner Vincent was rested and refreshed following a 12-hour marathon meeting three weeks earlier that brought an end to the month-long lockout. A groggy commissioner emerged from his office in the wee hours of the morning on March 19. Vincent was asked if baseball's seventh work stoppage since 1972 had done damage to the great American pastime. "I think it was damaged, and everyone who lived through this period believes the game was damaged," he said candidly. "But I believe that the recuperative power of the game is substantial. But I know there has been damage, and a number of us regret that."

The worst was yet to come.

For box scores, play-by-play and more, visit www.OpeningDay5050.com or use this QR code

1991

Complete Game? Don't "Count" on It.

The Game

Who:	Chicago White Sox 9, Baltimore Orioles 1
Where:	Memorial Stadium, Baltimore, MD
Attendance:	50,213
When:	Monday, April 8, 1991
Weather:	89 degrees (not a typo!)

Hall of Famers: White Sox manager Tony La Russa, 1B Frank Thomas, and C Carlton Fisk, Orioles SS Cal Ripken Jr. and P Mike Mussina

Game Highlights: It was all Chicago on this day. Pitcher Jack McDowell hurled a masterpiece, striking out 10, giving up four hits, walking only one, and completing the game with an efficient 124 pitches. On offense, White Sox 22-year-old outfielder Sammy Sosa began 1991 with career home runs numbers 24 and 25, accounting for five of Chicago's nine runs. Sosa would finish his career 16 years later with 609 home runs, ranking him No. 9 all time. Historically, 500 home runs made a player a first ballot lock for induction into the Hall of Fame. However, since Sosa first appeared on the ballot in 2013, he never received more than 19 percent of the votes. Election requires 75 percent. The cloud of steroid use hung over the heads of Sosa and other members of the 500 Home Run Club as evidence and details emerged during the decade that followed. Sosa denied ever using steroids. More in Chapter 2003.

The Story

Chicago's starting pitcher this day, 25-year-old Jack McDowell, was one of the most durable performers of his era. The White Sox staff led all of Major League Baseball in 1991 with 28 complete games, 15 by McDowell. He completed 38 of his 103 starts between 1991 and 1993, tops in the American League, pitching at least 250 innings each season. I couldn't help but flash back to the Opening Day 1977 experience when two future Hall of Famers, Jim Palmer and Bert Blyleven, completed 10 innings each in a 2–1 Texas win over Baltimore.

Completed.

The concept is so rare today that it requires some explanation. This is the idea of having the same pitcher throw a game's first pitch and last pitch. The starter *completed* it.

Consider this: Baseball-Reference.com lists the Top 1,000 pitchers of all time, ranked based on their number of complete games. None of the 1,000 are active pitchers. That bears reframing. Cy Young's all-time record of 759 complete games is not at risk. As of the start of the 2022 season, no active major-league pitcher had completed more than 30. McDowell finished his career in 1999 with a modest 62 complete games, tied for 683rd all time.

In 1971 the Baltimore Orioles starting rotation accomplished something that had happened only once before (1920 Chicago White Sox) and most certainly will never happen again. Four pitchers on the same team each won at least 20 games (the individual "win" for the pitcher has become another less-important statistic, but I digress). They combined for 81 wins in 1971, 70 of which they completed. I'd seen all of them on Opening Day in the seventies—Pat Dobson (1972), Dave McNally (1973), Jim Palmer (1974, '76, '77, and '79), and Mike Cuellar (1975).

That year, starting pitchers on the 24 major-league teams completed 1,082 games. Twenty years later, by 1991, starters on 26 major-league teams completed only 366. The complete game was fading. Fast. By 2011, 30 teams completed 172 and in 2019, only 45.

In the 1970s, a starting pitcher leaving before the ninth was giving his teammates in the bullpen something to do. In the 2020s, if a starting pitcher lasted past the sixth inning, he was giving his bullpen a much-needed break. The complete game is almost as dead as Tommy John's arm in the summer of 1974 before his landmark elbow reconstruction surgery.

A starter's pitch count has become the new nightly metric of durability, or lack thereof. Pitch count only became an official statistic in Major League Baseball in 1988. It did not take long for it to become an obsession. ESPN, for example, only began displaying pitch counts during MLB telecasts in 2014. That ever-present, constantly updated number convinced us fans that as a pitcher approached 100 pitches, his outing was nearing its end. If he lingered past that, he was living on borrowed time. But coaches, players, and front office staff were tracking it closely years before we saw it on a regular basis.

On Opening Day 1989, 46-year-old Tommy John, then with the New York Yankees, began his 26th and final season by throwing 107 pitches in seven innings to earn the win. Ten days later, 23-year-old teammate Al Leiter threw a whopping 163 pitches in eight innings of work, also earning the win. That year, starters would throw 140 or more pitches 55 times, including LA Dodger Orel Hershiser who topped the list at 169 in his meaningless season finale. He had offseason arm surgery and missed the 1990 campaign. Knuckleballer Tim Wakefield of the Pittsburgh Pirates set the official (post-1987) record in 1993 with 172 pitches in a single game, a mark that likely will never be broken. The unofficial record probably belongs to Nolan Ryan of the then-California Angels who reportedly threw 235 pitches over 13 innings against the Boston Red Sox. The more efficient opposing starter Luis Tiant threw fewer pitches but lasted until the 15th inning.

So what happened and why? Are players today just less durable? Hardly. Many books and essays have been written, analyzing and dissecting this evolution, attempting to package up simple categories of answers. We'll try three: mechanics, specialists, and money.

Mechanics

Rule changes and differences from decade to decade make generational, statistical comparisons unfair. For example, the availability of the designated hitter batting in place of American League pitchers since 1973 has impacted statistics for AL starters negatively versus their NL counterparts. But one change that universally altered the way pitchers needed to pitch in order to fool more hitters came in 1969. In response to the pitcher-dominant 1960s and a desire to generate more fan-favored offense, the pitcher's mound was lowered five inches (from 15 to 10), materially altering the trajectory of the ball, especially from the game's most dominant pitchers. It required the next generation to develop arm-wrenching, stressful breaking balls that required a more scientific approach to the profession, an approach rooted in mechanics, sometimes coming at a great price in patience and dollars.

"If your mechanics are good, you can throw 75 pitches without being taxed," Hershiser explained in 2009 to senior writer Tim Kurkjian of the now-defunct *ESPN The Magazine*. After 18 successful seasons, most with the Dodgers, Hershiser became a prominent baseball broadcaster with ESPN and later, Sports-Net LA. "But if your mechanics are not in order [as with some young pitchers], you could be worn out at 35 pitches. The light bulb goes on with a veteran pitcher about how to extend his career beyond injury and time by understanding the game."

His years on the field and in the booth gave Hershiser a respected perspective. He'd learned, and tried to convey, that throwing hard isn't always the answer, especially to longevity. "I'd tell our young guys that your best day is not your hardest day. That's a huge lesson to learn for young pitchers."

Specialists

The emergence of specialty roles out of the bullpen also weighed heavily on the transformation of the pitching staff. Managers were increasingly bringing in a specific relief pitcher to face a specific batter. Kurkjian summarized it with insights from Bud Black, an accomplished pitcher over 15 big-league seasons (1981–95) and experienced manager in San Diego and Colorado. "That's the biggest change," Black told Kurkjian. "We have 11-man, 12-man, 13-man pitching staffs today. We develop relievers in the minor leagues, college, and even high school. It never used to be that way."

"In the 1970s," Kurkjian continued, "Orioles manager Earl Weaver often would break camp with eight pitchers. And back then, when the game's best pitchers threw 25 complete games in a season, Weaver would let ace Jim Palmer finish what he started, asking, 'Who do you want pitching the ninth inning with a one-run lead, Jim Palmer or the ninth-best pitcher on the team?' But now, the ninth-best pitcher on the team might come out of the bullpen throwing 95 mph. And the ninth-best pitcher on the team might be making a lot of money."

Money

Major-league money has made Hershiser's message hard to get across to younger players. "Young guys today rely on stuff," Hall of Fame manager Tony La Russa told Kurkjian. "They are max effort on every pitch. And in the minor leagues, they're doing whatever they can to get from Double-A to Triple-A, so the stress level is higher. They're getting to the big leagues younger, there is maximum pressure to perform, and because of that, they are letting it fly. That's how young pitchers develop arm injuries and fatigue."

While player salaries throughout baseball are staggering, they are especially high for the game's best starting pitchers. In 2020, of the game's 10 highest paid players, seven were starting pitchers, each earning more than $30 million per season, not bad considering they play only once every five days! And don't cry for the game's best relief pitchers. They may play more frequently, and typically for only an inning or less, but MLB's best relievers are in the $10-20 million range.

In 1991 McDowell averaged just over 109 pitches per outing, good for fourth behind top dog Roger Clemens (average 116). Once he was arbitration eligible, McDowell joined the then-elite $5 million-per-year club. In 1996 he threw 3,439 pitches and earned roughly $1,570 per pitch. By 2019 the pitch counts of the game's top starters hadn't changed much, although there were many fewer pitchers averaging more than 100 pitches per outing. That season, 30-year-old Stephen Strasburg of the Washington Nationals threw 3,384 pitches (fifth in MLB), averaged 102 pitches per outing, and earned a little over $38 million ($11,328 per pitch or roughly seven times what McDowell earned 23 years earlier).

Monitoring pitch counts game by game and season by season has become its own unique and sometimes controversial science as teams seek to balance winning with protecting their massive investments. Leave him in? Take him out? Let him play? Sit him down?

Take for example the young Ross Stripling. The Los Angeles Dodgers invested heavily in developing Stripling over four seasons in the minor leagues. When he finally made his major-league debut in April 2016, the Dodgers enforced their predetermined 100-pitch limit even though *he was pitching a no-hitter* in the eighth inning! After the 26-year-old rookie issued a one-out walk and with his team protecting a 2–0 lead over the rival San Francisco Giants, manager Dave Roberts took the ball from Stripling and handed it to Chris Hatcher who immediately gave up a game-tying two-run homer. The Dodgers eventually lost in 10 innings.

The most controversial example came in 2012 when Washington Nationals general manager Mike Rizzo sat down his young star pitcher, Strasburg, in the middle of a pennant race and would not allow him to pitch in the playoffs. Strasburg had exploded into the majors in June 2010 as a 21-year-old phenom. Six weeks and 12 starts later he was heading for Tommy John surgery. After the arduous, year-long recovery, he enjoyed success in 2012 but was on a team-imposed pitch limit. In early September after a few more than 2,600 pitches and just shy of 160 innings, he was done for the year. Rizzo was widely, but unfairly, criticized as the Nationals made an early exit from the postseason. In retrospect, the decision is hard to second-guess. With Strasburg near the top of his rotation each year, Rizzo's Nationals finished atop the NL East three times in four years (2014–17) and won it all in 2019 behind World Series MVP Strasburg. After that disciplined shutdown, Strasburg's career trajectory continued upward, helping him to become one of the game's most dominant starters, and earning him more than $100 million from 2013–19.

Over those seven seasons, Strasburg started 194 games.

He completed two of them.

For box scores, play-by-play and more, visit www.OpeningDay5050.com or use this QR code

1992

Oriole Park at Camden Yards

The Game

Who:	Baltimore Orioles 2, Cleveland Indians 0
Where:	Oriole Park at Camden Yards, Baltimore, MD
Attendance:	44,568
When:	Monday, April 6, 1992
Weather:	Sunny and 60s

Hall of Famers: Orioles SS Cal Ripken Jr. and P Mike Mussina

Game Highlights: Both starting pitchers went the distance with Baltimore's Rick Sutcliffe outlasting Cleveland's Charles Nagy in near-record time: just two hours and two minutes! A two-run, bottom-of-the-order rally in the fifth inning gave Sutcliffe all he needed to earn the 17th shutout and 65th complete game of his career. Signed by the Orioles as a free agent during the offseason, the 36-year-old right-hander proved he still had plenty left. After his playing days were done following the 1994 season, he distinguished himself as a baseball commentator for ESPN and other networks for more than 20 years.

The Story

"From the small-town sandlots to the emerald patches in the nation's great cities, baseball fields are special places. Each one is the setting and the stage for an American rite of passage, and each is part of the fabric and fiber and mythology of the nation. The greatest of these green fields are hallowed places, pieces of Americana that live on in the minds of those who experienced them — Forbes Field, Wrigley Field, Ebbets Field, Fenway Park. These are baseball's forefathers, and in 1992, their descendant, Oriole Park at Camden Yards, baseball's newest tribute to the game and its traditional, old-fashioned values, opened its gates."

Jon Miller, Narrator
"Welcome Home: The Inaugural Season at Oriole Park at Camden Yards"

The dramatic words which began the hour-long commemorative video, spoken as only Hall of Fame broadcaster Jon Miller could, actually understated the significance of this Opening Day. Oriole Park at Camden Yards marked the beginning of a new era in the design, look, and feel of Major League Baseball venues. For the next few decades, this ballpark would be the standard against which every new baseball stadium would be compared. Courageous, thoughtful planning dismissed the cookie cutter, symmetrical stadiums of the 1960s and '70s, usually shared with an NFL team. Baltimore had resurrected the baseball-only park that was more than just a place to watch a game.

I knew Orioles president Larry Lucchino casually through work. He stayed on with the team after Edward Bennett Williams's estate sold the team to Eli Jacobs in 1989. Oriole Park was a personal passion for Larry. I remember politely asking early in the planning process if the stadium would be like the one they were building for the Chicago White Sox.

My naive question insulted him and afforded the opportunity to succinctly set me straight.

"The new Comiskey will be a stadium," he snapped back. "What we're building here is a ballpark."

During construction, Birdland and baseball fans up and down the East Coast couldn't wait to experience this modern marvel. As they traveled up and down Interstate 95 through Baltimore, they would peek to the west to catch a glimpse of the sport's first new retro park as it took shape around its meticulously restored anchor structure, the eight-story B&O Warehouse that would define the right-field side of Oriole Park.

This wasn't merely a team or city's Opening Day. The entire country was watching. From spots all around Camden Yards, Willard Scott did fun cut-ins all morning for NBC's *Today Show*. Charles Gibson was there, too, for ABC's *Good Morning America*. This was huge—Roundy's kind of event. Tickets for this Opening Day were as hot as any postseason game with buyers far outnumbering sellers and scalpers commanding 50 times face value.

"We wanted a ballpark that was reminiscent of ballparks we knew when we were growing up," Lucchino told Gibson's ABC audience. "Eli grew up in Boston and thought of Fenway. I thought of Forbes Field in Pittsburgh. There was a feel about the ballparks. They fit into their neighborhoods. There was something special about them."

The weekend leading up to Opening Day was filled with parties, parades, galas, and special events. The weather Monday afternoon was perfect for a larger-than-life ribbon cutting. The bright orange ribbon stretched all the way across the outfield. A cluster of dignitaries and former Orioles stood in center field, right where Babe Ruth's father once ran a saloon. Governor William Donald Schaefer did the honors as team owner Jacobs looked on. The two had feuded over the name of the team's new home. Schaefer preferred Camden Yards, a nod to the city's proud and rich history, while Jacobs preferred the more team-centric moniker, Oriole Park. Like good politicians, they compromised.

The Baltimore Symphony Orchestra was joined by the choir from Morgan State University for an emotional rendering of the national anthem worthy of the occasion. While the playing of the anthem is a pregame tradition at every major American sporting event, "The Star-Spangled Banner" has always stirred a unique civic pride in Baltimore. The poetic words were penned in 1814 by Francis Scott Key while he was a prisoner during the Battle of Baltimore aboard the British vessel *HMS Tonnant* where he was negotiating a prisoner exchange during the War of 1812. He was inspired as he watched his fellow Americans successfully defend Fort McHenry from a British bombardment near the entrance to Baltimore Harbor.

After the anthem, President Bush wasn't as sharp with his first pitch duties as he'd been three years earlier at Memorial Stadium. His casual toss forced catcher Chris Hoiles to glide to his left to scoop up the one-hopper.

Baltimore had lost its NBA team to Washington in 1973 and its NFL team to Indianapolis in 1984, in both cases, because the teams couldn't get new places to play. Baltimore wasn't going to let it happen a third time. For years there had been rumblings that Orioles owner Edward Bennett Williams might move the team to Washington, closer to his DC law practice. But by 1992, these Orioles weren't going anywhere. City and state leaders stepped up. Oriole Park at Camden Yards became a destination for baseball fans all over the country. Over the next decade, the Orioles averaged more than 3.3 million fans per year, consistently ranking among the top five teams in baseball in attendance even with sometimes mediocre teams.

This once-mighty franchise now had the mightiest of ballparks.

For box scores, play-by-play and more, visit www.OpeningDay5050.com or use this QR code

1993

Cal Ripken Jr.

The Game

Who: Texas Rangers 7, Baltimore Orioles 4
Where: Oriole Park at Camden Yards, Baltimore, MD
Attendance: 46,145
When: Monday, April 5, 1993
Weather: Overcast and 40s

Hall of Famers: Orioles SS Cal Ripken Jr., P Mike Mussina, and DH Harold Baines, Rangers C Ivan Rodriguez

---

Game Highlights: As fans arrived for Oriole Park's second Opening Day they found the Reverend Jesse Jackson leading a peaceful protest outside the ballpark, calling for increased minority representation in baseball front offices. Not enough had changed since that infamous Ted Koppel-Al Campanis interview on Opening Day 1987. Inside, a pair of two-run homers by Dean Palmer and Juan González headlined a five-run third inning for Texas off Baltimore starter Rick Sutcliffe, and that proved to be enough. The 23-year-old González would return to Oriole Park three months later with teammate Ivan Rodriguez to play in the MLB All-Star Game.

The Story

During my 50-year Opening Day streak, no player had a more profound impact on the game than Cal Ripken Jr. After the 1994 players strike canceled the World Series and nearly crippled the game, Cal was the game's unifying force. At the tribute following his final game in 2001, Commissioner Bud Selig reflected on Ripken's significance in 1995. "When baseball needed a hero, Cal Ripken was there for us."

Cal's incredible story could have been placed in this book almost anywhere between chapters 1983 and 2001. I spent Opening Day with him 19 times, more than anyone else. I placed his story here in 1993, not because of some heroic achievement or special personal memory (there were many). It's here because this was his first Opening Day without his dad in the dugout, and the first in six years without his little brother as a teammate. After the 1992 season, Cal Sr. and Bill were victims of the cold reality of the business of baseball. On Opening Day 1993, as a Ripken, Cal Jr. stood alone. It was a weird day.

If you were to map Ripken's most memorable moments on a master calendar, certain months would stand out. April would not be one of them. July, September, and October would command your attention.

During his 21-year career, Cal Jr. played in 19 All-Star Games, all but one in July, a month that also included his 2007 induction into the Baseball Hall of Fame.

He played in 28 postseason games, all but one in October, the month that also included the emotional 3,001st and final game of his career in 2001.

September memories were many including his milestone 400th home run in 1999 and the low-key, final, 2,632nd game of his consecutive game streak in 1998. September also included two of the most memorable regular-season games in baseball history: the nights he tied, and then broke, Gehrig's unbreakable mark of 2,130 straight games without a day off, September 5-6, 1995.

April had one memorable milestone: Cal Jr.'s 3,000th career base hit in 2000. There was another April memory, though he'd just as soon forget. His dad was relieved of his managerial duties just six games into the 1988 season. Cal Sr. returned a year later as third-base coach under manager Frank Robinson.

Yet almost every year for as long as Cal Jr. could remember, April featured the one day the Ripken family looked forward to more than any other: Opening Day.

Maybe not this year though.

Opening Day 1993 was awkward. The Ripken family probably wanted to get it over with as quickly as possible. In their own way, each needed to move on. For the first time in their lives, Cal Jr. and Bill were on opposite sides. Their dad was home with their mom, Vi, about 30 miles up the road, watching the game on TV. Six months earlier, after 37 years in various coaching roles with the Baltimore Orioles, he was the only member of manager Johnny Oates's staff not invited back. They offered him a demotion to minor-league instructor. He declined.

Two months later, Bill was released. He later found a job in Texas. Bill and Cal Jr. had played more than 600 games together in the middle of the Orioles's infield. While big brother was always the far superior all-around player, the Orioles had one of the best double-play tandems in the Majors from 1988–92 with Cal Jr. at shortstop and Bill at second.

From birth, the Ripken boys knew nothing but baseball. In his 1984 book, *Why Time Begins on Opening Day, Washington Post* columnist Tom Boswell wrote of Cal Sr., his wife, and kids, "Ripken uprooted his family nine times as a player, then nine more as a manager, taking them to every town. Yet, through all these dislocations, the family grew together, not apart. 'We made friends with each other because we were moving so much that we were always leaving our other friends,' says Cal Jr. now."

Bringing the Ripken trio together on the same team took more than a decade to develop. After 13 years as a minor-league manager, Cal Sr. became an Orioles coach in 1976. Cal Jr. was drafted by the Orioles in 1978 and made it to the majors just after his 21st birthday in September 1981. Billy was drafted by the Orioles in 1982. The younger brother became a good big-league player— the elder, one of the greatest of all time. In 1987 during their dad's only full season as manager of the club, Bill joined his brother and father at Memorial Stadium for a most memorable half season. After Robinson replaced Cal Sr. in 1988, the Ripken boys played on.

Both Bill and Cal Jr. acknowledged Opening Day 1993 was a strange day. "When there's a bullet hit to second base, you don't expect it to be your brother making the play," Cal Jr. told Jim Henneman of *The Sun*. "That made it real. It made it final in my mind."

"For several rewarding seconds," Henneman wrote, "Bill got top billing. During the pregame introductions he got a longer, louder ovation than his more famous brother."

"It was nice—real nice," said Bill. "It made me feel good, made me feel like the people liked the way I played here."

His brother thought it was nice, too. "I think it was an indication of their appreciation for the kind of player Bill is," he said. "It made me feel good, and I'm sure it made him feel good."

Baseball can be a generational game for families. The Ripkens did it their way. So did my family. My dad took me to baseball games when I was very young. His grandchildren and great grandchildren had similar experiences. Some of my sons' most memorable experiences had something to do with Cal Jr.

Kate and I had six children, including four boys. Each had their Ripken moment. In October 1991 six-year-old Brad (who was born just before Opening Day 1985) helped me entertain clients at the final game at Memorial Stadium. The Orioles capped "A Season to Remember" with a brilliantly choreographed postgame journey down memory lane. It included more than 100 retired Orioles reunited at their former home one last time, each trotting out to the position they once occupied during the glory days and six World Series seasons. The soundtrack from *Field of Dreams* filled the stadium, including the powerful voice of James Earl Jones. Stars of the past and present emerged not from a corn field, but from the Orioles dugout. At shortstop, 31-year-old Ripken joined his predecessors including Mark Belanger and Luis Aparicio.

I cried.

On August 6, 1995, nine-year-old Patrick was on my shoulders in the right-field bleachers, just below the four-digit banner across the third story of the B&O Warehouse. It kept track of the drama all summer long: 2050, 2051 . . . 2128, 2129, 2130 . . . In the middle of the fifth inning, the game became official. The Oriole Bird mascot released the final banner. The "0" became a "1" and Gehrig's unbreakable record was broken. The game stopped for more than 20 minutes to allow a national television audience and more than 40,000 fans in Oriole Park to celebrate. Adults cried freely—the entire Ripken family, the Oriole family, the baseball family. Cal's famous victory lap passed right in front of us.

Dad cried again.

And when it came time for Cal to say his final farewell at the end of the 2001 season, our youngest son, Greg, scored a memory and a sports collectible unlike any other. When the game was over, we left his now-16-year-old brother, Brad, upstairs with their grandfather Vin DeMarco (Kate's dad) while Greg and I wiggled our way as close to the field as we could for yet another memorable celebration. We got to within 10 rows of the field near third base. I recognized Ron Shapiro in the front row, a well-known sports agent who represented many of baseball's biggest stars, past and present, including Jim Palmer, Kirby Puckett, Joe Mauer, Eddie Murray, Cal, and others. I figured if a small 10-year-old could slither his way to the front row, he'd be safely within my line of sight and ensured a great view of the ceremony. I pointed out to Greg the gray-haired man in the front row wearing, as I recall, a brown jacket on the cool and windy evening. I assured my son he was safe. Although I had never met Ron, I suspect Greg thought he was a friend. I never told him otherwise.

Full disclosure. I am white. Greg is black. When Greg arrived at Mr. Shapiro's side, Ron turned around, looking for a parent for this lost little boy. He and I made eye contact. I made no acknowledgment Greg was my son, fearing Ron might send him back from his newfound front row viewing spot. Seeing no nearby black faces, Ron seemed to "adopt" Greg for the next several minutes. Greg's commemorative ticket from Cal's last game is most certainly the only one autographed by Eddie Murray, Cal Ripken Jr., and Dante Bichette, the Red Sox DH and four-time All-Star with the Colorado Rockies who also had just played his final game (Dante's son Bo Bichette made it to the majors with Toronto in 2019). All three visited Ron and his newfound friend Greg. I never had a chance to thank Ron.

Dad cried one more time.

Closer to home, my family's off-field encounters with Cal Jr. over the years spoke more to his status in the community. He generously gave of his time, often staying after games, signing autographs when most players had gone home. It devalued his autograph to collectors, but Cal didn't care. Each signature brought a big smile to a child.

Here are three such family encounters.

Fans respected Ripken's space. One night while living in Bel Air, Maryland, somewhere around 2002, Kate and I were dining at Scotto's, a favorite Italian place. He walked in with a business associate for dinner. During the entire time they were in the restaurant, not one person interrupted them or sought an autograph or photo.

Respect.

He was not so lucky at Disney World in November 1994. Touristy Florida is not Hometown, Maryland. Kate and I and the four boys (the two girls had not yet come along) were in the Magic Kingdom on a raft heading out to Tom Sawyer Island. We suddenly recognized familiar shipmates. Cal was holding his 18-month-old Ryan. Kelly had their five-year-old Rachel. They were enjoying a family vacation, not a book signing or photo op. We didn't say a word, not even our sons.

Ryan appeared to be asleep on Daddy's shoulder when some photo-hungry guy on the raft asked, "Can I hold him?" Dad politely declined. I, on the other hand, wanted to throw the guy overboard.

I was proud of my family's self-control. Respect. That other guy? Not so much.

Even our son Daniel, who didn't care much for baseball, had his Ripken moment three years after the Iron Man retired. Daniel was diagnosed with juvenile rheumatoid arthritis when he was just 11 years old. He spent years in a wheelchair but battled back thanks to medical breakthroughs and perseverance. In 2004 the Arthritis Foundation presented Cal Jr. with a Lifetime Achievement Award. Like so many arthritis sufferers, Ripken showed up for work every day, often playing through the pain of daily life. Sixteen-year-old Daniel had the privilege of walking, unassisted, across the stage to present the award, one Iron Man to another.

Yes, Dad cried again.

Respect is what the fans showed to Bill Ripken on Opening Day 1993 and to his brother throughout his career. The Ripken boys always reciprocated. Cal Sr. wouldn't have had it any other way.

As he concluded his farewell remarks to the fans in 2001, Cal Jr. said, "One question I've repeatedly been asked these last few weeks is: How do I want to be remembered? My answer has been simple: 'To be remembered at all is pretty special. I might also add that if I am remembered, I hope it's because by living my dream I was able to make a difference. Thank you.'"

For box scores, play-by-play and more, visit www.OpeningDay5050.com or use this QR code

1994

Country Boy Comes Home

The Game

Who:	Baltimore Orioles 6, Kansas City Royals 3
Where:	Oriole Park at Camden Yards, Baltimore, MD
Attendance:	47,549
When:	Monday, April 4, 1994
Weather:	Sunny and 60s

Hall of Famers: Orioles SS Cal Ripken Jr., P Mike Mussina, DH Harold Baines, and P Lee Smith

Game Highlights: Only one time during my streak did four future Hall of Fame players all contribute to a team's win on Opening Day. Orioles starter Mike Mussina gave up only two hits, and newly acquired free agent closer Lee Smith threw the game's final two pitches to earn the save. Smith was the only future Hall of Fame player I saw play on Opening Day for three different teams (Chicago Cubs in 1982, Boston Red Sox in 1989, and Baltimore Orioles in 1994). The position players this day who would eventually head to the Hall—Cal Ripken Jr. and Harold Baines—delivered two hits each. In addition to Smith, other members of Baltimore's offseason haul of free agents delivered on Opening Day including first baseman Rafael Palmeiro and third baseman Chris Sabo. Palmeiro's seventh-inning homer landed in the Camden Yards flag court beyond right field, while Sabo reached base twice. The new Orioles ownership group's winning bid at the August 1993 bankruptcy auction—more than $173 million—was, at the time, the highest price ever paid for a sports team in North America. Fans feared they wouldn't have enough left to compete for available players. They were wrong. In total, the team shelled out more than $40 million on free agent talent leading up to the 1994 season. If only there had been a 1994 postseason! When a players' strike ended the season in August with 50 games left to play, the Orioles were only two and a half games out of a playoff spot.

The Story

During most games over 40-plus seasons, Orioles fans have clapped and stomped their way through the seventh-inning stretch to the sound of John Denver's "Thank God I'm a Country Boy." After its debut at Memorial Stadium in the mid-1970s, the team made multiple attempts to try something different, and each time fans objected, sometimes more loudly than others. When financier Eli Jacobs took control of the club in 1989, the song was silenced. The stodgy and socially awkward Jacobs didn't think it was an appropriate song for the stretch, preferring instead the more traditional "Take Me Out to the Ball Game." Fans objected. Jacobs didn't care.

By Opening Day 1994, Jacobs was gone. "Country Boy" was back.

It actually made its comeback with a few weeks remaining in the 1993 season, just hours after Jacobs's reign ended. With his financial enterprise in ruins, Jacobs was forced to sell the Orioles to partially pay off creditors. He was more than $320 million in debt. On the afternoon of August 2, 1993, in a steamy New York City courtroom, New York art dealer Jeffrey Loria declined to continue bidding. An alliance formed between Baltimore lawyer Peter Angelos and Cincinnati investor William DeWitt prevailed, paying $173 million. Judge Cornelius Blackshear closed out the proceedings. Jacobs was done.

That night the Orioles played Milwaukee at Camden Yards. A mediocre outing by Baltimore starter Fernando Valenzuela had them trailing 5–3 heading into the bottom of the seventh inning. Jack Voigt led off with a home run and Sherman Obando singled. With one on and nobody out, Brewers manager Phil Garner started walking to the mound. With a rally underway, a pitching change in process, and Jacobs no longer in charge, front office veteran and head of public affairs Dr. Charles Steinberg had a nostalgic idea. After quickly checking with team president Larry Lucchino, he let it crank. "Country Boy" ignited the capacity crowd of more than 46,000. Three more Birds reached base and two more scored. The come-from-behind victory left fans giddy and started an eight-game winning streak.

Since I passionately enjoyed Harry Caray's unique rendition of "Take Me Out to the Ball Game" between 1979 and 1982, you'd think I would have aligned with Jacobs. But "Country Boy" had grown on me. I heard it often in the late '70s, but it never left an impression until the final game of the Orioles 1982 season. Baltimore entered the final weekend, needing a four-game sweep of first-place Milwaukee to give retiring manager Earl Weaver the sendoff he deserved and his seventh AL East crown. After taking the first three games of the series, Memorial Stadium was electric for the finale. Future Hall of Fame pitchers Jim Palmer and Don Sutton squared off on national TV in a win-or-go-home showdown. With the Orioles trailing 4–1 in the seventh, the loud speakers blared "Country Boy." The crowd was pumped up. Cab driver "Wild" Bill Hagy took them even higher with his well-known cheerleading from Section 34 above the right-field foul pole. Raising both arms over his head to form the letter "O," he contorted while spelling out the team name. More than 50,000 fans screamed each letter, "O-R-I-O-L-E-S . . . ORI-OLES!"

Harry Caray this wasn't, but it was pretty darn cool. This was not the atmosphere I remembered from most Baltimore ho-hum Opening Days in the '70s in front of 10,000 or more empty seats.

Hagy's exhortation during that final game in '82 wasn't enough. The Brewers scored six more runs, won the division, and fans bid a tearful farewell to the "Earl of Baltimore."

Jacobs's tenure (1989–93) wasn't the only time the Orioles messed with "Country Boy." In 1983 in front of more than 50,000 frigid fans on Opening Day, they unveiled a custom-made new tune called "That Magic Feeling," a failed attempt to reignite the "Orioles Magic" of the late '70s. In the next morning's *Baltimore Sun*, columnist Bob Maisel weighed in: "Instead of just sneaking it in, they had public address announcer Rex Barney say something like, 'For the last seven years or so, you've clapped to John Denver's record of "Thank God I'm a Country Boy," but in recent years we've sensed you are tiring of it and need a change.'"

They "sensed" wrong.

"The longer it went, the louder the boos," Maisel continued. "Before the Birds came up in the 8th, 'Thank God I'm a Country Boy' was back, people were clapping, singing, tapping their feet, yelling, having fun again, which is what a day at the ballpark is all about, right?"

Absolutely, Bob!

An extraordinary opportunity to make it right with the fans presented itself to the Orioles brass later that season. They arranged for John Denver to perform "Country Boy" live atop the Orioles dugout—during Game One of the 1983 World Series!

"Country Boy" has been a staple at Orioles games almost continuously since it reached the top of the charts in 1975. "The Orioles soon began playing it over the sound system at Memorial Stadium, although back then no one envisioned the enormous appeal the song would have for O's fans," reported the *Sun*'s Kevin Cowherd shortly after Denver's tragic death in October 1997.

"The whole thing started just by accident," said Bob Brown, the Orioles PR director from 1968–1989. "Frank Cashen (then the O's general manager) said, 'I'm tired of all this old-timer's music with the organs. Let's play something a little more current, try to get the kids interested.'"

"We experimented with a lot of seventh-inning stretch songs. When we got a (strong) fan reaction from 'Country Boy,' we tried it again and again. And every time we got the same reaction."

The Orioles strayed from "Country Boy" a few more times. According to Cowherd, it "was replaced by Rick Dempsey's video version of 'Old Time Rock 'n' Roll' as the seventh-inning stretch song in the second half of the 1986 season. Early in 1987, a variety of songs, including 'Twist and Shout' by the Beatles and 'Shout' by the Isley Brothers were used during the stretch."

"But by the middle of that year, 'Country Boy' was back," Cowherd continued, "and it remained a staple of the seventh inning until Eli Jacobs bought the Orioles in 1988. Jacobs decreed that the Andrews Sisters's version of 'Take Me Out to the Ballgame' would be played during the stretch. And despite widespread protestations from Orioles fans, 'Country Boy' was not played again during the seventh inning until Peter Angelos bought the team in 1993."

Perhaps another reason "Country Boy" grew on me had to do with love. During the 1983 postseason, I took my fiancée Kate, like me, a John Denver fan, to her first Major League Baseball game so she could see my Chicago White Sox play the AL East champion Orioles. While she did not yet quite understand this baseball thing, she figured any sport that encouraged 50,000 people to sing and dance with John Denver must be okay.

Fourteen years later in September 1997, she and I attended our sixth, and final, John Denver concert, this one a benefit performance for cystic fibrosis at the then-Baltimore Arena. That afternoon we took in the Orioles game against the Detroit Tigers at Camden Yards. The seventh inning included a surprise guest atop the O's dugout: John Denver himself!

Three weeks later he was gone. John was killed in a tragic accident when the experimental plane he was piloting crashed into the Pacific Ocean just off the coast of Monterey Beach, California. A generation later, fans continue to clap, sing, tap, yell, and have fun with "Country Boy" because, to quote Bob Maisel, that's "what a day at the ballpark is all about, right?"

For box scores, play-by-play and more, visit www.OpeningDay5050.com or use this QR code

1995

The Woman Who Saved Baseball, Strike 3!

The Game

Who:	Milwaukee Brewers 7, Baltimore Orioles 0
Where:	Oriole Park at Camden Yards, Baltimore, MD
Attendance:	46,523
When:	Monday, May 1, 1995
Weather:	60s and breezy

Hall of Famers: Orioles SS Cal Ripken Jr., P Mike Mussina, and DH Harold Baines

Game Highlights: The Orioles's bats on this day made Milwaukee starter Ricky Bones look like a Cy Young Award candidate (he wasn't!). The right-hander gave up only two hits in seven and a third innings. On the opposite side, Orioles ace Mike Mussina, who actually *was* a perennial Cy Young candidate, got roughed up during his team's home opener, giving up nine hits and five earned runs in just four innings. "To me, I'm halfway through spring training," the future Hall of Famer told Mark Maske of *The Washington Post*, describing the effect of the strike-delayed start to the 1995 season. "It's going to be spotty for a while until we get into the season . . . I'll come around." The late-March decision to end the strike resulted in a shortened preseason, a late start to the regular season, and many players being off-kilter. The 26-year-old Mussina did "come around," finishing sixth in the 1995 AL Cy Young voting. The Brewers collected three home runs this day, none off 32-year-old Jamie Moyer who took over for Mussina in the fifth and stayed for two and a third innings. Over 25 seasons playing for eight different teams, Moyer would give up 522 homers, more than any other pitcher. His dubious record is unlikely to ever be broken. No active pitcher is within 200 HRs of his all-time record.

The Story

For the third (and final?) time, Opening Day was delayed due to a work stoppage. Who ended it? Many say it was an underestimated Yankees fan.

On May 26, 2009, President Barack Obama read seriously and proudly the long list of accomplishments of Judge Sonia Sotomayor, his nominee to replace retiring Supreme Court Associate Justice David Souter. High on Obama's list was something she'd done 14 years earlier. "During her tenure on the District Court she presided over roughly 450 cases," Obama said plainly. As he continued, a smile came over his face. "One case in particular involved a matter of enormous concern to many Americans, including me: the baseball strike of 1994–95. In a decision that reportedly took her just 15 minutes to announce, a swiftness much appreciated by baseball fans everywhere, she issued an injunction that helped end the strike. Some say that Judge Sotomayor saved baseball."

Of all the accomplishments recited that day in the White House, this was the only one that garnered its own round of applause.

While the President's proclamation might have been a slight exaggeration, it would be correct to say the then 40-year-old Sotomayor, the youngest judge in the Southern District of New York back in 1995 who grew up in the Bronx just three miles from Yankee Stadium, did more in a quarter hour to end baseball's latest and most devastating work stoppage than had been accomplished by the players, owners, President Clinton, or Congress in more than a year.

Baseball's journey to her courtroom was long and painful. For the first half of 1994, the owners and players traded proposals aimed at reaching a new collective bargaining agreement. The owners were trying to solve their own business difficulties and lack of self-control by advancing concepts like revenue sharing and salary caps, while eliminating salary arbitration. This was playing out in an already toxic environment in which the players had won case after case, proving the owners had colluded to suppress and limit free agent signings in recent years. After the games of August 11, 1994, the players went on strike and did not return. For the first time in US professional sports history, the entire postseason was canceled, and no champion was crowned.

As the calendar flipped to 1995, the owners unilaterally reimposed the terms of the collective bargaining agreement which had expired more than a year earlier but added a nuance unprecedented in the history of baseball: they would prepare to play the 1995 season with replacement players, something the National Football League had done for three disastrous weeks during their strike-shortened 1987 season. "We are committed to playing the 1995 season," proclaimed acting commissioner and Milwaukee Brewers owner Bud Selig, "and will do so with the best players willing to play."

The parties were summoned to the White House in February by President Clinton for what turned into a lengthy, fruitless session with a federal mediator. At a late-night press conference, the President admitted, "Clearly they are not capable of resolving this strike without an umpire."

He asked Congress to step in, but Senate Majority Leader Bob Dole and House Speaker Newt Gingrich issued a joint statement saying Congress was "ill-suited to resolving private labor disputes."

Enter Judge Sotomayor.

As replacement players were training in Florida and Arizona, the players sued the owners in federal court. Some chauvinistic members of the owners' legal team were pleased when they learned the case would be heard by a female judge. They were in for a rude awakening.

The Associated Press summarized her approach:

"She used puns and waxed poetic. She confessed she was a fan. And then, with stern language and a piercing glare, she issued a ruling that might finally bring back baseball.

"If anyone doubted the importance of events in her Manhattan courtroom, she erased them quickly and with a rather unique opening: 'I can't help but to at least borrow some analogies from baseball as I start. The often-leisurely game of baseball is filled with many small moments which catch a fan's breath. There is, for example, that wonderful second when you see an outfielder backpedaling and jumping up to the wall and time stops for an instant as he jumps up and you finally figure out whether it's a home run, a double or a single off the wall or an out.'

"Then she got to the heart of the matter, demonstrating, with only four days' preparation time, a detailed grasp of how the business of baseball works.

"'This strike . . . has captivated the public's attention,' she said. 'Given the popularity of the sport, it appears that any delay on my part . . . would halt the continuation of the negotiating process.'

"She told lawyers for striking players and the owners that they could salvage the 1995 season and use the progress as a catalyst to reach a new labor agreement. Then she scolded the owners' lawyers, staring as she said the possibility of an agreement 'will be greatly diminished if this season is lost because of the unfair labor practices of the owners.'

"'I hope that none of you assumed . . . that my lack of knowledge of any of the

intimate details of your dispute meant that I was not a baseball fan,' she said. 'You can't grow up in the Bronx without knowing about baseball, particularly from a family where their claim to fame is that every member of it has a different team that they have rooted for.'"

Lawyers for the owners had underestimated the situation. After her opening remarks, even before they presented their case, they knew this day was not going to end well for them.

"In her two and a half years on the bench," reported James McKinley in the next day's *New York Times*, "United States District Court Judge Sonia Sotomayor has earned a reputation as a sharp, outspoken, and fearless jurist, someone who does not let powerful interests bully, rush, or cow her into a decision. She lived up to that billing yesterday morning when the fate of major-league baseball was thrust upon her. After a two-hour hearing in which she grilled both sides on the fine points of labor law, she took only 15 minutes to issue an injunction that could break the deadlock in the baseball strike."

Her preliminary injunction ordered the owners to restore free agency and arbitration and prohibited the use of replacement players. Days later, the Second Circuit Court of Appeals upheld her ruling. With no other way to play the 1995 season, the owners had no choice but to relent. The again-empowered players returned to work while a new collective bargaining agreement (CBA) was hammered out.

Fourteen years later, at the time of her Supreme Court nomination, *TIME Magazine* looked back on her historic ruling. Judge Sotomayor told *TIME*'s Sean Gregory, "The owners misunderstood the case law, and many of their arguments were inconsistent. One side can't come up with new rules unless they negotiate it with the other."

"A few sports columnists," Gregory continued, "offended by the speed with which she reached her decision, offered odd indictments of Sotomayor. 'I'm sorry she's not male, so I could say what I really think,' wrote [76-year-old] Furman Bisher of the *Atlanta Journal-Constitution*. 'I haven't the time or disposition to deal with NOW [the National Organization for Women] right now.'

"However, the legal community for the most part still has high praise for her judgment. 'It was the correct ruling,' says Rick Karcher, sports law professor at the Florida Coastal School of Law. 'She assured that fair collective bargaining would take place under the labor laws.'"

The only other significant pro-labor figure involved in the delayed Opening Day 1995 was, ironically, one of baseball's owners, a relative newcomer to baseball ownership, Baltimore's managing general partner Peter Angelos. When the owners, led by Selig, voted overwhelmingly to proceed with replacement players, Angelos and other members of the Orioles ownership group like author Tom Clancy, boldly refused. Their stance won high praise from players and labor-friendly fans. The contrast of experiences across the country on Opening Day was notable. In cities like New York, Cincinnati, Pittsburgh, and elsewhere, unforgiving fans booed the home team, staged protests, and angrily threw dollar bills at players. Larger numbers showed their disgust by simply staying home.

In Baltimore, however, Camden Yards was sold out, once again, as it had been for almost every game for the prior three seasons. And while fans' retaliation led to a 20-percent drop in attendance across the country, Oriole Park stayed generally full for the next four years.

Angelos invited the owner of that day's opponent, the Milwaukee Brewers, to attend Opening Day in person. Bud Selig respectfully declined.

For box scores, play-by-play and more, visit www.OpeningDay5050.com or use this QR code

1996

Baseball Bill Clinton

The Game

Who:	Baltimore Orioles 4, Kansas City Royals 2
Where:	Oriole Park at Camden Yards, Baltimore, MD
Attendance:	46,818
When:	Tuesday, April 2, 1996
Weather:	Sunny, windy, 50s

Hall of Famers: Orioles SS Cal Ripken Jr., P Mike Mussina, and 2B Roberto Alomar, plus Orioles general manager Pat Gillick

Game Highlights: With a new general manager (Pat Gillick), new manager (Davey Johnson), and 14 players who were not on the 1995 Opening Day roster, the Orioles relied on a couple of very familiar faces to earn the win. Cal Ripken Jr. drove in three of Baltimore's four runs with a two-run single in the first inning and another in the third, while starting pitcher Mike Mussina earned the win, giving up only two runs in seven innings. Newly acquired closer Randy Myers earned the save. Jesse Orosco delivered a shutout inning in relief, pitching in his 755th major-league game. The 39-year-old left-hander would go on to appear in nearly 500 more games over the next eight seasons to finish with baseball's all-time record for games played by a pitcher. His mark of 1,252 appearances (all but four in relief) may never be broken. No active pitcher has more than 800.

The Story

Like Ronald Reagan in 1984 and George H. W. Bush in 1992, President Bill Clinton was running for re-election in 1996, and that could only mean one thing: first pitch ceremonies in Baltimore on Opening Day!

While Clinton didn't initially fit into the sports fraternity of his immediate predecessors, he did blaze his own trail to Baltimore during his first term. He was living out the boyhood dreams of a kid who grew up as a baseball fan, played a little church league ball, but was better at playing the saxophone than playing second base.

Clinton spent his childhood in Arkansas about 500 miles south of St. Louis, baseball's southernmost city, throughout most of the 1950s and '60s. He'd listen to Harry Caray's radio broadcasts of Cardinals games and occasionally pick up the powerful signal of WLS, radio home of the more distant Chicago Cubs. He would later become a Cubs fan during the 1970s when he started dating, and later married, Illinois native Hillary Rodham.

The men who occupied the Oval Office for a dozen years ahead of Clinton had more notable sports résumés. Ronald Reagan played football in college and, as a 30-year-old actor, portrayed legendary Notre Dame running back George Gipp in the 1940 film *Knute Rockne: All-American*. Reagan also famously recreated Chicago Cubs broadcasts for a radio station in Des Moines, Iowa, in the 1930s. Bush was well known to have played baseball at Yale. Even the man who followed Clinton in the White House, George W. Bush, had played Little League baseball and served as managing general partner of the Texas Rangers (1989–94).

What Clinton might have lacked in sports pedigree, he more than made up for once he took office. His first-of-their-kind Opening Day appearances in 1993 and 1996, an effort in early 1995 to help settle the baseball strike, and the boyish enthusiasm he brought later that year to Oriole Park the night Cal Ripken Jr. broke Lou Gehrig's record for consecutive games played, were noteworthy. In 1997 he presided with Acting Commissioner Bud Selig over baseball's historic recognition of Jackie Robinson. In 1998 Clinton's signature drove the final nail in the coffin of baseball's antitrust exemption with respect to issues between players and owners.

Clinton began to build his baseball brand less than three months after taking office in 1993. While continuing a time-honored tradition, he added some new wrinkles to eight decades of Presidential Openers. Ever since William Howard

Taft converted the White House stables into a parking garage for automobiles, Presidents had traveled by chauffeur-driven limousine on Opening Day. For the Orioles's 1993 home opener, Clinton had a different idea. He made the one-hour trip from DC's Union Station to Baltimore's Camden Station by commuter rail. Like most other first-time visitors to Oriole Park, the second-youngest American President in history was awed by the experience. He toured the Orioles's clubhouse and watched the visiting Texas Rangers take batting practice. Unlike any of his predecessors, he elected to wear the home team cap and jacket, winning over the local fans who cheered his high floating toss to Baltimore catcher Chris Hoiles. Of Clinton's delivery, *Sun* columnist John Steadman opined politely, "... he resembled a boy who grew up playing the saxophone." During his inning in the TV booth, he gushed with excitement. "Opening Day is a way for every American to recover his childhood. You've given me back mine."

Less than two years later, Clinton stepped in to try to end the work stoppage that had already canceled the 1994 World Series. Opening Day 1995 was at risk. Of greater political significance, baseball's spring training camps in Florida and Arizona were scheduled to open in late February, two swing states Clinton lost in 1992 but looked to be in play in 1996. The President knew he was powerless in this situation but needed to create the impression he was trying. The parties made no progress during the day-long session at the White House.

By September, play had resumed and the entire baseball world was focused on Oriole Park the night Cal Ripken Jr. was set to break Gehrig's unbreakable record. Clinton wanted to soak up every minute of it. By the third inning, the Commander in Chief was making the rounds to broadcast booths. He spent the third inning with Chris Berman and Buck Martinez on ESPN, reminiscing about growing up a Cardinals fan. About this extraordinary event, Berman told the President, "It wouldn't be a night like this in baseball if you weren't at the park."

An inning later, Clinton found his way to the radio booth where he joined the Hall of Fame voice of the Orioles, Jon Miller. After a Bobby Bonilla homer put Baltimore up 2–1, Ripken took the first three pitches from California Angels starter Shawn Boskie. "Boskie can't walk Cal on this night, can he?" Miller asked his esteemed guest, rhetorically. Ripken had homered the night before in the record-tying game, electrifying the Camden Yards crowd. "Send the order down there, will you," demanded Miller, assuming some mythical Presidential power.

Conventional wisdom would have glued the bat to Ripken's shoulder on the next pitch. But this was no conventional evening. "If he throws one down the middle here, even at 3–0—"

The President interrupted Miller with a prediction.

"He'll swing at it!"

Seconds later, Ripken drilled that next pitch into the left-field seats. The ballpark exploded. So did the President.

"Yes!" he shrieked. For an instant, the leader of the free world sounded a lot like a nine-year-old Cardinals fan in Hope, Arkansas. And just like the other 46,000-plus people who had packed every nook and cranny of Camden Yards, he stood and cheered for the Iron Man.

By Opening Day 1996, Baseball Bill had hit his stride. Since a rainout on Monday forced the game to be moved to Tuesday, some rearranging of the President's schedule tightened things up a bit. Instead of limo or commuter rail, the First Fan hopped into Marine One on the South Lawn of the White House and landed at Fort McHenry in Baltimore minutes later. His chopper jostled the politically powerful welcoming committee: the mayor, governor, members of the Maryland congressional delegation, and more. And with a nod to their ongoing work toward a new collective bargaining agreement, Acting Commissioner Bud Selig and Players Union Chief Donald Fehr were also at the fort to show the President they weren't fighting anymore, at least not in public. The parties were still operating under the terms of the CBA that expired in December 1993, the terms of which were restored by injunction of Judge Sotomayor in May 1995.

After a 10-minute drive to Oriole Park, Clinton was again hanging out at Cal Ripken's locker. Out of respect for the political importance of Missouri's 11 electoral votes (only once since 1904 had anyone won the presidency without carrying Missouri), Clinton made sure to spend equal pregame time in the clubhouse of the visiting Kansas City Royals.

His ceremonial first pitch was more confident than his debut in 1993. He shook off the orange streamers from his ankles that lingered from the pregame festivities and lobbed a strike to catcher Chris Hoiles.

Clinton's cameo in the baseball strike drama of 1994–95 and his 1996 Opening Day engagement probably didn't sway many voters, but it's worth noting Clinton again carried swing state Missouri and reliably blue Maryland in November. He also flipped Florida and Arizona from red to blue en route to a convincing 1996 victory over Bob Dole.

Less than two months after Clinton's second inauguration in 1997, the owners and players formally agreed to a new CBA, setting in motion for the fans a period of lasting labor peace. And a month later on the 50th anniversary of

Jackie Robinson's historic first game with the Brooklyn Dodgers, Clinton again took center stage with Acting Commissioner Selig and Robinson's widow, Rachel. More on this incredible night in chapter 2002.

On January 20, 1997, the day of Clinton's second inaugural, one of the best-known St. Louis Cardinals of Clinton's youth, Curt Flood, lost his battle with cancer. When 20-year-old Flood arrived from Cincinnati in 1958 to play for St. Louis, Clinton was only 11 years old. More than a decade later, encouraged by his idol Jackie Robinson, Flood challenged baseball's reserve clause in 1969, setting in motion an uprising that would forever change the game.

Free agency took hold in the late '70s, but it took 20 more years to make it official. It seemed fitting that it was President Clinton who on October 28, 1998, signed Public Law 105-297 of the 105th Congress—officially, the Curt Flood Act of 1998—revoking baseball's antitrust exemption for labor matters, once and for all.

For box scores, play-by-play and more, visit www.OpeningDay5050.com or use this QR code

1997

"Peanuts, get your ··· poison!"

The Game

Who:	Baltimore Orioles 4, Kansas City Royals 2
Where:	Oriole Park at Camden Yards, Baltimore, MD
Attendance:	46,588
When:	Wednesday, April 2, 1997
Weather:	60s and breezy

Hall of Famers: Orioles 3B Cal Ripken Jr., P Mike Mussina, and 2B Roberto Alomar, plus Orioles general manager Pat Gillick

Game Highlights: My, how the game had changed! On Opening Day 1977, Bert Blyleven and Jim Palmer each pitched 10-inning complete games in two hours and 34 minutes. Twenty years later, on Opening Day 1997, the Orioles and Royals each relied on a starter and four relievers over eight and a half innings that took three hours and 15 minutes. Eight more pitchers. Three fewer half innings. Forty-one additional minutes. Another big change was the meaning of finishing second. On Opening Day 1977, the Orioles were coming off a second-place finish in 1976 which earned them exactly nothing. On Opening Day 1997, the Orioles were coming off a second-place finish which earned them a spot in the newly expanded postseason as a wild-card team. They defeated the Cleveland Indians in the 1996 American League Division Series before falling to the New York Yankees in the ALCS. As much as things change, some things remain the same. On defense, Cal Ripken Jr. moved to third base after 14 seasons at shortstop, but on offense, nothing had changed. Ripken homered and doubled twice to pace the Baltimore offense. Like any Opening Day win, the victory gave the Orioles the satisfaction of starting the year in first place, a position they would not relinquish all season en route to their second straight appearance in the ALCS. It marked only the sixth time in major-league history a team spent the entire regular season in first place.

The Story

In the 15 years since college, I had advanced through a series of progressively better jobs in sports, entertainment, media, and marketing. Four months before Opening Day 1997, I made my sixth and final career move to Comcast Cable (better known today as Xfinity). To oversimplify one aspect of the change, I went from constantly entertaining others at games to occasionally being entertained. The good news that day was that although I was not entertaining anyone, nor was I anyone's guest. I was able to get five tickets, enough for me, Kate, and three of our five kids. The bad news? I no longer had access to special seating, a welcome refuge on foul weather Opening Days.

The weather that day was fine. The Orioles had politely postponed Opening Day in deference to Mother Nature, so I optimistically encouraged my wife to load up Brad, Patrick, and our youngest son, Greg, and meet me at the ballpark. Brad was two days shy of his 12th birthday, Patrick almost 11, and Greg almost 6. Nine-year-old Daniel didn't care much for baseball, so he stayed home with a babysitter along with his two-year-old little sister Mary. After three birth children, we continued to expand our family, adopting Greg in 1993 and Mary in 1994.

By Opening Day 1997, the older boys genuinely liked baseball, although Brad's interest would wane in future years. Both were anxious to continue to indoctrinate their extremely active youngest brother. And since they were home-schooled at the time, getting them out of class for Opening Day was a little easier than it had been for me and Roundy in the 1970s.

Since game time wasn't until 3:00 p.m. and we had no pregame social obligations, I went to the office in the morning and told Kate I would meet them at the will call window at the north end of the Camden Yards Warehouse at 2:00 p.m., a plan I would later regret. I dutifully left the office an hour before our scheduled rendezvous for the 30-minute trip. Opening Day traffic snarls were predictable, but I had failed to take into account that thousands of parking spaces had been wiped out this year due to construction of the Baltimore Ravens new stadium next to Oriole Park. Usually available nearby garages were at workday capacity, so I progressed farther and farther north. One after another I passed signs reading Garage Full.

My stress level was rising, not because I might miss the first inning, but because I knew my wife was waiting not so patiently with three excited and energetic little boys and no game tickets. They'd been left in my name, not hers. After finally ditching my '93 Honda Accord in a very shady lot, I huffed and puffed my way back to the ballpark, jogging, running, and dodging cars and pedestrians. When I arrived, it was a tense reunion with the family an hour later than planned, but at least the tickets were still there. Before we could make our way to the turnstiles, the national anthem began. We stood silently and respectfully. For the next two minutes, I was spared a public scolding thanks to the "Star-Spangled Banner."

Once inside, we wound our way down Eutaw Street basking in sunshine, the iconic warehouse to our left, and the playing field to our right. The anxiety of the past 90 minutes was replaced by the heavenly aroma of Boog's Barbecue.

This was Opening Day!

I didn't dare suggest we stop at Boog's so that I could get something to eat. Kate and the boys had managed hot dogs and chips while waiting. Onward we marched to the upper deck above the first baseline. After traversing the ramps and climbing the stairs, we arrived at our assigned row, and it was "only" the second inning. We climbed over already seated fans to the five empty seats in the middle of the section, repeating the usual:

"Excuse me please . . ."

"Sorry . . ."

"Thank you . . ."

"Sorry . . ."

"Excuse me please."

"Thank you."

"Sorry."

Seated at last. I exhaled and wiped the perspiration from my brow, a moist memory of my crosstown sprint. Brad announced he was hot, too, so he tucked his cherished black-and-orange Orioles jacket under his seat, a decision he would later regret. Patrick pounded his glove, convinced the next foul ball was coming his way, about a mile and a half from home plate. And Greg was just happy to be there.

Then Kate suddenly had an epiphany.

PEANUTS!

It was quickly followed by a motherly panic attack. You see, when we adopted Greg, we learned all about peanut allergies, and his was potentially fatal. Of course, we religiously carried an EpiPen and would never let him ingest or even touch peanuts. I thought he could safely sit on my lap or hers. But at that moment, it seemed to Kate that we were sitting in the official peanut section of Oriole Park. There were discarded shells all around. I guess in previous visits with Greg we'd managed to be more isolated. But not today. Maybe perceptions were heightened because we arrived late and folks had settled into their game day routine, or that we had just climbed over many of them. Whatever the reason, she insisted we find somewhere else to sit.

On multiple occasions over the past 15 years, we'd enjoyed special seating. I had no such access today. Those days were over. She wasn't buying it. I was sent to find an upgrade.

As I embarked on my one-man mission for safer seating, I wondered who might have extra tickets in their pocket. It was known to happen from time to time in my previous life that someone would hold onto tickets too long. While I supposed I could possibly scrounge up a pair, finding five seemed unlikely. Might I get lucky? Since this season opener was supposed to have been played the day before, I wondered if the schedule change might have caused a VIP no-show?

I talked my way to the reception desk on the club level but could get no further without a ticket or pass. All I could do was drop a few names, ask if they could contact my former coworkers, and pray for a favorable response.

Several minutes later, an HTS marketing manager emerged, amused at the misfortune of her former boss. A few of their suite guests were making an early departure. We were in luck! I trekked back to the upper deck and retrieved the family. Brad was overjoyed to learn we were heading to a suite, but his mood suddenly soured when he scraped his beer-drenched jacket off the ground.

We managed to enjoy the rest of Opening Day from the safe, calm serenity of a suite.

Over the next 20-plus years, Greg would become the family's most ardent, lifetime Orioles fan. When Baltimore advanced later that year to the ALCS against Cleveland, Greg and I sat in safety behind home plate, disappointed when the Orioles lost to the Indians. Seventeen years later, we sat in virtually the same seats for the 2014 ALCS against Kansas City but were disappointed again. The occasions are frozen in time in a framed side-by-side photo set, a family treasure.

His passion for Baltimore sports extends across the Camden Yards parking lot. Greg bleeds Orioles orange every summer and Ravens purple every winter.

And he avoids peanuts every day.

For box scores, play-by-play and more, visit www.OpeningDay5050.com or use this QR code

1998

Ken's Column

The Game

Who: Kansas City Royals 4, Baltimore Orioles 1
Where: Oriole Park at Camden Yards, Baltimore, MD
Attendance: 46,820
When: Tuesday, March 31, 1998
Weather: 91 degrees at game time. That's not a typo!

Hall of Famers: Orioles 3B Cal Ripken Jr., P Mike Mussina, DH Harold Baines, and 2B Roberto Alomar, plus Orioles bench coach Eddie Murray and general manager Pat Gillick

---

Game Highlights: With the highest payroll in baseball ($72-plus million) and the most veteran batting order in the game (average age of non-pitchers 33.2; the San Diego Padres were a distant second at 31.1), Orioles fans were hopeful the team that general manager Pat Gillick had assembled might be the one to not just return Baltimore to the ALCS as they had done the previous two seasons, but to win the World Series for the first time in 15 years. Rookie field manager Ray Miller (Baltimore's eighth Opening Day skipper in 14 seasons) was not a big fan of the hoopla surrounding Opening Day. He also wasn't a big fan of the way those veteran bats performed today, mustering only five hits and one run. Utility player Larry Sutton singled, doubled, and drove in three of the Royals four runs. Mike Mussina delivered eight solid innings but took the loss.

The Story

I mentioned in the Introduction this book contains 50 percent memories and 50 percent research. For each chapter the research included game day and day after articles in local newspapers. The exercise provided two striking insights. First, year after year, without exception, local newspapers delivered at least two predictable blocks of Opening Day copy: a talented columnist offering a colorful pregame piece and a know-nothing feature writer describing their experience wandering the grounds, interviewing fans about this special event as if such an article had never been written before. Second, a surprising number of today's most prominent sports media figures cut their teeth in the Baltimore-Washington area: Michael Wilbon, Tony Kornheiser, Christine Brennan, Buster Olney, Tim Kurkjian, Sally Jenkins, Richard Justice, and Ken Rosenthal to name a few.

Before arriving on the national stage covering baseball for *The Athletic*, Fox Sports, and MLB Network, Rosenthal spent 13 years at *The Baltimore Sun* (1987–2000), earning Maryland Sportswriter of the Year honors five times. On Opening Day 1998 he penned one of those game day gems, a version of which could run on any Opening Day in any major-league city. In less than 1,000 words, he perfectly captured so many of the highlights, memories, and emotions of these pages: Camden Yards, weather, Boog Powell, nods to Cal and other future Hall of Famers, Presidents, Rex Barney, Baltimore's managerial carousel, the not-yet-fallen stars of the steroid era (Mark McGwire, Barry Bonds, Rafael Palmeiro), and best of all, fond memories of Opening Days past.

His words that day were pure poetry. Under the headline of "Opening Day never gets old with many happy returns," Rosenthal re-energized this writer's journey at roughly the halfway mark with a magnificent, concise highlight reel. A portion follows.

Opening Day is a Baltimore tradition, a civic celebration, an electric moment in a city where baseball is king and Camden Yards is the throne.

It is a special section in the newspaper, wall-to-wall radio and TV coverage, a media horde of about 500 descending on the day's hero.

It is bunting at the ballpark, pomp and circumstance, the president throwing out the first pitch when he's not running away to Africa.

Opening Day is the sight of the warehouse, the smell of Boog's, the action on Eutaw Street.

The gates of the greatest ballpark on earth swinging open.

The warm smiles of the ushers, welcoming back old friends.

Opening Day is Chapter One of a 162-game mystery.

The 2,479th installment of Cal Ripken's streak.

And 3,038 in a row at home for the Orioles' other Iron Man, 73-year-old umpires attendant Ernie Tyler.

Opening Day is [cancer survivor] Eric Davis starting in right field on the first day of the rest of his life.

It is Boog Powell, Joel Stephens and thousands of others, waging their own courageous fights against cancer.

It is a day to remember Rex, watching from his own skybox.

And a day to embrace new PA announcer Dave McGowan.

Opening Day is Mike Mussina's first appearance at Camden Yards since his glorious performance in the 1997 postseason.

And Armando Benitez's first appearance since Tony Fernandez took him over the right-field wall.

It is a day to raise the flag on the Orioles' first division title since '83, with the team's best manager since Earl Weaver [Davey Johnson] sitting home in Winter Park, Fla.

Think Davey is watching?

Opening Day marks the beginning of the Ray Miller Era, with Mount Angelos dormant.

"My manager searching is over," the owner told USA Today, ominously.

Opening Day is a new beginning for bench coach Eddie Murray. A second chance for pitching coach Mike Flanagan.

It is bullpen coach Elrod Hendricks' 30th opener in an Orioles uniform -- only 14 took place without him.

Opening Day marks the Orioles debuts of warhorses Joe Carter, Doug Drabek, Norm Charlton and Ozzie Guillen.

And maybe the beginning of the end in Baltimore for Rafael Palmeiro and Roberto Alomar.

It is a day to gasp at the most expensive baseball team ever assembled, playing right here in lil' ol' Bawlmer.

And a day to grumble at the price of tickets, concessions and the new caps, redesigned especially for you.

Opening Day is a parachutist dressed as the Oriole Bird, aiming for second base and landing in the parking lot.

It was a good omen -- the Orioles won their last World Series the year it happened, 1983.

Opening Day is a dramatic 10th-inning home run by Bostons Tony Conigliaro in '75, playing his first game since the beaning that forced him to miss the entire '68 season after three years away from the game. [*]

It is Dave McNally's three-hit shutout of Milwaukee in '73, complete with two homers by Frank Robinson and a 4-for-4 day by Don Baylor -- two doubles, a triple and a homer.[*]

Opening Day is a clean score book.

A day that begins with every team unbeaten. A day that ends in a box score.

It is a 12-0 loss to the Brewers in 1988, the Orioles swearing it was only one defeat, when actually it would be 21.

It is a three-run homer by Cal Ripken off Roger Clemens in "89 after Boston Globe columnist Dan Shaughnessy predicted The Rocket would throw a no-hitter.

Opening Day is Brady Anderson playing hurt, B. J. Surhoff grinding out an at-bat, Ripken diving to stab a grounder.

It is Davis raising the roof, Mike Bordick making every play, Alomar taking your breath away.

Opening Day is an afternoon game, a reminder of simpler times and a cellphone extravaganza for the suits who broke away from the office.

It is a two-hour, 20-minute masterpiece or a three-hour, 45-minute mess.

It is a talk-show controversy waiting to happen.

Opening Day is fathers and sons, mothers and daughters, and grandparents telling you about the very first Orioles opener in 1954.

It is a day to break out your old glove.

To remember the first game you ever attended.

To remember the game that broke your heart.

Opening Day is the dawning of spring, the renewal of life, the beginning of time whatever.

Opening Day is a ballgame.

Play ball.

[*] – Author's note: In Ken's defense, in 1998 he did not have the convenience and completeness of today's Internet at his fingertips while writing this column. Roughly 25 years after the facts, he came darn close to nailing the details of Opening Days 1973 and 1975. As described in Chapter 1975, it was *Carl Yas-*

trzemski who hit the game-winning homer in the *12th*. Tony C's dramatic shot that day came in the *5th*. And in '73, it was *Brooks* Robinson who homered twice. Frank had been traded to the Los Angeles Dodgers in late 1971.

For box scores, play-by-play and more, visit www.OpeningDay5050.com or use this QR code

1999

Yet Another Expansion Team (Grrrrr!)

The Game

Who:	Baltimore Orioles 10, Tampa Bay Devil Rays 7
Where:	Oriole Park at Camden Yards, Baltimore, MD
Attendance:	46,733
When:	Monday, April 5, 1999
Weather:	50s and windy

Hall of Famers: Orioles 3B Cal Ripken Jr., P Mike Mussina, and 2B Roberto Alomar, plus Orioles bench coach Eddie Murray, general manager Pat Gillick, and Devil Rays 3B Wade Boggs

Game Highlights: This marked the first Opening Day since 1983 in which Cal Ripken's streak of consecutive games played was irrelevant. The Iron Man quietly ended the string with a week left in the 1998 season. On this day he left the game with back spasms in the third inning, a clear sign his body was starting to say enough is enough. The Devil Rays began their second season by getting to Orioles ace Mike Mussina for four runs in his five innings of work, including a home run by newly signed free agent DH Jose Canseco. Wade Boggs began the final season of his 18-year career with a pair of base hits. The 12-time All-Star would join the elite 3,000-hit club later in the season, punching his ticket to Cooperstown. The Baltimore bats and relievers made the most of the Orioles's otherwise inexperienced opponent with homers by Albert Belle and Brady Anderson en route to the win.

The Story

With construction now complete for the beautiful new football stadium, parking was more plentiful on the south side of Oriole Park for Opening Day 1999. The Baltimore Ravens had played their first game in PSI Net Stadium just a few months before. The city felt more complete with two big-league facilities and teams to occupy them. The Ravens had filled a void in a city that endured 12 years without an NFL team after the Colts moved to Indianapolis.

This marked my 30th consecutive home opener somewhere, 24th in Baltimore, and 8th straight at Camden Yards. After a surge of civic pride while passing the Ravens's stadium, my feelings started to slide to jealousy as I entered Oriole Park. I saw opposing uniforms I'd never seen before and felt bitter and angry. I had nothing personal against the expansion Tampa Bay Devil Rays or any of their players. As they began their second season, the franchise simply represented the latest slap in the face to baseball fans in the nation's capital.

In the 28 years since the Washington Senators were dragged off to Texas against my will, Major League Baseball saw fit to expand its roster of cities three times, adding six new teams. Each time, an ownership group from Washington or Northern Virginia (just a stone's throw across the Potomac River) submitted an impressive proposal. Each time, other cities got picked.

In 1977, Canada was awarded its second team with the Toronto Blue Jays joining the 1969 expansion Montreal Expos north of the border. The other "new" MLB city in 1977 was Seattle. The arrival of the Mariners filled a void created in 1970 when a Wisconsin car dealer bought the bankrupt Seattle Pilots, moved them to Milwaukee, and renamed them the Brewers. Bud Selig delivered for his hometown, filling a void created five years earlier when his beloved Braves moved to Atlanta.

In 1993 Denver and Miami got teams as the Colorado Rockies and Florida (now Miami) Marlins joined the National League. Five years later, Phoenix was awarded the Arizona Diamondbacks while Florida got its second team of the decade, these Devil Rays.

I had embraced other teams since the Washington Senators became the Texas Rangers in 1972. My loyalty moved to the Rangers for a time, then to the White Sox, and now to these Orioles. But the city of my birth still lacked a team. My void had yet to be filled.

The states which had hosted baseball's spring training for generations, Arizona and Florida, now had three teams combined, Canada had two, and even

Colorado had a team, while baseball had been restored in Seattle and Milwaukee. All the while, the supposed most powerful place in the world, America's capital city lacked the great American pastime.

Yes, I was jealous and angry.

Our hopes had been dashed before, not just by being left at the expansion altar in '77, '93, and '97. Washington interests had agreements in place to buy and move the San Diego Padres (in 1973) and Houston Astros (in 1985), only to have the deals fall apart. "Teams and politicians played footsie with Washington, often using the city as leverage to better their own situations and obtain new ballparks," wrote retired *Washington Post* sports editor George Solomon, reflecting on the empty years (1972–2004) in October 2019 during the days leading up to Washington's first World Series appearance since 1933. "The San Francisco Giants were freezing in Candlestick Park, the Chicago White Sox had wandering eyes, and the Cleveland Indians were dying in an 80,000-seat stadium."

On March 9, 1995, Major League Baseball announced Tampa and Phoenix had beaten out Northern Virginia and Orlando and would begin play in 1998. In a morning-after rant, readers could appreciate the sarcasm and feel the frustration flowing from the fingers of *Washington Post* columnist and native Washingtonian Tom Boswell.

"*So, on this fine bright-eyed morning in the hub of the free world, you probably think that Northern Virginia is 'next in line' for an expansion team, don't you bunky? That's what Bud Selig and the Executive Expansion Sub-Committee Council on the Long Range Hustle are whispering in everybody's ear.*

"*And you probably believe them.*

"*Don't bother. We're just a market — that's to say a pawn. When it's the proper fiscal play to gobble us, we'll be swallowed.*

"*But don't hold your breath. For nearly a quarter century, Washington has been an invaluable tool to baseball for extortion. Why would the sport wish to find a less valuable role for us to play?*"

Boswell continued. "*If the Devil Rays, or Manta Rays, or whatever Tampa Bay calls its new nine, don't draw flies in their $138 million dungeon, then the first region you'll hear mentioned is Northern Virginia.*"

I'm with you, Boz! Keep going!

"*When the Senators played their final game in 1971, you couldn't have found one person on earth who would have believed Toronto, Seattle, Miami, Denver, Phoenix and Tampa Bay would all get expansion teams before the nation's capital.*

"*They've put a team in the middle of the desert. They've put a team in the Rocky*

Mountains where there are more bears within a 200-mile radius than humans. They've put two teams in Florida and a second team in another country since the Senators existed. Why, they've even put a second team in the state of Washington – after the pathetic Pilots left – since we had a ballclub here in the real Washington."

Washington's baseball team left RFK Stadium following the 1971 season. Its football team moved to a new home in suburban Maryland in 1997. And yet RFK had not yet been torn down. Although empty, it still stood, like so many other Opening Day images, as perhaps a beacon of hope for DC baseball fans growing tired of the drive to Baltimore.

For box scores, play-by-play and more, visit www.OpeningDay5050.com or use this QR code

2000

Mike Hargrove

The Game

Who:	Cleveland Indians 4, Baltimore Orioles 1
Where:	Oriole Park at Camden Yards, Baltimore, MD
Attendance:	46,902
When:	Monday, April 3, 2000
Weather:	70s, cloudy and breezy

Hall of Famers: Orioles 3B Cal Ripken Jr., DH Harold Baines, P Mike Mussina, and 2B Roberto Alomar, Indians 1B Jim Thome plus Orioles 1B coach Eddie Murray.

Game Highlights: Coming off a breakout season in 1999, Cleveland's 27-year-old ace Bartolo Colón got the better of Baltimore's top gun, Mike Mussina. The two had finished fourth and second, respectively, in the previous season's AL Cy Young Award voting. Speedy Cleveland leadoff man Kenny Lofton's solo homer off Mussina in the sixth proved to be the winning run. A six-time All-Star, Lofton would finish his 17-year career with 130 home runs and 622 steals, ranking No. 15 all time. No other active player has more than 400. This would be Mussina's sixth and final Opening Day start with the Orioles, tying a club record set in 1980 by fellow Hall of Famer Jim Palmer. After 10 years in Baltimore, Mussina would spend his final eight seasons in the Bronx with the New York Yankees. Cal Ripken Jr.'s first-inning double off Colón drew the Iron Man to within eight hits of his 3,000-hit milestone.

The Story

Signs of middle age vary widely. For me, the list included things like close inspection of hair color and quantity, kids becoming teenagers and no longer laughing at my jokes, eagerly anticipated trips to the hardware store, and getting nostalgic about *everything!* That included looking out on the field and seeing men *managing* baseball teams who, it seemed to me, had been *playing* just a few years earlier. Okay, maybe 25 years earlier. At age 39, this was my view of middle age on Opening Day 2000 as Orioles fans gave a hardy welcome to the team's new manager, Mike Hargrove.

He can't possibly be old enough to be an accomplished major-league manager, I thought for a wishful second. *He's only . . .*

Eleven years older than I am.

Ugh.

Hargrove wasn't the first man I'd seen play, and then later, manage. He was the Orioles's fifth manager in seven Opening Days since Peter Angelos bought the team in 1993. I'd seen one of Hargrove's predecessors, Davey Johnson, play for the Orioles in 1972 and then manage the Birds from 1996–97. But I hadn't followed Davey as a player as closely as I had Hargrove during his playing days in Texas. Davey's last Opening Day as a player in Baltimore was my first, on a cold, wet, Sunday afternoon 28 years earlier.

My boyhood hero, slugger Frank Howard of the Washington Senators, had two less-than-heroic stints as a major-league manager in the early 1980s which, thankfully, I never witnessed. He did seem to pop up as a coach quite frequently on my Opening Days: for the Milwaukee Brewers (1978), New York Mets (1982), and Tampa Bay Devil Rays (1999).

While dutifully traveling with Roundy to Baltimore each Opening Day in the mid-1970s, my heart remained with the Texas Rangers (née Washington Senators). The team that played in a modified minor-league stadium in Arlington, Texas, in 1972 was just as dreadful as the one that played in DC's RFK Stadium in 1971. Yet they still were *my* team. Unable to watch them on TV or listen to their games on the radio, I was left to track them diligently in *The Sporting News*, that weekly publication with all the baseball box scores I mentioned in Chapter 1977.

Each year, one by one, familiar names would disappear from the Rangers's roster. Howard was sold to the Detroit Tigers. Pitcher Dick Bosman was traded to Cleveland. Cut by cut, it was a form of torture.

Two one-time Senators blossomed into All-Stars in Texas: shortstop Toby Harrah and outfielder Jeff Burroughs. By 1974 the Rangers added impressive new names to play for 46-year-old manager Billy Martin who had guided the Minnesota Twins to a division title in 1969 and had done the same with the Detroit Tigers in 1972. The Rangers picked up future Hall of Fame pitcher Ferguson Jenkins from the Chicago Cubs as well as other big-name veterans such as six-time All-Star third baseman Jim Fregosi and former American League batting champion Alex Johnson. With right-handed All-Star first baseman Jim Spencer on the roster and the American League now in its second season with the designated hitter batting for the pitcher, Martin spent a roster spot in 1974 on 24-year-old Hargrove, a left-handed hitting first baseman.

One Saturday that summer, Roundy took me to Baltimore to see *my* Rangers. Hargrove was only 40 games into his major-league career and was not in the starting lineup that night. His name had been showing up in those aforementioned box scores on a pretty regular basis for weeks, collecting two-or-more hits nearly a dozen times, ranking him among the league leaders in batting average.

Jenkins was facing Baltimore left-hander Mike Cuellar that night in what turned out to be anything but a pitcher's duel. In the top of the ninth inning after Fregosi cut the Baltimore lead to 6–4 with an RBI single, Martin sent Hargrove (and his blistering .358 batting average) to face right-handed reliever Bob Reynolds with two men on base and nobody out. Hargrove grounded into a force out, the next two Rangers struck out, and the game was over. Disappointed, Roundy and I headed for the exits.

On our way to the car, not far from where we'd met Boog Powell on Opening Day just two months earlier, I spotted Texas pitcher Jim Bibby who would be starting the next afternoon. Rangers pennant in hand, I sprinted over and asked for an autograph. As he signed, Roundy snapped the picture.

Scribble. Click. With the cherished Bibby photo opportunity complete and his autograph in hand, Hargrove's groundout was quickly forgotten.

As for the 1974 Rangers, rarely had a team accumulated so many individual honors in a single season without making the playoffs. Hargrove took home the American League Rookie of the Year Award, Burroughs was named AL MVP, and Jenkins rebounded from a disappointing 1973 season in Chicago to finish second in the AL Cy Young voting while earning AL Comeback Player of the Year. And for leading his team to only the second winning season in the 14-year history of the franchise, Martin was named AL Manager of the Year.

I saw Hargrove play a few more times in the '70s, including Opening Day 1977, when he singled and scored off Jim Palmer in the Rangers' 2–1 win.

After five seasons with the Rangers, Hargrove was traded to San Diego. His departure from Texas after the 1978 season coincided with my defection from the Rangers to the White Sox. I lost track of him for most of the next two decades until he reappeared as manager of one of the most dominant teams in baseball in the late 1990s, the Cleveland Indians. He led the talent-rich club to five straight AL Central division titles and two American League pennants. Yet the Indians unceremoniously dismissed Hargrove four days after falling to the Boston Red Sox in the 1999 American League Divisional Series, another disappointing postseason effort.

Cleveland general manager John Hart explained the firing at the time. "If anything," he said, "it sends the message this club is serious about going to the next level."

That "next level" proved elusive for Cleveland and for Hargrove. Hart stayed only two more years in Cleveland. In the decades that followed, the club advanced to the World Series only one time—losing to the Chicago Cubs in historic fashion in 2016. Hargrove had few healthy weapons in Baltimore, and his teams finished in fourth place each of his four years at the helm (2000–03), although he was the first Orioles manager since Earl Weaver (1969–82) to last more than three full seasons. "Grover" later managed two more losing seasons in Seattle (2005–06) and abruptly walked away from the game for good midway through the 2007 season.

For box scores, play-by-play and more, visit www.OpeningDay5050.com or use this QR code

2001

The Orange Carpet

The Game

Who:	Baltimore Orioles 2, Boston Red Sox 1 (11 innings)
Where:	Oriole Park at Camden Yards, Baltimore, MD
Attendance:	46,547
When:	Monday, April 2, 2001
Weather:	Cloudy, breezy and cold

Hall of Famers: Orioles 3B Cal Ripken Jr. and 1B coach Eddie Murray and Red Sox P Pedro Martinez.

Game Highlights: Fans were treated to an absolute masterpiece: a pitchers' duel featuring two of the game's finest. The newest Oriole, four-time All-Star and 1996 American League Cy Young Award winner Pat Hentgen against the man who would win the award three of the next four years, Boston's Pedro Martinez. Each man gave up only one run. Martinez completed seven innings, while Hentgen lasted into the ninth. Neither was around in the bottom of the 11th when Baltimore's Brady Anderson drove in Jerry Hairston with the winning run. The city was still basking in Super Bowl glory. Just two months earlier, the Ravens had defeated the New York Giants for Baltimore's first football title in 30 years. It had been "only" 17 years since that bizarre Opening Day week in 1984 when the city honored its 1983 World Series winners just days after losing its NFL team to Indianapolis. And just like 1984, the Orioles had a new television home in 2001. Comcast SportsNet had replaced Home Team Sports.

The Story

Every major-league city has its own unique Opening Day rituals and traditions. Some enjoy the adrenaline rush of a military flyover. Others cover the outfield with a field-sized American flag, unfurled by heroes and first responders. For decades in Washington, DC, the President usually threw out the ceremonial first pitch. In *every* city, it's the only day of the regular season when everyone in uniform gets introduced to the crowd—every coach and every player. They emerge from the dugout one by one, first the visitors, then the home team. Excited fans react. Players slap hands like Little Leaguers as they line up between home plate and either first or third base.

But in Baltimore, it's different.

For more than a quarter century at Camden Yards, after the visitors are introduced and lined up between *second* and third base, attention turns from the visiting dugout to straight away center field, and the far end of The Orange Carpet.

Not to be confused with the celebrity runway of similar name associated with Nickelodeon's annual Kids' Choice Awards, The Orange Carpet at Oriole Park splits the outfield in half each Opening Day, stretching about 300 feet from second base to the outfield wall where it meets a festive arch of orange and white balloons.

Out of sight, the players process, single file, from their clubhouse halfway around the ballpark to the bullpen, where they wait patiently until their names are called. Dramatic music and fireworks accompany the unveiling of each player. The Orange Carpet has become an iconic entryway where Orioles fans cheer their favorites, welcome new players, and watch carefully to see if nervous rookies complete the run without tripping.

Although he had not yet decided to retire, fans knew Opening Day 2001 might very well be the final time they would see 40-year-old Cal Ripken Jr. make his way down The Orange Carpet. The ovation for him was memorable. For 24-year-old rookie Jay Gibbons, this anxiety-filled "Welcome to the big leagues" ritual was equally memorable. He made it without incident.

According to the players, it's an Opening Day unlike any other. After a stellar career, mostly in Cleveland and Toronto, five-time All-Star Joe Carter played the final Opening Day of his career as an Oriole. Best remembered for his heroic, walk-off home run to win the 1993 World Series for the Blue Jays, Carter had never experienced anything quite like this. "We really got the orange-carpet treatment," he told Peter Schmuck of the *Baltimore Sun* after Opening Day 1998. "I've been through 14 Opening Days, but I've never been involved in one with this much hoopla and excitement."

Brad Brach spent three seasons in San Diego before joining the Orioles in 2015 and earned his way into the All-Star Game in 2016. Remembering his first Orange Carpet experience, Brach reflected later, "It's a really special day. It's great for the fans, but as a player," he added with great sincerity, "getting to run down that Orange Carpet is truly an honor."

"Running down the Orange Carpet was an incredible feeling," recalled former Oriole Mike Bordick in a 2019 interview with PressBoxOnLine. Bordick played seven seasons in Oakland before replacing Ripken at shortstop in 1997. "It's like a dream. There's this incredible amount of anxiety because it's Opening Day. You put all that time into spring training, and then boom, there is this huge amount of hoopla."

The pre-staged orange trappings debuted in 1997, but the tradition was born a year earlier as a patriotic surprise. On Opening Day 1996, fans thought it was odd to see the Kansas City Royals dutifully take their positions between *second* and third base as their names were called, not along the third baseline. The Orioles's coaches were quietly introduced from the Baltimore dugout and trotted out toward second base. Suddenly, five members of the Camden Yards grounds crew frantically rolled out a red carpet from the outfield toward second base. The red, white, and blue balloon arch appeared out of nowhere. President Bill Clinton was in the house, and the decorations needed to match the occasion. Patriotically clad junior cheerleaders rushed to their positions along the runway.

Fittingly, Cal Jr.'s younger brother Bill was the first player ever to make such an Opening Day entrance. Hall of Fame broadcaster and Master of Ceremonies Jon Miller welcomed Bill back to Baltimore after three years of exile in Texas and Cleveland.

After the non-starters were introduced, Miller welcomed home another former Oriole, new manager Davey Johnson. Davey played for Baltimore from 1965–72 and later managed the New York Mets (1984–90) and Cincinnati Reds (1993–95). The energized Johnson sprinted from center to second faster than any of his players.

"This is the Opening Day I'll remember," he said later that day. "I've had capacity crowds in New York and big crowds in Cincinnati, but this was definitely special. It gave me chills. I'm not one to show much expression, but I could hardly hold it in."

Memorable? Special? For someone, Opening Day always is.

For box scores, play-by-play and more, visit www.OpeningDay5050.com
or use this QR code

2002

Mariano Rivera: The Final 42

The Game

Who:	Baltimore Orioles 10, New York Yankees 3
Where:	Oriole Park at Camden Yards, Baltimore, MD
Attendance:	48,058
When:	Monday, April 1, 2002
Weather:	Spectacular! 60s and breezy

Hall of Famers: Yankees manager Joe Torre, SS Derek Jeter, P Mariano Rivera, and P Mike Mussina (yes, now a Yankee!)

Game Highlights: For the second time in 13 years, the game's most decorated starting pitcher, Roger Clemens, was sent home from Baltimore on Opening Day on the losing side. In 1989, he had already hit the showers when the Orioles beat his Red Sox in 11 innings, although Cal Ripken Jr.'s three-run home run off Clemens in the sixth helped lead to the 5–4 win. The 39-year-old now-Yankee had just won the sixth of his record seven Cy Young Awards in 2001, but labored this afternoon, lasting just four and a third innings, giving up eight earned runs.

The game also marked the first regular-season Yankees game on their new cable channel, YES Network. Back in New York, viewers heard analyst Jim Kaat's pregame description of the Orioles's anemic run production of recent seasons that coincided with the diminished role of now-retired Ripken. "For the last few years, they've had a 'low Cal' offense," he told broadcast partner Michael Kay. "This year, they have a 'no Cal' offense." At least for this one day, Cal's successor at third base, Tony Batista, provided all the calories the Orioles needed: a grand slam off Clemens in the bottom of the fourth inning.

The Story

It seemed only fitting that the New York Yankees began their 100th season in the city from whence came the most famous player in franchise history, Babe Ruth. The Babe surely spent time as a boy in what was now center field of Oriole Park where his dad once owned a saloon. Since the opening of Camden Yards, transplanted New Yorkers flocked to Baltimore from throughout the Mid-Atlantic whenever the Bronx Bombers were in town. Others enjoyed the two-and-a-half-hour ride on Amtrak's Acela from Midtown Manhattan.

My boss had bought a larger-than-usual bunch of tickets, knowing demand to see the visiting team would be quite high. I was happy to get just one! For my 33rd consecutive Opening Day, it seemed for the first time that the home team's fans might be outnumbered. When the relief pitchers emerged from the dugout for their walk to the left center-field bullpen, thousands of fans in Yankee caps and pinstripe jerseys came to their feet and cheered, although a few heckled closer Mariano Rivera. Just five months earlier, "Mo" had blown the save opportunity in Game Seven of the World Series in the Arizona desert. Those few fans were quickly silenced by the overwhelming majority who seemed more appreciative and respectful. The game's most dominant closer, Rivera had led the majors in saves two of the previous three years and averaged 42 saves (remember that number) over the previous five seasons, during which time the Yankees won four American League pennants and three World Series. The more obnoxious few wondered what Mariano had done for them lately!

On Rivera's back was something you didn't see too often in Major League Baseball anymore.

Number 42.

Only five years earlier at an emotional ceremony in New York marking the 50th anniversary of Jackie Robinson's debut with the Brooklyn Dodgers, Major League Baseball took the unprecedented step of retiring his jersey number for all teams for all time. Players wearing number 42 at that time, many in honor of Robinson, were allowed to wear it for the rest of their careers. And for the final 10 years of his Hall of Fame career (2004–13), Rivera stood alone, an honor he took seriously and wore proudly.

On April 15, 1997, the baseball world stopped, quite literally, to pay homage to the legacy of the man who in 1947 had the talent, courage, and self-control to become the first African American invited to play Major League Baseball. After the fifth inning of a scoreless game, Commissioner Bud Selig, Robinson's widow,

Rachel, and President Bill Clinton took center stage at Shea Stadium where the Mets were hosting (who else?) the Los Angeles Dodgers in front of a national television audience. Selig led off with brief remarks and a bombshell announcement. "Throughout its long history, Major League Baseball has operated under the premise that no single person is bigger than the game—no single person other than Jackie Robinson. In his life, and in the remarkable legacy he left for all Americans, Jackie Robinson was, and remains, bigger than the game. Jackie's entry into baseball 50 years ago today will forever remain baseball's proudest moment.

"In honor of Jackie," Selig continued, "Major League Baseball is taking the unprecedented step of retiring uniform number 42 in perpetuity. Those players who currently wear 42 . . . in tribute to Jackie may continue to wear the number for the remainder of their careers. However, number 42, from this day forward, will never again be issued by a major-league club."

The stunned, capacity, mostly white crowd erupted with approval. Selig concluded, "Number 42 belongs to Jackie Robinson for the ages."

"It is hard to believe that it was 50 years ago at Ebbets Field that a 28-year-old rookie changed the face of baseball and the face of America forever," Clinton told the crowd. Even though on crutches, still recovering from knee surgery, he exuded a confidence we hadn't seen four years earlier at Oriole Park. "Jackie Robinson scored the go-ahead run that day. And we've all been trying to catch up ever since."

"This anniversary has given us an opportunity as a nation to celebrate together the triumphs of the past and the social progress that has occurred," Rachel concluded. "It has also given us an opportunity to reassess the challenges of the present. It is my passionate hope that we can take this reawakening and feeling of unity and use it as a driving force so that each of us can recommit to equality of opportunity for all Americans."

Her words continue to resonate decades later.

On the night of Selig's announcement in 1997, 13 major-league players still wore the number 42. Four of them took the number to new teams in the twilight of their careers: Mo Vaughn, Butch Huskey, José Lima, and Mike Jackson. By Opening Day 2002, only four 42s remained, and two years later only Rivera. That same year Selig announced that April 15 of every season would be Jackie Robinson Day, and by 2009, all uniformed personnel in baseball would mark the occasion by wearing No. 42.

If Reggie Jackson hadn't changed his mind before the Yankees 1977 season, the number 42 might not have been available to Rivera when he arrived. It would have been enshrined in Monument Park at Yankee Stadium attached to Reggie's name. After Jackson signed with New York in November 1976, he announced he would honor Robinson and wear 42 in pinstripes. His proclamation drew rage from the New York media, especially those sympathetic to Yankee-hating fans of Robinson's Brooklyn Dodgers, who considered Jackson's gesture a sacrilege. Before the 1977 season started, he opted instead to honor the all-time home run king Hank Aaron who had just retired following the 1976 season. Reggie's number 44 was retired by the Yankees in 1993, two years before Rivera's Bronx debut.

Rivera's jersey assignment was rather random. As a 25-year-old rookie who spoke very little English, the young Panamanian knew hardly any American or baseball history. It wasn't until his third season, upon learning of Selig's proclamation, that the Yankees's No. 42 realized he had some homework to do.

"I was really naïve when it came to statistics, the people that had played the game," Rivera recalled to MLB.com's Mark Feinsand in April 2020. "I was just happy to play the game and do the best I could to help the team win. People were talking about Jackie, making such a big move to retire the number, so I decided I better learn about him and understand what he was all about, what he did."

While acquiring historical context, Rivera also acquired a devastating cutter, a pitch that fooled opposing hitters for the next 17 seasons. He often called the sudden emergence of his cut fastball in 1997 a gift from God. A humble man of great character and faith, Rivera went about his business over the years without flash or fancy. He set all-time records for saves in the regular season (952) and postseason (42—that number, again!), starred on five World Series championship teams, and appeared in 13 All-Star Games, earning the game's MVP honors in 2013.

By announcing before the start of the 2013 season his plan to retire at season's end, it afforded each city he visited that summer the opportunity to plan special tributes, perhaps none more special than in Los Angeles. By now, Rivera was well aware of the storied Yankees-Dodgers rivalry. The two teams met in the World Series six times during Robinson's too-brief 10-year career. As part of the pregame ceremonies, he heard from Rachel Robinson. "You have worn the number with class and dignity," she said, "and I believe you have added to the historic significance of that number. I'm sure that if Jack had seen you play, he'd have been proud to have had his number worn by you.

"Although," she added with a smile, "he probably would have wanted it to be for a team other than the Yankees."

Five years later Rivera became the first baseball player in history to earn the vote of 100 percent of the Hall of Fame electors, arguably the greatest of the all-time greats.

As he was getting ready to join Robinson in Cooperstown, Rivera talked with ESPN about his acquired respect for the "other" 42.

"The legacy of Mr. Jackie Robinson, to me, was something special. You know (me) being a minority, someone coming from Panama, and what he did for us . . . to remain firm in the belief that what he was doing would be something special. I took that real serious. I took that as a challenge. It was a blessing. It moved me to always do my best so I can make Mr. Jackie Robinson proud of me. That was my challenge. I wanted to do whatever it takes to keep the legacy that Mr. Jackie Robinson left us."

For box scores, play-by-play and more, visit www.OpeningDay5050.com or use this QR code

2003

The Steroid Era

The Game

Who:	Baltimore Orioles 6, Cleveland Indians 5 (13 innings)
Where:	Oriole Park at Camden Yards, Baltimore, MD
Attendance:	46,257
When:	Monday, March 31, 2003
Weather:	30s, blinding snow in the third, followed 15 minutes later by bright sunshine!

Hall of Famers: None (as of March 2022)
Future HoFers?: Indians P CC Sabathia? (eligible 2025)

Game Highlights: Indians 22-year-old left-hander CC Sabathia held Baltimore in check through seven innings, allowing only two earned runs. However, five Baltimore relievers outlasted the Cleveland bullpen in extra innings, giving up only one run in their seven innings of work. Orioles Gary Matthews Jr. ended the game with a two-out, bases-loaded single in the bottom of the 13th. Later in the season, Sabathia would make the American League All-Star team for the first of seven times during his 19-year career, primarily with the Indians and Yankees. He pitched more than 3,500 innings, making him one of the last great workhorses the game may ever know. He finished in the top five among AL Cy Young Award candidates five times and won the award in 2007.

The Story

Opening Day 2003 marked the approximate and very unofficial halfway mark of Major League Baseball's steroid era. Remarkably, this would be the first season players would be subjected to any sort of testing for the performance-enhancing drugs (PEDs). It had been 15 years since the pumped-up young Bash Brothers, Jose Canseco and Mark McGwire, powered the Oakland A's to the first of three consecutive World Series appearances, yet it would be another 15 years before more rigorous testing, strict enforcement, and harsh consequences would allow baseball to confidently claim that, with respect to performance-enhancing drugs, it had restored the integrity of a game played by imperfect people.

The use of PEDs by many players had been rumored for years, but there were few public admissions of guilt, virtually no physical evidence, and a wide array of convincing denials, fueled by a baseball media machine willing to play along. That was about to change. From 2003 to 2013, multiple federal investigations, whistle-blowers, and public results from expanding testing programs combined to cast a dark shadow over a generation of players, bloated statistics, and tainted titles. Eventually, several of the game's biggest, statistically worthy stars were denied enshrinement by the voters into the National Baseball Hall of Fame.

It was fittingly ironic that, for a time on this Opening Day at Oriole Park, the fans—quite literally—could not see what was happening on the field in front of them. A brief but intense snowstorm in the third inning caused Orioles right fielder Jay Gibbons to lose sight of a fly ball, leading to a 15-minute snow delay. Years later we would learn Gibbons was one of several players on the Orioles's roster in the early 2000s tied to PEDs. And as the public's eyes were opened in the years that followed, the Orioles would get a disproportionate amount of attention as the steroid story unfolded.

In Ken Burns's 2010 documentary film *The Tenth Inning* (a fitting epilogue to his 1995 masterpiece *Baseball*), *ESPN The Magazine* editor Gary Hoenig summed up the conflicted attitude of so many sports journalists of the era when it came to the steroid story. "You're sort of contradicting your own desires, not only personal, but professional," he admitted. "On the one hand, you're thinking, 'Gee, I should find out about this.' Then, on the other hand, you're thinking, 'Do I *really* want to find out about this? I mean, I'm not really here to tear sports down for fans. I'm here to make sports joyous for fans.' So you're living a contradiction."

That contradiction was center stage in the summer of 1998. Baseballs had been flying out of ballparks at a suspiciously high clip since the days of the Bash

Brothers, but the epic battle in '98 between McGwire, by then with the St. Louis Cardinals, and Sammy Sosa of the Chicago Cubs, electrified the sports world. Both men shattered Roger Maris's 37-year-old single season record of 61 home runs: Sosa with 66 and McGwire with 70! Barry Bonds upped the ante with 73 in 2001 en route to a career total of 762, seven more than Hank Aaron's all-time record.

In August 1998 Associated Press reporter Steve Wilstein observed a bottle of androstenedione on visible display in McGwire's wide-open locker. At the time, "andro" was a little-known over-the-counter product already banned by the International Olympic Committee and NFL where drug testing was now routine, but it had not yet been banished by baseball. Wilstein reported what he saw and was vilified for it. Cardinals manager Tony La Russa suggested Wilstein be banned from the locker room. Even a few fellow journalists jumped on the bandwagon, pointing out andro was not illegal in baseball. They were too wrapped up in the thrill of the Maris chase.

"There was not an embracing of the issue, that we have a problem, and we need to solve this problem," Wilstein recalled when interviewed for *The Tenth Inning* a dozen years later. "There was no sense in baseball that this was the tip of the iceberg, that we need to look further to see who else is using performance-enhancing drugs. It was more, 'Bury our heads in the sand, and maybe it will go away.'"

It didn't go away. More and more "clean" players were insisting on testing, but the players' union under Executive Director Donald Fehr objected. Interviewed for *The Tenth Inning*, Fehr arrogantly and naively proclaimed, "The notion that we would willingly surrender to our employer as the price of a job, all the protections we insist on from the government is a rather extraordinary notion."

There was nothing "extraordinary" about it. According to the American Management Association, by 1996, 81 percent of US employers subjected their employees to drug testing, including the federal government itself. Perhaps fueled by his victory in the 1994–95 strike, Fehr had clearly lost touch with the world around him and was leading the union down a dark path.

Also interviewed for *The Tenth Inning*, revered Hall of Fame broadcaster Bob Costas said emphatically, "The players association did a horrible job in this case. They should have seen this early on and said, 'Wait a minute. How can we expect some of our players to compete at a competitive disadvantage? . . . to either use (PEDs) to keep up, or don't use and, inevitably, fall behind? Who is it that we represent? The guilty or the innocent?'"

In 2003 highly confidential "survey" testing of players began. A new, four-year collective bargaining agreement between the owners and players had been reached in August 2002, just hours before the strike deadline. It was a historic CBA, the first reached without a strike, and the first to include random testing of major-league players for steroids. However, there were strings attached.

Testing in 2003 was intended only to measure the actual scope of the issue and nothing more. Results would never be made public (or so they thought), and there would be no punishments for a positive test. If more than 5 percent of players tested positive for a banned steroid, tougher testing and penalties would follow in 2004. In November MLB announced the 5 percent threshold had been exceeded. SI.com, *The New York Times*, and other media outlets would report years later that the confidential 2003 list included more than 100 players. Dozens of names were leaked including some of the game's biggest stars.

Year after year the issue continued to make headlines. The conversation shifted from professionals enhancing or prolonging their careers, to younger athletes emulating the pros, putting their health, *and lives*, at risk. Every relevant government entity got involved, including congressional committees, the DEA, FBI, FDA, IRS, and more. Baseball players learned painful lessons about privacy and confidentiality. There were no more secrets. From 2003–13 every time a steroid lab or similar business was investigated or raided, another client list would surface that included athletes from track and field, football, and baseball. Informants came forward from MLB locker rooms, trading information for immunity. Even a few players, under oath, came clean with details not only about themselves, but about other players.

The most significant example of a player exposing fellow players was Canseco. After his steroid-infused playing career fizzled, perhaps the most disliked man in baseball wrote a tell-all book published in early 2005. He detailed his own 20-plus years of steroid use and described how he taught other players the "benefits" of doing the same. But the most shocking part of his book? He named past and current players he claimed were using steroids.

Bolstered by a blizzard of national media attention, *Juiced: Wild Times, Rampant 'Roids, Smash Hits, and How Baseball Got Big*, became a *New York Times* best seller, fueled dozens more inquiries and investigations, and triggered routine denials.

The ritual became all too common, regardless of the source or target. The oft-repeated script included most of the following:

1. Accusation.
2. Vehement denial.

3. Discredit the accuser.

4. Repeat the denial.

5. Evidence.

6. Discredit the evidence.

7. Acknowledge it *might* have happened but don't know how. Maybe an accident? (Example: "I did not knowingly allow an illegal substance into my body.")

8. Blame a medical professional, trainer, or teammate for providing steroids instead of vitamins.

9. Admit to making mistakes.

10. Apologize to teammates, family, and fans.

11. Move on.

12. Accept your next big money contract.

Owners and general managers were increasingly concerned they might be spending tens of millions of dollars on free agent players whose market value was based on inflated statistics, and whose playing days might be numbered. Non-steroid-using players were outraged by the unfairness of competing for jobs on an uneven field. Both demanded a more aggressive approach. As the parties negotiated a new CBA that would take effect for the 2003 season, the owners demanded, and the players association reluctantly agreed to, a testing plan.

Over time, random tests became more frequent, the list of covered substances expanded, testing became more sophisticated, and most importantly, punishments became more severe. In 2005 a player would be suspended just 10 games for his first failed test and wouldn't miss a full season until his fourth infraction. By 2014 the slash line was 80/162/life. The first failure cost a player 80 games. Second time? Miss a season. Third time? You're done. The consequences were grave, especially for a younger player for whom a half season off the field caused proportionately greater financial pain and could permanently derail a career.

When it came to Hall of Fame consideration, by 2007 the increasingly enlightened voters punished the players who passed the statistical performance tests with flying colors but flunked the "integrity, sportsmanship, character" considerations specified in the Baseball Writers' Association of America Rules for Election. In the history of the game, fewer than 300 players have been elected out of more than 15,000 who have played. Members of the 500-home-run club were once considered automatic. All 15 who hit 500 or more home runs and played in the 1970s or earlier are in the Hall, most elected in their first year of eligibility: Hank Aaron, Babe Ruth, Willie Mays, Frank Robinson, Harmon Killebrew, Reggie Jackson, Mike Schmidt, Mickey Mantle, Jimmie Foxx, Willie McCovey, Ted Williams, Ernie Banks, Eddie Mathews, Mel Ott and Eddie Murray—legends all. Yet of the 13 who joined the club in the 1990s or later, only four have been elected: Frank Thomas (2014), Ken Griffey Jr. (2016), Jim Thome (2018), and David Ortiz (2022). Two are not yet eligible as of 2022: Albert Pujols, and Miguel Cabrera. The writers have made clear the other seven—McGwire, Sosa, Bonds, Rafael Palmeiro, Manny Ramírez, Gary Sheffield, and Alex Rodriguez—are not welcome in Cooperstown because of their connection to PEDs.

The "survey" testing of 2003 reportedly identified many of the game's biggest stars, and none missed a game as a consequence. Fifteen years later things looked quite different. Between 2017 and 2019 only 13 active players (*total over three years!*) were suspended for PED violations according to Baseball-Almanac.com, all first-time offenders, and each missed 80 games without pay.

There was only one big name on the list: eight-time All-Star second baseman Robinson Canó. His 2018 suspension came during the fifth year of a 10-year, $240 million contract and cost him nearly $12 million! With five years left on his contract, you'd think an 80-game punishment would be a deterrent to future steroid use! Sadly, no. In November 2020 Canó became a two-time offender and was suspended for the 2021 season. It cost him another $24 million.

"A superstar who now will warrant only scorn," wrote Ken Rosenthal, now senior baseball writer for *The Athletic* after Canó's second suspension. "Canó has ruined his good name and almost certainly can forget about election to the Hall of Fame, an honor that seemed likely before his first suspension and still might have been possible if he had not received his second.

"It's fair to debate whether voting members of the Baseball Writers' Association of America should make moral judgments on Hall of Fame candidates," Rosenthal continued. "But when a player proves to be a cheater, not once but twice, the authenticity of his career is thrown into question.

"It's sad," he concluded, "for a player of Canó's talent might have made it to Cooperstown without PEDs. But it's also infuriating, because of the lies Canó lived during at least a portion of his career, and the lies others told on his behalf."

The Canó story clearly is now the exception, not the rule. In 1998 the baseball world pounced on a reporter who dared to question the credibility of a hero's accomplishment. Nearly a quarter century later, the next generation of reporters is challenging the credibility of the next generation of flawed heroes.

Of the 13 position players on the Orioles 2003 Opening Day roster, four were later linked to PEDs: Gibbons, Gary Matthews Jr., David Segui, and Jerry Hairston Jr. From 2004 to 2005, Palmeiro, Sosa, Miguel Tejada, and Jason Grimsley would join the team, all proven or admitted steroid users. By contrast, the list of 31 players suspended between 2014 and 2020 included no Baltimore players.

Times had changed.

Baseball's crackdown on PEDs took too long to start and too long to implement. And while a few still make bad decisions and pay a high price, the steroid era finally appears to be over.

For box scores, play-by-play and more, visit www.OpeningDay5050.com or use this QR code

2004

Thank You, Peter Angelos

The Game

Who:	Baltimore Orioles 7, Boston Red Sox 2
Where:	Oriole Park at Camden Yards, Baltimore, MD
Attendance:	47,683
When:	Sunday, April 4, 2004
Weather:	Freezing! 40s plus strong wind from center field

Hall of Famers: Red Sox P Pedro Martinez and DH David Ortiz

Game Highlights: Optimism for the 2004 season emanated from both dugouts this night. Boston had bolstered its pitching staff with five-time All-Star Curt Schilling joining Opening Night starter Pedro Martinez at the top of the rotation in hopes of a deep postseason run. Red Sox Nation was wondering if this just might be the year they would finally break the "Curse of the Bambino." Where better to begin the quest for their first World Series title since trading away Babe Ruth to the Yankees after the 1918 season than Baltimore, Babe's birthplace? A national television audience joined the fun to see Baltimore's expensive new roster energize the local fan base, a feeling markedly absent the past six losing seasons. Ownership shelled out big bucks during the offseason to lure several free agents including Atlanta's three-time All-Star catcher Javy Lopez, Oakland's 2002 American League MVP shortstop Miguel Tejada, and Texas's slugging first baseman Rafael Palmeiro, back for his second stint with the Orioles. All three shined on Opening Night. Lopez hit his first pitch as an Oriole off Martinez into the left-field seats and later doubled home Tejada and Palmeiro in the seventh.

Less than six months earlier in Game Seven of the 2003 American League Championship Series, then-Boston manager Grady Little allowed Martinez to face a few too many batters in the eighth inning. Four Yankee hits and three runs later, the game was tied, New York eventually won in 11 innings, and Little was fired. In the opposing dugout that night in the Bronx was Joe Torre's respected bench coach, Lee Mazzilli. On Opening Night 2004, Mazzilli had the same field-level view of Martinez, this time from the Orioles's dugout as the team's new manager.

The Story

Lee Mazzilli's first day as a major-league manager began with a phone call from his mentor, Joe Torre, and a pregame clubhouse visit from a man he'd never met before, Orioles owner Peter Angelos.

For the past four seasons, Mazzilli had learned much from Torre whose Yankees had won six of the previous eight American League pennants and four World Series. The Hall of Famer's pregame message to his mentee-turned-division-rival was simple: Be yourself and trust your convictions.

It's unlikely the 74-year-old Angelos could have related to the same advice. He had never aspired to be like anyone but himself, for better or worse, and the only convictions he trusted were his own. Over the years he was branded by sportswriters as a meddler, not trusting the recommendations of those he'd hired to run the ballclub. In hiring Mazzilli, however, Angelos had been hands-off, approving the recommendation of the search committee led by his co-general managers, Jim Beattie and Oriole pitching great Mike Flanagan. A season and a half later, Angelos was more hands-on when Mazzilli was fired after a three-week summer losing skid.

In 1993 this personal injury lawyer's group outlasted Jeffrey Loria at a bankruptcy auction, and Angelos became managing partner and principal owner of the Baltimore Orioles. It marked the return of local ownership of the franchise for the first time since National Brewing Company President Jerry Hoffberger sold the team to Washington, DC lawyer Edward Bennett Williams in 1979. Sportswriters, fans, fellow owners, and others have been trying to figure out Peter Angelos ever since. Most have failed.

One writer who tried harder than most was *Sports Business Journal* correspondent Bruce Schoenfeld, who interviewed more than 40 people in 2013, most off the record, about one of the most unique owners in sports, a contrarian who didn't fit the mold. Schoenfeld brought to the effort a more objective lens than any local sportswriter. He talked to past and current players, front office executives, politicians, law firm associates, childhood friends, and family members. Everyone, it seemed, spoke to Schoenfeld but Angelos himself, who did not respond to Schoenfeld's invitations to participate.

Schoenfeld's cleverly written piece titled "The Complicated Peter Angelos" took a "man in the mirror" approach. His 5,000-word essay seemed to get deep into Angelos's head. In 2021, eight years after it was published, I asked Schoenfeld to summarize his findings. He declined. "I don't know that you can," he said.

"He's a very complex man."

"What matters most to Peter Angelos?" Shoenfeld asked Angelos rhetorically in the 2013 article. "Those close to you don't hesitate. It's the Law Offices of Peter G. Angelos, P.C., first, and everything else after. The firm you started in 1961 isn't just your place of business. It defines you. 'He's a lawyer,' says (Andy) MacPhail, who ran the Orioles's baseball operations from 2007 to 2011, 'who happens to own a baseball team.'

"That sets you apart from the dark suits who fill the seats at the owners meetings," Schoenfeld continued, "but it's hardly all that sets you apart. You look around at the corporate titans who have become rich by tilting the playing field and taking advantage of the working man on behalf of the moneyed interests, and you feel the bile rising. They're fat cats, tycoons, Republicans. You're a battler, a laborer, a Democrat. Better than they are? Smarter, more honorable, more worthy of admiration? Damn right you are."

In his earliest days as Orioles owner, Angelos took bold steps to strengthen his franchise, winning over players and local fans while infuriating his fellow owners. Fans were worried that by spending so much to buy the team, he wouldn't have money left to invest in players. They were wrong. During their first offseason under Angelos, the Orioles spent more than $40 million on free agents, a significant amount by 1994 standards. A year later when Acting Commissioner Bud Selig and the other owners announced plans to have strike-breaking scabs replace major-league players for the 1995 season, the labor-friendly Angelos refused. Once the strike ended, angry fans in other cities showed their disgust with players and owners by staying away in droves, but not Oriole Park. Blue-collar Baltimoreans and well-heeled travelers continued to flock to Camden Yards to experience the game's best ballpark and appreciate baseball's most expensive lineup.

"Alone among the 28 franchises, yours supported the players during negotiations, most visibly by refusing to authorize replacements," Schoenfeld's "man in the mirror" told Angelos. "You'd taken labor's side against management all your life. Never had a corporate client, you like to brag. 'Peter hates corporate America,' says a former associate who spent much of his adulthood working for your firm. 'This is a guy who wore short-sleeve shirts to work with a tie. He had his office in a blue-collar section of Baltimore. He was a peasant. A peasant who got rich and bought a baseball team.'"

By 1996 the Orioles had brought in two of the best leaders in baseball, field manager Davey Johnson and general manager Pat Gillick. Both men were winners everywhere they'd been and had World Series championships on their résumés with the New York Mets and Toronto Blue Jays, respectively. The Orioles flourished, advancing to the American League Championship Series in both 1996 and 1997.

After four years the honeymoon was over, as one by one the legends and Hall of Famers departed. Hall of Fame broadcaster Jon Miller went home to San Francisco after the 1996 season following 13 glorious years in Baltimore. A year later Johnson elected not to return, and Gillick departed once his contract expired a year after that. Pitcher Mike Mussina continued his Hall of Fame career as a New York Yankee in 2001, and Cal Ripken retired at the end of that season.

By the time the 2004 campaign got underway, Orioles fans had endured six consecutive fourth-place finishes. Only the expansion Tampa Bay Devil Rays were worse. In spite of the 1994–95 players strike, attendance at Oriole Park averaged more than 44,600 per game from 1992–97. From 1998–2003 it dropped 14 percent. To local sports media and fans, the once-proud Orioles's franchise was disappearing before their eyes, and they largely blamed Angelos. He generally refused to engage with his media critics except to occasionally set the record straight when he felt the public had been misinformed.

Meanwhile, farther south, another group of fans and sportswriters was growing more hostile. Washington was still without a team of its own, and the trip to Baltimore was becoming harder to justify. Efforts to return Major League Baseball to the nation's capital were gaining momentum, and Angelos was leading a one-man crusade to derail it.

"It's not going to work," he was quoted by Tom Heath in *The Washington Post* in November 2002. "If you put a team in the Washington area, it would make it impossible for either team [Baltimore or Washington] to generate the revenues to be competitive in the divisions in which they play.

"Washington has the Capitol," he continued. "It has the White House, Congress, the Smithsonian. It has the government office, museums and the Mall. What else does it want?"

Many in Washington at the time would gladly have traded Congress and the White House for a baseball team!

In late 2001 the owners voted 28–2 to contract Major League Baseball from 30 teams back to 28, just three years after the expansion Devil Rays and Arizona Diamondbacks had completed their inaugural seasons. The struggling Minnesota Twins and Montreal Expos were on the chopping block. Legal action in Minneapolis forced the Twins to honor their stadium lease, effectively nixing the owners' plan. Major League Baseball took ownership of the Expos and spent the next three years looking for a new home for the team. Washington was on the short list.

Angelos relentlessly continued his crusade right up through Opening Day 2004 and beyond. Yet by the end of the season, the battle appeared over. On September 29, 2004, one day before the 33rd anniversary of the last Washington Senators game, it was official. The Expos would be moving to DC for the 2005 season.

Angelos wasn't done yet.

"When Major League Baseball relocated Montreal's Expos to Washington, it made one huge mistake," Schoenfeld's "man in the mirror" reminded Angelos in 2013. "Commissioner Bud Selig announced that the deal was done before working out how you would be compensated for encroachment on your broadcast territory. MLB underestimated you."

"They thought Peter would be reasonable," remembered Joe Foss, who helped orchestrate Angelos's purchase of the club in 1993 and served as the team's COO for the next 14 years, "and Peter had absolutely no intention of being reasonable. He felt that he had a responsibility to protect the economic value of his franchise for himself and his minority owners."

And his hometown.

Even though all 29 of his fellow owners voted to approve the relocation of the Expos, they still had to finalize a plan to compensate Angelos. After six months of negotiations, he accepted financial guarantees worth hundreds of millions of dollars, including a disproportionate share of a new regional sports channel. It would control the television rights of both the Orioles and the new Nationals franchise for 20 years or more. In return, he agreed to something he had vowed he would never accept: a team in Washington.

Hoffberger, whose legacy of local ownership Angelos restored in Baltimore, had also once struggled with the prospect of peaceful coexistence between Baltimore and Washington. According to Hoffberger's April 13, 1999, obituary in *The New York Times*, "When the Griffith family, owners of the Washington Senators, expressed opposition to the sale of the St. Louis Browns to Baltimore investors in 1953, Mr. Hoffberger offered to have his brewery sponsor Senators games. That deal helped soften the Senators's opposition to a nearby competitor for their fan base."

The price Washington owners would one day pay to soften Angelos's opposition was somewhat higher than a beer sponsorship.

Opening Night 2004 was my 29th opener in Baltimore. It was also my last.

For Opening Day 2005, I was going home.

Thank you, Peter.

For box scores, play-by-play and more, visit www.OpeningDay5050.com or use this QR code

2005

Baseball's Back!

The Game

Who:	Washington Nationals 5, Arizona Diamondbacks 3
Where:	RFK Stadium, Washington, DC
Attendance:	45,596
When:	Thursday, April 14, 2005
Weather:	Perfect!

Hall of Famers: Nationals manager Frank Robinson

Game Highlights: For a team that played 22 of 81 "home" games each of the past two seasons in Puerto Rico, and the first nine games of 2005 on the road, these former Montreal Expos were just happy to settle down in a stadium they could call home for the next three years. The new Washington Nationals provided more than enough offense this night in front of more than 500 national media representatives and an emotional, nostalgic, and electrified sellout crowd. Nationals starting pitcher Liván Hernández, 1997 World Series MVP for the Florida Marlins, took a 5–0 lead into the ninth inning before needing relief help from 22-year-old closer Chad Cordero. Veteran third baseman Vinny Castilla, who had spent most of his big-league career with the Colorado Rockies, was just a single away from becoming the second Nationals player in eight days to hit for the cycle. Center fielder Brad Wilkerson had done it in the season's second game at Philadelphia. Diamondback reliever Lance Cormier ended the historic bid when he delivered his first pitch to Castilla's back. The young right-hander was lustily booed by the home crowd that was quickly relearning the nuances of fandom after 33 seasons without baseball. Castillo would finish with a double, triple, homer, and four RBI.

The Story

I had been planning this night for more than six months, but it was a night nearly 34 years in the making.

After Major League Baseball announced on September 29, 2004, they would be relocating the Montreal Expos to Washington, DC for the 2005 season, I was overcome with nostalgic joy. *The Washington Post* shared my emotional letter to the editor the following week:

The return of baseball stirs up a lifetime of memories.

I remember the transistor radio under my pillow and the voices of Shelby Whitfield, Tony Roberts, and Ron Menchine. I remember watching games on Channel 9 with Warner Wolf and Ray Scott. I was 11 when I attended the last Senators game with my dad. I begged him to let me go out on the field with everyone else as all hell broke loose. Dad said no. I cried myself to sleep that night.

We journeyed to Baltimore for many years whenever the Texas Rangers came to town, but that interest eventually faded. Once I made a banner and hung it from the mezzanine of Memorial Stadium. It said: "Go Senators!" A big picture of it appeared the next day on the front page of the sports section of the Washington Star.

I remember Dad taking me to Rinaldi's Cleaners near the White House one Saturday morning. That's where the teams' uniforms got laundered. Old Mr. Rinaldi let me try on the jerseys of Frank Howard and Reggie Jackson; the jerseys were bigger than I was.

Memorial Stadium's gone now. So are the Star and Rinaldi's. And, yes, Dad's gone too. But he'll be with us in April when I take his grandchildren to RFK. Baseball's back!

MICHAEL ORTMAN
Ellicott City

On April 14, 2005, I had a promise to keep. Only three of Roundy's grandchildren were available to join me and Kate: Daniel (16), Greg (13), and Mary (10). The other three were not living at home at the time. We took Metrorail to RFK Stadium, a mode of transportation that didn't exist in 1971. A friend in the Nationals's makeshift front office helped me buy, at face value, five of the hottest tickets in DC sports history. Scalpers were getting more than $1,000 per ticket, and the crowd was a "who's who" in the nation's capital. Among the more than 45,000 fans able to get tickets for this historic event, relatively few attended that chaotic finale in 1971. After all, there were only 14,460 of us that night. Many of them, like Roundy, had long since passed away.

We arrived about 4:30 p.m., two and a half hours before game time, and security lines were already quite long. President Bush was expected to join the celebration. I couldn't wait to get through the metal detectors to lay my eyes on something I hadn't seen in a very long time: my personal field of dreams. As we waited, the kids were very tolerant of my childish chatter.

"I'll never forget . . ."

"There used to be a peanut vendor who . . ."

"I remember the time . . ."

"We used to park our car over there . . ."

Daniel even politely asked why, if the new team was playing in the same stadium as the old team, they didn't have the same name—Senators. I explained that local politicians didn't like the old name since Washington did not have elected representation in the United States Senate. Besides, during the first half of the 20th century, they used the names "Senators" and "Nationals" (or "Nats" for short) interchangeably, so for this new team, Nationals worked.

In the decades since a *real* baseball game had been played at RFK, I had attended at least 100 soccer or football games here but ignored more than a dozen baseball exhibitions. I had memories of many Senators games including my first frigid Opening Day in 1970, sitting high above third base as part of a capacity crowd. I also remembered sitting much closer to the field, just beyond first base for that sparsely attended finale in 1971.

Once inside, but before climbing to the upper deck, I insisted we visit the front row of Section 211 where Roundy and I sat on September 30, 1971. Thanks to our early arrival, no ushers impeded the pilgrimage.

As the five of us entered the lower bowl of this vintage 1960s multipurpose stadium, I felt like actor Ned Beatty as Rudy's dad entering Notre Dame Stadium and seeing the band of the Fighting Irish for the first time.

"This is the most beautiful sight these eyes have ever seen."

The city government spent more than $18 million to quickly get the 44-year-old dump ready again for baseball, and MLB schedulers put the Nats on the road for the season's first two weeks to buy the work crews more time for the makeover. They slapped sufficient lipstick on this pig to last three seasons. They even repainted (in white) three specific seats in the upper deck, the landing spots of monster home runs hit by Frank "Hondo" Howard more than a generation ago.

Whoever had purchased those Opening Night seats in Section 211 had not yet arrived, so we made ourselves comfortable. I pointed to center field and explained to the kids about the two-part sign that scrolled from the upper deck the night of the final game, chastising Senators owner Bob Short who was taking our team to Texas. SHORT. STINKS.

For a moment I paused and thought about the people of Montreal. Somewhere in French-speaking Canada was a little boy who attended the Expos finale but had no Opening Day this year.

I then pointed to the upper deck above third base and told Kate, "That's where Roundy and I sat for Opening Day 1970." I tried to explain to the kids how there used to be football seats where left field and center field were this night. Those sections shook during the rowdy Super Bowl years under Joe Gibbs.

Sufficiently reconnected, we zigzagged our way to the upper deck, grabbed a bite and a beverage, and scaled the steps to the 14th row of Section 550, just shy of the very top. Uniformed military stood watch, alternating their gaze between the growing crowd inside the stadium and the throng they could see over the wall, waiting outside. The kids passed some of the pregame time letting these Air Force spotters know their oldest brother also wore a uniform. Brad was in his second year at West Point. "Go Army. Beat Air Force!" Mary proclaimed.

As angry as we had been at Major League Baseball over the years for failing time and again to restore baseball in Washington, tonight, all was almost forgiven. The Nationals still had no owner, so this was MLB's team. They staged a memorable pregame ceremony that connected 1971 to 2005 almost as if only a single offseason had passed.

Picking right up where he left off 34 years and eight days ago on Opening Day 1971, my former boss, 77-year-old public address announcer Charlie Brotman introduced the coaches and players: first the visiting Arizona Diamondbacks, then the home team Nationals. The ovation was deafening. RFK was shaking. Servicemen and women unfurled an American flag that spanned the outfield, and opera star Renée Fleming provided an inspiring rendition of the "Star-Spangled Banner" as four F-16 jets rumbled across the sky.

There had been rumors a few still-living Washington Senators would participate in the festivities. What played out in the moments that followed spanned generations.

Former Senators pitcher Joe Grzenda emerged from the Nationals's third-base dugout. Grzenda was, quite literally, the last man standing on September 30, 1971. That night, with the Senators protecting a 7–5 lead in the ninth, Yankees outfielder Bobby Murcer hit a ground ball to Grzenda who flipped to first baseman Tom McCraw for the second out. McCraw had put the Senators ahead in the bottom of the eighth with a two-out, pinch hit single. (Coincidentally, McCraw was in the Nationals dugout this night, serving as the team's 2005 hitting instructor.)

Grzenda never got to throw another pitch that night in 1971 as angry fans poured onto the field. Players fled to their locker rooms for safety, the umpires called the game a forfeit in favor of New York, and Grzenda held onto that baseball for 33 years, 6 months, and 14 days. On Opening Night 2005, he handed it to the President of the United States.

George W. Bush took the mound and threw a strike to catcher Brian Schneider.

RFK shook again.

The scriptwriters perhaps saved the best for last. Brotman, who had introduced President Bush at his second inaugural less than three months earlier, resumed his baseball duties, introducing a cast of former Washington Senators. He had no trouble with pronunciations. He had introduced each of them decades before.

One by one, they emerged from the dugout, each wearing a Nationals warm-up jacket and a baseball glove, almost as if they were ready to play. Seven-time All-Star Mickey Vernon, 87, made his way to first base. Vernon's career stretched from 1939–1960 including a two-year pause to serve in World War II. The much-younger Roy Sievers, only 78, had a longer journey to the outfield. The 1949 AL Rookie of the Year was joined by Fred Valentine and Jim Lemon (who managed the Senators in 1968). Then came the younger guys who played here at RFK in the 1960s and '70s: former Howard University baseball coach and founder of the Major League Baseball Players Alumni Association, Chuck Hinton, slick fielding shortstop Eddie Brinkman, pitcher Jim Hannan, and the starter of that final game in September 1971, Dick Bosman.

They saved the best for last.

With the crowd already in a nostalgic frenzy, 68-year-old Frank Howard, the ever-humble Hondo, limped his way to left field. The triumphant soundtrack from *The Natural* filled the stadium. If I had closed my tear-filled eyes, I would have seen the lights atop RFK exploding as Howard, not Roy Hobbs, rounded the bases.

RFK was shaking. Grown men were crying.

Before the crowd could catch its breath, the cast of lesser-known young men joined their elders. Vernon welcomed 26-year-old Nick Johnson to first base. Hinton greeted Vinny Castilla at third. Cristian Guzmán introduced himself to Brinkman at short, and Brad Wilkerson was overshadowed by the still-larger-than-life Howard in left. The Senators then removed their mitts and handed them over.

The baseball gloves, like this night, belonged to the Washington Nationals.

The celebration continued for most of the next two and a half hours until the postgame fireworks had subsided. This city hadn't seen a major-league game in more than a generation, but these fans were clearly ready to resurrect Washington's storied baseball past, turn the page, and help write the next chapter.

"This is closure for me, it really is," the 61-year-old Bosman told Jeff Barker of the *Baltimore Sun*. "That last game here was chaotic. You just knew something was going to happen, and it turned into mayhem."

Among the World Series–like throng of sportswriters in the Nationals's locker room after the game was Tim Brown of the *Los Angeles Times*. He observed plainspoken veteran relief pitcher Joey Eischen sharing his first impressions with *Washington Post* columnist Tom Boswell.

"Eischen looked at a Washington reporter," Brown wrote, "and explained, 'Ya'll's baseball fans never left. Baseball did.'

"And then it came back."

For box scores, play-by-play and more, visit www.OpeningDay5050.com or use this QR code

2006

Alfonso Soriano

The Game

Who:	New York Mets 7, Washington Nationals 1
Where:	RFK Stadium, Washington, DC
Attendance:	40,530
When:	Tuesday, April 11, 2006
Weather:	70s and sunny!

Hall of Famers: Nationals manager Frank Robinson and Mets pitchers Tom Glavine and Pedro Martinez
Future HoFers?: Mets OF Carlos Beltrán? (eligible 2023)

Game Highlights: Five of the eight position players voted to start the 2006 All-Star Game for the National League were in the starting lineups for the Nationals's 2006 home opener. The problem for Washington? Four of the five played for the New York Mets. Shortstop José Reyes, catcher Paul Lo Duca, center fielder Carlos Beltrán, and third baseman David Wright combined for eight hits this day, scoring four runs and driving in six. The potent Mets offense also included first baseman Carlos Delgado, acquired in the offseason from the Florida Marlins. Delgado reached base twice and scored. New York would coast to the National League East title in 2006. The fifth NL All-Star? Nationals newly acquired star left fielder Alfonso Soriano collected one of only three Nationals hits, a meaningless home run in the seventh. Rookie third baseman Ryan Zimmerman, who had hit his first career home run a week earlier at New York, also singled.

The Story

By Opening Day 2006 the euphoria of the Nationals's inaugural season had worn off. Major League Baseball was still dragging its feet, not yet naming a new owner for the franchise, and the team languished in mediocrity after a fifth consecutive offseason without a future vision. The glint of optimism spawned by a shocking 51–30 start in 2005 was muted by a depleted roster for 2006 and a 2–5 start on the road. The home opener was typical of the season that lay ahead—a forgettable pitching matchup, a good but less-than-capacity crowd, and a single, shining star in a losing effort: Alfonso Soriano.

There were no stars on the pitcher's mound this day. The matchup was a powerful reminder of how spoiled I had been. Almost every year for the past 36, Opening Day starting pitchers had included the best of the best: five future Hall of Famers (Mike Mussina, Jim Palmer, Fergie Jenkins, Pedro Martinez, and Bert Blyleven); nine others who won Cy Young Awards (Mike Cuellar, Vida Blue, Mike Scott, LaMarr Hoyt, Mike Flanagan, Roger Clemens, Rick Sutcliffe, Bartolo Colón, and CC Sabathia); and countless others with at least an All-Star Game appearance. This day we got Ramón Ortiz for Washington and Brian Bannister for New York. Ortiz's career would span 12 seasons on eight teams. He led his league in home runs surrendered in 2002 and losses in 2006 and would retire with a forgettable 4.95 career ERA. Bannister was worse. He would hang it up after just five seasons with a 5.05 ERA. But today, the Nationals made Bannister look like an All-Star.

Soriano's solo shot in the seventh provided the day's only offense for Washington. It was his third home run of the young season, a year that would see him win the hearts of hungry fans in Washington, be voted to start the 2006 All-Star Game, and put up historic numbers on offense. And just as Opening Day was a microcosm of the season for the Nationals, so too was 2006 a mini-version of Soriano's career. He changed teams twice, changed positions once, earned some individual accolades, and put up numbers on offense that were great but not good enough.

Soriano was a superstar on a team that had none. A rare talent who possessed both power and speed, he joined the Nationals in December 2005 when Nats general manager Jim Bowden sent popular outfielder Brad Wilkerson and two others to the Texas Rangers for Soriano. The arbitration-eligible second baseman had played in four consecutive All-Star Games representing the American League. He emerged from the arbitration process in February 2006 with a one-year, $10-million contract to play for the Nationals.

Soriano's professional baseball career began in Japan in the late 1990s before signing with the Yankees organization. Once in the majors, he put up excellent numbers in 2001, yet finished third in Rookie of the Year voting (behind Ichiro Suzuki and CC Sabathia). In 2002 he was the best hitting second baseman in the American League with 39 homers and 102 RBI. Soriano led the league in runs, hits, and stolen bases, yet finished third in Most Valuable Player voting (behind juicers Miguel Tejada and Alex Rodriguez). After another stellar season in 2003, Soriano was sent to Texas in exchange for Rodriguez and cash. Two more All-Star seasons later, he was shipped off to Washington.

When told during spring training by Nationals manager Frank Robinson he would be moving from second base to left field, Soriano was more than unhappy. He flat out refused. But with 10 million reasons in 2006 to reconsider and an even bigger payday looming in free agency, the speedy slugger decided to accept the change.

By July 2006 the mood around the Nationals was more upbeat. Major League Baseball accepted $450 million from local developer Ted Lerner to own the team. The Lerner family outlasted seven others in a process that had dragged out for nearly two years since MLB decided to move the Montreal Expos to Washington in September 2004. On July 21 the Lerners staged a second Opening Day of sorts, a grand reopening, promising a better game day experience for the next season and a half at 45-year-old RFK before moving to a shiny new ballpark. Lerner family members, front office executives, players, and coaches greeted fans at every entrance, even 70-year-old manager Robinson.

"Frank was only supposed to be at the gate for 30 minutes, but he stayed an hour," said an appreciative Mark Lerner, Ted's son and the team's managing partner.

At another entrance was an emotional and excited Soriano, connecting face to face with his DC fans. Most assumed that with the Nationals deeply entrenched in last place in their division and the trading deadline looming in just 10 days, the All-Star's brief stay in Washington was nearing an end. "Everybody says: 'Stay. Please don't go,'" he told Tom Boswell of *The Washington Post* of his pregame "meet and greet" experience. "The team knows how I feel. I love DC. It's a great city. I believe in my friends here. I'd like to stay. I'm waiting."

The inspired Nationals won their next six games at home and re-energized the fans. Soriano led the charge, reaching base 15 times in 28 plate appearances, hitting two home runs, and stealing two bases. He would finish the season with

46 homers and 41 steals, making him only the fourth player in major-league history to reach the 40–40 milestone. The careers of the other three—Jose Canseco (1988), Barry Bonds (1996), and Alex Rodriguez (1998)—were stained by evidence of steroid use. Add his 41 doubles, Soriano's 2006 performance stands alone. He remains the only player in baseball history to top 40 in all three categories in a single season.

Alfonso said he'd like to stay in Washington. He got his wish (for a few months, anyway). The 2006 trading deadline came and went, and Soriano remained a National for the rest of the season, allowing DC fans to celebrate his historic milestone. After hitting home run No. 40 in Philadelphia on August 19, he stole base No. 40 at RFK four weeks later.

Bowden was criticized by many for *not* trading Soriano in July for future talent. But in November after Soriano signed an eight-year $136 million deal with the Chicago Cubs, the Nationals were awarded two compensatory draft picks in 2007. They used the second of those picks to select right-handed pitcher Jordan Zimmermann who would become a two-time All-Star, a stalwart in the starting rotation of the Nationals's first-ever playoff team in 2012 and author of the team's first no-hitter in 2014.

As for Soriano, after six and a half productive seasons in Chicago, the Cubs traded him in July 2013 to the Yankees, the same team that welcomed him to the big leagues nearly 14 years earlier. He was released a year later.

In 16 seasons Soriano hit more than 400 home runs and stole nearly 300 bases, a set of numbers that earned many others Hall of Fame consideration. He ranks 11th all time with a power-speed number of 339.71, a metric crafted in 1980 by baseball stats guru Bill James, recognizing the rare combination of home runs and stolen bases by the same player. Of the 10 ranked ahead of him, two have been punished by Hall voters for using performance-enhancing drugs (Bonds and Rodriguez) and Carlos Beltrán had yet to appear on the ballot as of 2022. Six of the other seven have been inducted in Cooperstown: Rickey Henderson, Willie Mays, Joe Morgan, Andre Dawson, Hank Aaron, and Craig Biggio.

But not Alfonso Soriano. He got no love from the voters. His lack of clutch hitting in the postseason with the Yankees (2001–03) and Cubs (2007–08) was notable (.213 average and only four home runs in 186 postseason plate appearances). Combined with his legacy of poor fielding, especially early in his career at second base, Soriano's time on the Hall of Fame ballot lasted as long as his career with the Washington Nationals. He first appeared on the ballot in 2020, receiving less than 2 percent of the vote. A player needs 75 percent to get into the Hall and 5 percent to stay on the ballot in subsequent years.

He was done after just one season.

 For box scores, play-by-play and more, visit www.OpeningDay5050.com or use this QR code

2007

Farewell to RFK

The Game

Who: Florida Marlins 9, Washington Nationals 2
Where: RFK Stadium, Washington, DC
Attendance: 40,389
When: Monday, April 2, 2007
Weather: 70s and sunny!

Hall of Famers: None (as of March 2022)
Future HoFers?: Marlins 3B Miguel Cabrera? (eligible five years after retirement)

Game Highlights: Marlins starter Dontrelle Willis reminded fans why he was National League Rookie of the Year in 2003 and NL Cy Young runner-up in 2005. On Opening Day 2007 he gave up only one earned run in six innings while the Marlins tagged Washington starter John Patterson for six runs in four. Dmitri Young, who would be Washington's token representative in the 2007 All-Star Game, drove in Ryan Zimmerman with a double in the sixth. Dan Uggla and Miguel Cabrera homered for Florida and Hanley Ramírez collected four hits. The Nationals and Marlins would battle all season for last place in the NL East, a painful start for two rookie managers, Washington's Manny Acta and Florida's Fredi González. The Marlins would edge out the Nationals, finishing 18 games behind the first-place Philadelphia Phillies and two games behind the Nats.

The Story

My college sophomore son Patrick was able to skip afternoon classes and join his old man for RFK Stadium's final Opening Day. By this time next year, Nationals Park would be complete, and RFK would be a permanent memory. Today was about celebrating the present—a father-son outing, spectacular weather, and a fresh start for our Nationals—and began a season-long reflection on the past.

In spite of a 33-year absence of Major League Baseball, this 46-year-old venue was full of fond family memories. I'd attended hundreds of events here, mostly soccer and football games, a few seasons of baseball, and even a memorable Beach Boys concert. Many of their classic song titles and lyrics fit well with memories of this old barn.

"Good Vibrations" happened during football playoff games and whenever the Dallas Cowboys were in town. Fans moved in unison and caused the lower bowl to shake.

"Wouldn't It Be Nice" if the baseball gods would allow baseball to return. It was!

"I Get Around" this stadium with ease, from working the press box in the '80s announcing international soccer matches and United States Football League games, to shuffling to new seat locations season after season, each time Roundy was able to upgrade his football season tickets.

After nearly 40 years here, there was one constant: "Fun, Fun, Fun."

The fun began in 1968 when my parents provided my first tastes of pro football and baseball at DC Stadium. It was renamed Robert F. Kennedy Memorial Stadium in early 1969, less than a year after the assassination of the former attorney general and US senator. Every pro football game at RFK was sold out from 1968 through 1996 when the team moved to FedEx Field just eight miles to the west in suburban Maryland. Because RFK was hollow under the lower bowl, the stadium literally shook, especially during the winning seasons and Super Bowl years under future Hall of Fame coaches Vince Lombardi (1969), George Allen (1971–77), and Joe Gibbs (1981–92).

After the Senators left in 1971, Roundy tried to fill the summer void with an occasional pro soccer game. Soon after Brazilian star Pelé joined the North American Soccer League (NASL) in 1975, his New York Cosmos came to RFK to play the Washington Diplomats in front of what was then the largest crowd ever to attend a soccer game in the United States. Roundy and I were among the

35,620 fans that steamy summer afternoon.

Eight years later I was old enough to get myself to the stadium (and buy my own beer) as part of another huge soccer crowd for a late June game of the NASL's short-lived Team America. The game happened to include a free post-game concert by the Beach Boys. It's not clear how many of the 50,108 people thought they were buying concert tickets with a free pre-concert soccer match, or vice versa. President Ronald Reagan's Interior Secretary James Watt had banished the Beach Boys from performing on the National Mall on the Fourth of July, saying their music might attract the "wrong element."

Subject for another book.

Soccer at RFK also held special memories for our daughters, Mary and Theresa. Kate and I gushed with pride in 2003 when the girls each got to make a ceremonial "first kick" at a Women's United Soccer Association game. On the receiving end of their crisp passes were World Cup stars Abby Wambach and Mia Hamm of the Washington Freedom. It was Theresa's ninth birthday, and she even got special scoreboard recognition.

But of all the games and memories, one family story gets told over and over and spans generations from 1971 until 1996. I'm sure on this Opening Day 2007, Patrick's eyes rolled as I told it one more time.

The story begins on September 30, 1971, when Roundy took his 11-year-old son (me!) to that last Washington Senators game at RFK. Near the end the fans poured out onto the field, tearing up the turf. Wanting a grassy souvenir of my own, I looked up at my dad and said, "Let's go out on the field, Dad, and tear up some turf!"

"No, no, no, Son," he replied. "It's too dangerous."

As I recollected in that 2004 letter to the editor of *The Washington Post*, I cried myself to sleep that night in 1971.

More than 25 years later, on December 22, 1996, I took my 10-year-old son (Patrick!) to the last raucous pro football game at RFK. As Washington neared the end of its thrashing of Dallas, we wound our way to the lower bowl around the 30-yard line to what had been Roundy's season ticket seats. We greeted the two police officers who sat next to him for years. I hadn't seen them since Dad passed away more than two years earlier. They expressed their condolences.

With the Cowboys on the losing end of a 37–10 score, RFK was filled with joy, not anger. The fans poured onto the field. I'd seen this before, although the mood was less festive. I looked down at Patrick and said, "Let's go out on the field, Son, and tear up some turf!"

"No, no, no, Dad," he replied. "It's too dangerous."

History sometimes has a weird way of reversing itself.

I made eye contact with the officers, in search of a favor. They nodded. I then looked back at Patrick and said, "Then you need to stay here with my friends. I have some unfinished business to attend to."

The large chunk of right field, or rather the south goal line, extracted that afternoon from RFK, was boxed and shared with family members, one chunk of which remains in our basement fan cave.

Some fans never grow up.

Opening Day 2007 boiled up nearly 40 years of memories, so many of which shaped my fanaticism and friendships for generations. One more Beach Boys lyric came to mind.

"God only knows what I'd be without you!"

We were about to find out.

For box scores, play-by-play and more, visit www.OpeningDay5050.com or use this QR code

2008

Mr. Walk-Off, Ryan Zimmerman

The Game

Who:	Washington Nationals 3, Atlanta Braves 2
Where:	Nationals Park, Washington, DC
Attendance:	39,389
When:	Sunday, March 30, 2008
Weather:	Chilly! 40s and breezy

Hall of Famers: Braves pitchers Tom Glavine and John Smoltz, 3B Chipper Jones and manager Bobby Cox

Game Highlights: While the Philadelphia Phillies won the NL East every year from 2007 through 2011, this night belonged to the teams who would each finish more than 20 games behind the 2008 World Series champion Phillies, teams whose dominance had passed or was yet to come. The Atlanta Braves had ruled the East for more than a decade, winning the Division title 11 straight times (1995–2005). The Washington Nationals would win the Division four times between 2012 and 2017 plus the 2019 World Series. But on Opening Night 2008, Atlanta and Washington had the entire baseball stage to themselves for the grand opening of Nationals Park. The home team delighted their packed house with a pair of first-inning runs, a highly unlikely start considering Atlanta starter Tim Hudson shut down these same Nationals all four times he faced them in 2007, surrendering only two runs in 30 innings. Future Hall of Fame third baseman Chipper Jones cut the lead to 2–1 with a fourth inning solo home run off starter Odalis Pérez. Neither team managed another hit until the ninth. Atlanta's Jeff Francoeur doubled, advanced to third on a groundout, and scurried home with the tying run when Nationals catcher Paul Lo Duca couldn't handle a Jon Rauch slider. That set the stage for a dramatic ending to the grand opening party: a two-out, bottom-of-the-ninth, game-winning home run by 23-year-old third baseman Ryan Zimmerman.

The Story

By 2008 my previous Opening Days had provided a few lessons in proper planning for the unique experiences that accompany capacity crowds, new ballparks, Presidential pregames, and the like. This would be the eighth time I would see the President throw out the ceremonial first pitch and the second time I would help christen a new baseball cathedral: Camden Yards in 1992 and tonight at Nationals Park. The most important lesson learned over the years about nights like this one? Arrive very early.

I also had learned that if you cared about the game's outcome, you sometimes needed to stay very late. Three times during my streak, the Orioles had won on Opening Day in walk-off fashion, but never like this night.

With sons Patrick (21) and Greg (16), I exited the Navy Yard Metro station about 4:00 p.m., more than four hours before game time, anxious to experience the neighborhood around the ballpark. We had not realized the "neighborhood" did not yet exist. Nationals Park was surrounded by vacant lots, abandoned buildings, and a few pop-up businesses staffed by opportunistic entrepreneurs. It was an area with a hopeful future but not much of a present. With a global financial crisis in full swing, it would be many more years before construction would catch up with the plan envisioned in 2004 when the city agreed to pay for a stadium on the banks of the Anacostia River.

We were among the first through security and had plenty of time to wander around this modern marvel. Since Oriole Park set the standard for retro ballparks 16 years earlier, baseball had opened 13 new venues; two more were under construction in New York City and another in Minneapolis. We connected with other awestruck friends who were equally impressed and proud of our team's new home. As we continued to explore, I made the boys stop on the upper deck for a photo of them with the Navy Yard in the background. Better known as the supposed setting for the CBS television show *NCIS*, it's where their great-grandfather, Louis Ortman (Roundy's dad) worked for 40 years as a machinist in the Navy's munitions factory. After World War II he was honored by Navy Secretary John Sullivan for his commitment to helping to train less experienced workers.

The energy in the ballpark was much like it had been three years earlier for the team's first game at RFK, but instead of nostalgia, this night would create new memories. President George W. Bush was back to handle first pitch duties. When he emerged from the dugout, he was greeted by two men who were not at that inaugural game in 2005: Bush's pregame battery mate and second-year manager Manny Acta and the Nationals promising young third baseman Ryan Zimmerman. On Opening Night 2005, Zim was midway through his final season at the University of Virginia before becoming the Nationals's first draft pick that June.

The beginning of this night belonged to Acta and Bush. The ending belonged to the Z-Man.

About two and a half hours after Bush's first pitch, Zimmerman stepped to the plate in the bottom of the ninth with the score tied at 2–2. Less than half the sellout crowd had braved the cold to stay until this dramatic moment. ESPN's Jon Miller was telling the national TV audience what a clutch hitter young Zimmerman was. "Last year, he made his hits count," Miller explained. "Despite only 91 RBIs, 18 of them were game-winning RBIs!"

Exactly four seconds later, Zimmerman lined Peter Moylan's next pitch into the hands of a fan in the front row above the left-center-field wall, and the ball game was over.

While watching their team lose more than win the previous two seasons, Nationals fans embraced Zimmerman as the face of the franchise, a reliable hitter who could deliver excitement during otherwise down times. He already had ended games with home runs three times, plus three more game-ending RBI singles.

Among the exuberant fans who stayed and were rewarded was William F. Yurasko, sitting in the mezzanine level above the third baseline. After witnessing the fourth walk-off home run and seventh walk-off RBI of Zimmerman's young career, only one thing came to mind for the 31-year-old blogger. "I was screaming it, 'Ryan Zimmerman is Mr. Walk-Off, Ryan Zimmerman is Mr. Walk-Off,'" he would tell *Washington Post* columnist Dan Steinberg more than seven years later. Steinberg had diligently researched the first use of the now-permanent nickname.

Yurasko couldn't wait to make his nightly post. Under the headline which repeated the words he'd screamed just a short time earlier he wrote, "Ryan Zimmerman sent a telegram to the baseball world this evening: 'I am Mr. Walk-Off.'"

The moniker stuck and in the seasons that followed, Zimmerman added more glue. By Opening Day 2021, Zimmerman would accumulate 16 walk-off hits including 11 home runs. Only seven players have done it more often: Jim Thome 13 times; and Babe Ruth, Stan Musial, Mickey Mantle, Jimmie Foxx, Frank Robinson, and Albert Pujols 12 times each. All are in the Hall of Fame except Pujols, and the curators in Cooperstown are surely saving space for Albert's plaque when he becomes eligible in the late 2020s.

Zimmerman's career would include many milestones. The runner-up for 2006 National League Rookie of the Year, he would go down in history as the only first-year player ever to drive in more than 100 runs and *not* win the Rookie of the Year Award (Miami speedster Hanley Ramírez won by a razor-thin margin). Zimmerman would appear in two All-Star Games (2009 and 2017) and established a new record for home runs by a Washington baseball player with 283 (through 2021) with the Nationals, besting Frank Howard's mark of 237 with the Washington Senators. Fittingly, Zim would hit the first World Series home run in team history in 2019 and would savor his most cherished walk-off later that month: walking off the post-parade stage on the National Mall with a World Series trophy.

For box scores, play-by-play and more, visit www.OpeningDay5050.com or use this QR code

2009

Harry Kalas, RIP

The Game

Who: Philadelphia Phillies 9, Washington Nationals 8
Where: Nationals Park, Washington, DC
Attendance: 40,386
When: Monday, April 13, 2009
Weather: 50s and breezy

Hall of Famers: None (as of March 2022)
Future HoFers?: Phillies 2B Chase Utley (eligible in 2024)

Game Highlights: While the Philadelphia Phillies came into the day still celebrating their 2008 World Series championship, this Opening Day would prove to be unlike any other, as the Phillies would end up playing the game with the heaviest of hearts. Meanwhile, the struggling Nationals were still looking for their first win of 2009 after losing their first six games in Miami and Atlanta. With 46-year-old pitcher Jamie Moyer starting for the Phillies, Nationals fans were hopeful. But a pair of Washington errors led to three unearned runs in the first five innings, wasting an otherwise decent outing for Nats starter Daniel Cabrera. The baseball left the yard frequently (three home runs for each team), including a ninth inning, two-run shot by Washington's Ryan Zimmerman off All-Star closer Brad Lidge. But Lidge quickly retired the next three batters to earn the save, just as he had six months earlier in the decisive Game Five of the World Series. The Nationals fell to 0–7, a perfect start to a season that would see Washington lose more than 100 games for the second straight year.

The Story

I lingered too long at a pregame social event, so by the time I got to my seat on Opening Day 2009, the Phillies had already been introduced and were lined up along the third-base line as I slid past standing fans to get to a seat in the middle of Section 116. After the Nationals were introduced, public address announcer Jerome Hruska shared shocking news that rocked the baseball world.

His voice cracked with genuine, personal emotion as he requested a moment of silence for Harry Kalas. The legendary voice of Phillies baseball for nearly four decades had died of a heart attack just a short time earlier in his broadcast booth at Nationals Park.

Pregame moments of silence are always somber and respectful. This one was jarring. I was stunned, as were many around me. As I looked down at the Phillies players less than 100 yards away, it was clear these men were deeply shaken. Many Phillies fans unable to get tickets for their team's banner-raising and ring ceremonies at Citizens Bank Park a week earlier had made the trip to Washington to extend their celebration. As I glanced around, it was clear most of the Philadelphia fans already knew of Harry's sudden passing and had been sharing it among themselves, jersey to jersey. News must have traveled fast by phone, texts, and word of mouth over the previous hour. Many Nationals fans, only four full seasons into baseball's rebirth in their city, knew of the legend of "Harry the K" and were stunned. They were respectful but not fully aware of the emotional bond between the Philly faithful and Harry, the only voice of the Phillies most had ever known.

Back in Philadelphia, radio listeners heard the news with even more emotion from one of Harry's broadcast partners, Scott Franzke.

"The Philadelphia Phillies have lost their voice."

Nationals management was prepared to call off the game and send more than 40,000 fans home if the Phillies felt they could not play under these extraordinarily difficult circumstances. "There's no manual for what to do in these circumstances, that close to the beginning of the game," Nationals president Stan Kasten shared with Chico Harlan of *The Washington Post*. "Ultimately it was our call, but we wanted to know the wishes of the Phillies before we decided, and I'm sure we would have acceded to their wishes if they felt strongly—and especially if the [players] felt strongly."

Phillies president David Montgomery said the team was appreciative of the Nationals's sensitivity, "but Harry would have wanted us to play."

Few announcers were as close to the players as Harry Kalas was to his Phillies, then in his 39th season at the microphone. When he slapped a distinctive moniker on a player, it stuck, and each one loved it. Just ask "The Man" Chase Utley or Hall of Fame icon of the 1970–80s Michael "Jack" Schmidt! Later in his career, players welcomed Harry into locker room celebrations, most notably after winning the 1993 National League pennant, to lead a chorus of his signature song, Frank Sinatra's version of "High Hopes." Harry's rendition is still played at Citizens Bank Park after every home win.

"Where else would he go but in a ballpark and in the announcer's booth?" asked an emotional John Kruk that night on *Baseball Tonight*. Kruk, at the time, was an ESPN analyst who also played for the Phillies from 1989–94 and was a member of that '93 pennant winner. Like most Phillies players of that era, Kruk was very close to Kalas. "That's where he belonged. That's where his life was."

Harry's rich baritone voice, fine-tuned by good whiskey and bad cigarettes, resonated both inside and outside Philadelphia. On the national stage, Kalas had served as the voice of *Inside the NFL* since 1975 and as the primary voice of NFL Films after the passing of John Facenda in 1984. Even non–sports fans couldn't escape Harry's voice on commercials for everything from soup to trucks to video games.

The dark logic of the fitting location of Harry's passing, so clearly expressed by Kruk, was also baseball poetry. The first baseball team he fell in love with as a 10-year-old boy was the Washington Senators.

Harry grew up on the south side of Chicago. One rainy afternoon in 1946, his dad took him to Comiskey Park for a game between two middle-of-the-pack teams, the host White Sox and the visiting Senators. Harry and his dad sat right next to the visitors' dugout. He would tell the story often of his chance encounter with Washington's All-Star first baseman and best player of that era. "Because of the rains, the field was covered," Harry explained. "There was no batting practice, so the players really didn't have anything to do. Mickey Vernon popped out of the dugout, saw this wide-eyed kid (*me*), picked me up, took me into the dugout, gave me a baseball, introduced me to his teammates, and thus began my love of baseball and the Washington Senators."

Harry's love of the game and his one-of-a-kind voice combined to deliver a Hall of Fame career. After six seasons with the Houston Astros, Harry joined the Phillies in 1971 as they opened their brand new Veterans Stadium. In a city not known for welcoming outsiders, he became as much a part of the fabric of Philadelphia as cheesesteaks and the Liberty Bell. From 1971–97 Harry partnered on Phillies broadcasts with adored former Phil and fellow Hall of Famer Richie

"Whitey" Ashburn. Neil Hartman's narration of Comcast SportsNet's tribute to Harry described their antics in words that stirred nostalgic hearts. "Kalas and Ashburn rivaled any long-running Broadway act. They performed from April to September for 27 years, and their shows, like the games themselves, were never predictable." When the Phillies won the World Series in 1980, then-current MLB broadcast rules precluded home team announcers from calling the games. The outrage from Phillies fans led to a rule change less than two years later. So when the Phillies won it again in 2008 over Tampa Bay, just five months before his passing, Harry finally had the opportunity he had been dreaming of for a lifetime.

His call of Brad Lidge's final pitch of the World Series has been repeated by Phillies fans ever since. "The 0–2 pitch, SWING AND A MISS! STRUCK HIM OUT!!! The Philadelphia Phillies are 2008 World champions of baseball!"

Kalas's outgoing, gregarious personality was contagious. He loved talking baseball with anyone. In recent years, that included the Washington Nationals's hero-worshipping stadium announcer Hruska, the memorable voice that broke the news to us of Harry's passing.

"When I was six years old, I made recordings of myself calling Yankees games," Hruska says modestly. "When I got the Nationals job in 2007, I was the youngest stadium announcer in baseball. Whenever the Phillies came to town, Harry and I would have dinner. I was awestruck. Harry was my idol. And for him to take me under his wing and talk baseball? I can't describe it. It was unbelievable!"

More than a decade later, Hruska still remembers every detail of that painful Opening Day.

"We had just finished our pregame production meeting. There was some commotion down the hall. I asked my boss what was going on. He said, 'Medical issue. One of the announcers.'"

Hruska sprinted toward the Phillies broadcast booth. When he saw Harry, his Eagle Scout instincts took over. Hruska dropped to his knees and began performing chest compressions on his fallen hero until the paramedics arrived minutes later.

Harry was gone.

The shaken Hruska returned to his post where he was drawn into the "What should we say?" conversations. As the ballpark's voice, his perspective mattered. Together with the teams' communications departments, they cobbled together appropriate words to form a script that would honor Harry's special place in the game. They would then ask for a moment of silence.

But Hruska was still struggling. "I'm not sure I can do this," he told his boss. "I just had my hands on the chest of my hero, and now I have to tell 40,000 people he's gone?"

Like Harry's broadcast partners and the Phillies players, Hruska overcame the emotional hurdle.

That night in Philadelphia, Michael Barkann opened a somber postgame telecast on Comcast SportsNet, choking back tears, with a tribute fans in any city would appreciate. "This program is not about the game that just finished. There are 162 of those. This program tonight is about the sounds of summer. The soundtrack of our lives. Burgers sizzling on the grill. Children shrieking with joy at a swimming pool. Seagulls and waves at the shore. And always nearby, the voice of our summers. The voice of Phillies baseball. Harry Kalas. Hall of Fame voice. Great Man. That voice is silent tonight."

 For box scores, play-by-play and more, visit www.OpeningDay5050.com or use this QR code

2010

John McNamara

The Game

Who:	Philadelphia Phillies 11, Washington Nationals 1
Where:	Nationals Park, Washington, DC
Attendance:	41,290
When:	Monday, April 5, 2010
Weather:	Spectacular! 70s and sunny

Hall of Famers: Phillies P Roy Halladay and Nationals C Ivan Rodriguez
Future HoFers?: Phillies 2B Chase Utley? (eligible 2024)

Game Highlights: This game marked the National League and Philadelphia Phillies debut of pitcher Roy Halladay. During 11 seasons north of the border, Halladay dominated the American League. But after approving an offseason trade from Toronto because he wanted to play for a contender, the 33-year-old delivered notice on Opening Day that his best was yet to come. He stymied the Nationals, allowing only one run in seven innings. The following month Halladay would pitch a perfect game at Florida. In October, in the first playoff game of his brilliant career, Halladay pitched only the second postseason no-hitter in baseball history (Roundy was at the first; see Chapter 1970) and became only the fifth pitcher to win the Cy Young Award in both leagues.

On this Opening Day, things stayed interesting for a while. Just minutes after accepting his 2009 National League Silver Slugger and Gold Glove Awards, third baseman Ryan Zimmerman doubled home the Nationals only run of the day. Starter John Lannan kept pace with Halladay for three innings, taking a 1–0 lead into the fourth. That's when the Phillies lit him up, sending 11 men to the plate and scoring five, including a two-run homer by Ryan Howard, the National League's 2005 Rookie of the Year and 2006 MVP. Even Halladay got in on the fun with an RBI single. A grand slam by Plácido Polanco in the seventh sent most remaining home team fans to the exits, leaving behind the Phillies's "phaithful" to celebrate in Nationals Park. It was a common scene in Washington during Philadelphia's five-year stretch of NL East Division dominance (2007–11) when tickets were tight in South Philly and plentiful in DC, just a two-hour train ride away.

The Story

Over the past 40-plus years, I have been fortunate to stay in touch with so many sports media types I grew up with in the '70s. One was Beth Huffman who in 1980 became the first female sports editor of Notre Dame's student newspaper *The Observer*. She went on to work in college athletics and later as a sportswriter at the *Philadelphia Inquirer* before transitioning to corporate marketing and communications in the legal profession. This Opening Day she'd taken Amtrak to Washington to see her Phillies and experience Nationals Park for the first time.

Another sportswriter friend from the '70s was John McNamara. It was tough to connect with John over the years, even at games, because he was working. For 40 years, from high school through college and beyond, John stuck with his passions: sports and writing. We made plans, though, to connect on this Opening Day. With President Obama scheduled for first pitch duties, Beth and I arrived early to beat the security crunch. I excused myself from pregame social activity, told Beth I'd meet her at the seats, and journeyed to the upper deck to see John.

He came down from the press box high atop Nationals Park for our rendezvous on the concourse. It was the first time we'd seen each other in years. The high five and hug were so genuine. Decades melted. As we shared life experiences, we gazed down as fans filed into one of baseball's newest shrines, a spectacular aerial view I had not yet experienced during the ballpark's first two seasons.

"Did you think you'd live long enough to see this?" John asked sincerely.

"I had my doubts," I answered back.

"We all did," he added soberly of our long wait for baseball's return. "But look at this! Look at us," he added with a smirkish grin.

Little did we know at the time, I was standing with a man who would be recognized more than eight years later on the cover of *TIME Magazine's* 2018 Person of the Year issue. The storied publication honored "The Guardians and the War on Truth." More than 50 journalists were murdered in 2018. John was one of five shot and killed on June 28, 2018, in his newsroom at the *Capital Gazette*.

In the weeks that followed this senseless assault in Annapolis, it seemed less painful to dwell on the past with a smile than to try to make sense of the present.

John and I were a year apart in high school, but we had so much in common: DC sports junkies to the core trying to figure out if maybe, someday, someone might actually pay us to do what we love—write or talk about sports. During the

1977–78 school year, we *were* the sports section of our high school paper.

Our passion that spring was the basketball team general manager Bob Ferry had assembled, the Washington Bullets, with players like Kevin Grevey, Phil Chenier, Wes Unseld, Elvin Hayes and Bobby Dandridge. When the Bullets defeated the Supersonics in Seattle for an unlikely NBA title, the opera was over, coach Dick Motta's figurative "Fat Lady" sang, and nowhere on the planet were there two teenagers more excited than me and John.

I went off to Notre Dame. He stayed and became editor of the high school paper, and then a year later, John was off to the University of Maryland. During those summers we would play keg softball on Sunday afternoons near his house in Bethesda. The Barwood cab drivers with whom we played had only one strict rule: if you knocked over someone's beer in the field, you were automatically out!

I remember fondly a basketball showdown between our universities in January 1981. I'm not sure if ND's student radio station WSND had any listeners, but it *did* have a small travel budget, and they paid my way for a weekend trip "home" to call this game. We arranged to have the beat reporter from the Maryland student newspaper, sophomore John McNamara, as the on-air halftime guest. For a 19-year-old to have such a prestigious assignment was almost unheard of in college journalism at the time, but John had earned it.

Even though Notre Dame's visiting student radio crew was exiled to the rafters of Cole Field House, just to be in the building working this nationally televised contest between two of the country's top ranked teams had us pinching ourselves!

"Are we really here? Is this really happening?"

We were like kids in a candy store! John was in his element as he would be so many more times over the next 30-plus years. He made the trek upstairs that afternoon from what I assume was a comfy courtside seat assigned to *The Diamondback*, donned the WSND headset, and we started talking like the world was listening. It was a classic college basketball matchup with Lefty Driesell vs. Digger Phelps, plus some of the greatest players in each school's history: Albert King, Kelly Tripucka, Ernie Graham, Orlando Woolridge, Buck Williams, John Paxson, Greg Manning, and Tracy Jackson all in the same game. John could have talked Terps hoops for hours. We were almost disappointed that the second half had to be played.

Little did we know at the time, this "halftime radio guest" thing at a Maryland basketball game was something John would do with the Terrapins's legendary broadcaster Johnny Holliday dozens more times in the decades that followed. John was immensely trusted and respected by the coaches. His reporting was fair and honest. John's tenure included Maryland's 2002 National championship. Hall of Fame coach Gary Williams was a guest of honor at John's memorial service on the College Park campus and wrote the foreword for John's last book, *The Capital of Basketball*.

I dug into *The Diamondback* archives and read John's pregame and postgame coverage of that 1981 game. Not surprisingly, it was polished, well written, and concise. Absent were the snide or unnecessarily clever remarks that frequently flow from the fingers of student journalists while they're still learning how to report and not opine. And from the tributes following his passing written by many of his mentees over the years, it seems that quality served him well. His lack of ego made him a marvelous reporter and probably kept him from being a columnist. Heaven knows John always had an opinion, but I can't imagine he'd be very comfortable knowing large numbers of people were waking up every morning wondering what it was. His writings were almost always about someone or something else, not about his view of the world.

If you had scrolled through his Facebook feed during his final years, you would have found quotes by someone else, John applauding another person's achievement (especially those with a connection to DC sports), or sharing somebody else's excellent work. One such "share" is rather chilling in retrospect. In 2017 John shared a *Washington Post* piece on gun violence which he described as "A sobering look at the gun problem in the DC area, told by following the trail of one gun. A good argument for greater gun control if ever there was one ..."

You'd almost never see John show off his own work. A rare exception came a month before he was killed when he shared his piece on the aforementioned Bob Ferry on the 40th anniversary of that Bullets title.

In August 2016 Washington Senators legend Frank "Hondo" Howard was finally inducted into the Nationals Park "Ring of Honor." John was one of the few people I knew who could truly appreciate the significance of honoring a man who last played in DC in 1971. Like me, John had saved his ticket stub from that awful September night when Hondo hit the last home run ever by a Washington Senator. I invited John to join me at Nats Park the night of Howard's induction. He had other plans, but his prompt response was concise, well written, and included a pointed retort.

"Hondo should have been in there years ago! What gives?"

Vintage John.

Since John couldn't join me, another DC baseball loyalist, Notre Dame classmate Tom Jackman (TJ), shared that nostalgic "Hondo" night in 2016. Like John, he had been a friend since the '70s, was a die-hard fan of the Washington Senators, loved journalism, and stuck with it for life. When I was writing about Notre Dame sports, TJ was more of a news junkie, skills he refined at *The New York Times* and *Kansas City Star* before landing at *The Washington Post* in 1998 where he would become a Pulitzer Prize–winning crime reporter. John and TJ were similar men from different parts of my life who never met.

Eerie irony: The *Post* assigned TJ to cover John's murder.

A couple of months later, a small group of John's friends and family gathered one quiet Saturday morning outside the center-field gate of Nationals Park. His widow, Andrea Chamblee, had somehow convinced the Lerner family to allow her to carry out a wish John had whimsically expressed a year earlier—to have his ashes placed at Nationals Park. The request was not unique, but the approval was. A team representative escorted us to the seats just above the outfield wall where Andrea shared beautiful words about John's life. "I never thought they'd let us do this," she said. "They allowed it not because of how John died, but because of how he lived. He was a sportswriter."

Andrea was pleased with the spot the Nationals had selected: the flower box atop the left-field wall. "This is the perfect spot. John told us to watch out for Juan Soto," she said of the team's then-19-year-old rookie left fielder who made his major-league debut just six weeks before the shooting. "He said Soto is going to be the next Bryce Harper!"

A year later Soto and the Nationals were in the midst of their storybook run through the postseason. I was at Game Four of the National League Championship Series, coincidentally with TJ. The Nationals led the best of seven series, 3–0, and we were hoping for a sweep and a trip to the World Series. I wanted to capture the night with a very specific photo. During the top of the third inning, I wandered out to Sections 105–106 where Andrea had placed John's ashes. I explained the situation to the usher and the access I needed.

"I'm sorry," he responded dutifully, "but without a ticket for this section, I can't let you do that." He then immediately turned the other way as if to say, "Go for it." I took my cue and scurried down the steps, squatting at the front of the section. I briefly explained my mission to the fan in the front row aisle seat who could not have been more gracious.

Tap tap. Mission accomplished. A photo of the begonias in the foreground and a very focused Juan Soto right behind. On the way back to my seat, I made eye contact with that usher. I just smiled and nodded. So did he.

About two hours later, Nationals reliever Daniel Hudson closed things out with a 1-2-3 ninth inning, including a flyout to Soto. The ballpark erupted. Players and fans were jumping, hugging, screaming, crying. For the first time in 86 years, a Washington baseball team was going to the World Series.

As the Nationals players slipped on their "National League CHAMPIONS" caps and the grounds crew hastily assembled a stage near second base for the postgame ceremonies, a euphoric Jackman turned and said, "This is all I need. Whatever happens from here on, happens."

As the celebration continued, I was haunted by John's words from Opening Day 2010.

"Did you think we'd live long enough to see this?"

I'm sorry you didn't, my friend, but good to know you're keeping an eye on all of us.

For box scores, play-by-play and more, visit www.OpeningDay5050.com or use this QR code

2011

Edward DeMarco

The Game

Who:	Atlanta Braves 2, Washington Nationals 0
Where:	Nationals Park, Washington, DC
Attendance:	39,055
When:	Thursday, March 31, 2011
Weather:	40s and drizzly

Hall of Famers: Braves 3B Chipper Jones and Nationals C Ivan Rodriguez
Future HoFers?: Braves 1B Freddie Freeman? (eligible five years after retirement)

Game Highlights: After enduring five last-place finishes in six seasons since baseball's return to Washington, ever-hopeful Nationals fans were starting to see a light at the end of the tunnel by Opening Day 2011. All those bad seasons led to good draft picks who were blossoming into promising players: Jordan Zimmermann, Drew Storen, Danny Espinosa, and others. Phenom Stephen Strasburg exploded onto the big-league stage with a stunning 14-strikeout performance in his June 2010 debut. But after just 12 starts, he faced season-ending elbow surgery that would cause him to miss most of 2011, while 18-year-old Bryce Harper would spend 2011 seasoning in the minor leagues. High-profile free agents were taking notice though and Washington was paying accordingly, inking free agent right fielder Jayson Werth to a seven-year $121 million contract, at the time, one of the biggest in history.

Still, that light at the end of the tunnel was dim on Opening Day as expectations for 2011 were muted. The cold and miserable weather matched Washington's offensive output, spoiling a decent pitching performance by 36-year-old starter Liván Hernández and four relievers. Brian McCann singled home Chipper Jones in the first, and Jason Heyward homered in the second for the game's only runs.

The Story

No matter the city, Opening Day is the one time each regular season when you can count on local celebs and VIPs to be at the ballpark. In the nation's capital, that includes politicians, lobbyists, bureaucrats, agency heads, and national news anchors, among others. Most are casual fans who attend only a few games each season. Many are seeking to influence or be influenced (or just plain under the influence!). A few are well known and recognizable. Most are not.

For example, Edward DeMarco, a die-hard Nationals fan and partial plan season ticket holder from the day the team arrived in Washington, is a familiar face only to his friends, family, and regular viewers of C-SPAN 3. Mr. DeMarco was a conscientious, career civil servant and one of the country's leading experts on the mortgage industry and housing policy. A calm, knowledgeable, levelheaded, nonpartisan agency head is a rare breed in Washington but was so necessary to help lead the country out of the 2008 housing crisis. In 2009 he was entrusted by President Obama to head the Federal Housing Finance Agency.

On March 31, 2011—Opening Day—Mr. DeMarco was summoned to testify before the US House of Representatives Financial Services Subcommittee on Capital Markets, Insurance, and Government-Sponsored Enterprises (GSEs) to report on the financial condition of the housing GSEs, Fannie Mae, and Freddie Mac—something he frequently was called upon to do. As conservator of Fannie and Freddie, his agency was responsible for assisting troubled homeowners while minimizing further calls on taxpayers who had already bailed out mortgage securities holders at a cost well in excess of $100 billion.

The hearing was scheduled to begin at 10:00 a.m. and last two and a half hours. It would be tight, but with first pitch slated for 1:10 p.m., DeMarco thought he might make it on time.

At 12:30 p.m., with the interrogation of DeMarco now complete, California Republican Gary Miller, who already had exceeded his allotted time, asked Committee Chair Scott Garrett of New Jersey for an additional minute. Anxious to leave, DeMarco politely held his position at the witness table. Miller simply wanted to publicly wish his political rival, Massachusetts Democrat and the Committee's Ranking Member Barney Frank, a happy 71st birthday. After bipartisan applause but before the chair could draw the hearing to a close, it was Frank's turn to further extend the proceedings.

First pitch was slipping away! DeMarco's foot was nervously tapping a gym bag hidden under the table. It contained his Nationals jersey and other game day gear.

"Mr. Chairman, if you would yield briefly?" Frank asked.

"I will yield, yes," Garrett replied.

"I would just like to add," Frank continued, "Mr. DeMarco's testimony was exactly what we need from witnesses. It was responsive. It was aimed at helping us legislate, and I not only want to express my appreciation, (but) I hope other people will follow his example."

After accepting hearty congratulations for his most excellent performance on the hot seat, DeMarco quickly packed his papers, reached under the table to fetch that gym bag, and scurried down the hall to the men's room to shed the suit and tie. A meticulous planner, he had wisely packed the layers needed to survive what promised to be a frigid Opening Day. A car was waiting just outside the Rayburn House Office Building, and the driver followed DeMarco's instructions exactly.

"Nationals Park please. Quickly!"

The trip was a little over a mile straight down South Capitol Street. At 12:50 p.m. DeMarco hopped out of the Chrysler's back seat and sprinted to the center-field entrance and then through a metal detector. Without a Presidential first pitch, security was lighter than years past. He went straight to the nearby Red Porch bar where a cold beer was waiting.

After a stress-filled three hours, it was the least I could do for my brother-in-law.

"Eddie Baby," I exclaimed!

"Orti Baby," came the customary response.

His wife, Garland, and sister Kate (my wife) joined the festivities. Minutes later, Liván Hernández's first pitch to Jason Heyward: a called strike. Another Opening Day was underway.

Ed and I became friends during the summer of 1978 between high school and college. We were the real life "Odd Couple"—my Oscar Madison to his Felix Unger—best friends living in different worlds. He graduated from Notre Dame in three and a half years before earning his master's and PhD in economics. I had to take nine credits during summer school in 1981 to barely graduate on time. When he was in the library on Friday or Saturday nights, I could usually be found at a game or social event clinging to a fake ID. And while he was circulating in the highest levels of economic thought and academia, I was hanging out in stadiums and arenas.

Our respective journeys to the Nationals were quite different, too, but once the team landed in 2005, we were kindred spirits. He spent his early childhood in New England, growing up a Red Sox fan. He wound up at Notre Dame, in part, because Carl Yastrzemski went there. Of course, I grew up a Washington Senators fan.

One of our fondest Nationals memories is from September 23, 2007, the last-ever Nationals game at RFK. The team was planning a lower-key pregame ceremony compared to what we experienced upon baseball's historic return in April 2005. It promised to be a more upbeat farewell than the one in 1971. We'd heard it would involve a few local Senators alumni including my hero, Frank "Hondo" Howard.

On the way to the ballpark, I got a call from Tom Ward, head of sales and marketing for the Nationals. The team was planning a postgame ceremony and he was in search of a last-minute, willing participant. Each player would give a lucky fan or sponsor the jersey off their back. Since someone had canceled, my company was a sponsor, and no one else was able to make it on such short notice, Tom offered the spot to me. I asked if I could re-gift the opportunity to someone who was an even more invested fan than I was. He agreed to allow Ed to participate.

The ceremonies, pregame and post, were a weak attempt to replicate what the Orioles had done so masterfully in 1991 for the final game at Memorial Stadium (see Chapter 1993 and story about my son Brad). But unlike Baltimore, Washington didn't have 37 continuous years of baseball memories to draw from, or three World Series titles. It was still a thrill to see Hondo limp out to third base and greet his successor as the face of DC baseball, Ryan Zimmerman, and to see Dick Bosman throw one more pitch from the RFK mound.

After the Nats beat the Phillies and while they uprooted home plate to ship it off to the new ballpark, players lined up along the third baseline, unbuttoning their jerseys. Eager fans lined up along first. Ed stood near the end of the line, while our families huddled in the stands near home plate. We started counting off players, hoping to figure out whose jersey might find its way to the DeMarco home. Standing at only 5'5", whatever jersey Ed got would be too big. At 6'0", All-Star closer Chad Cordero's would come closest.

One by one each player handed his jersey to an adoring fan and then headed to the locker room. As the lines got shorter, we couldn't control our laughter. Ed was about to meet Nationals pitcher Jon Rauch. At 6'11", Rauch was the *tallest player in Major League Baseball history!* Hecklers, especially his family, encouraged Ed to immediately don the giant's jersey. Unwilling to be humiliated on the field, Ed earnestly thanked Rauch for a great season (his 88 relief appearances in 2007 led the National League). Both smiled and walked away.

Once outside the stadium, we insisted Ed try it on. Seeing him in that jersey conjured up memories of the summer of 1969 and the Frank Howard jersey experience I described in Chapter 1976 and included in the 2005 letter to the editor of *The Washington Post*. Just as Hondo's once fit me, so too did Jon's fit Ed. It was bigger than he was!

Over the past 40-plus years, we've enjoyed countless family events: holidays, weddings, funerals, graduations, and reunions. The Nats always provided that special escape from everything else, especially during our annual trips to spring training. Oftentimes we'd be at the same Nationals games but not sitting together. Yet we'd still find a way to connect, especially on Opening Day.

For box scores, play-by-play and more, visit www.OpeningDay5050.com or use this QR code

2012

Let Teddy Win!

The Game

Who:	Washington Nationals 3, Cincinnati Reds 2 (10 innings)
Where:	Nationals Park, Washington, DC
Attendance:	40,907
When:	Thursday, April 12, 2012
Weather:	50s and cloudy

Hall of Famers: None (as of March 2022)
Future HoFers?: Reds 1B Joey Votto (eligible five years after retirement)

Game Highlights: Closer Brad Lidge was hoping to do the same thing on Opening Day 2012 at Nationals Park that he had done here in 2009: earn the save for his team. The difference? In 2009 he was able to close out the 9–8 win for his Philadelphia Phillies. This day Lidge blew the chance to finish off the Reds for his new team, the Washington Nationals, giving up two runs in the ninth to send the game to extra innings. The two-time All-Star had signed a one-year, $1-million contract during the offseason but would appear in only 11 games before being released by Washington. The Nationals manufactured a run in the bottom of the 10th to win. Ryan Zimmerman rounded the bases after being hit by a pitch, moved along by a Jayson Werth single, a groundout, and a wild pitch. Starter Gio González was impressive in his Nationals debut, shutting out the Reds for seven innings. Acquired in an offseason trade with the Oakland Athletics, González would team with Jordan Zimmermann and a healthy Stephen Strasburg to anchor a pitching staff with the National League's lowest ERA, leading Washington to the best record in baseball and the city's first postseason appearance since 1933.

The Story

The race for US President was in full gear in the spring of 2012 with Mitt Romney closing in on the Republican nomination to challenge Barack Obama. And even though Obama chose to become the first incumbent President in more than 30 years to *not* participate in an Opening Day first pitch ceremony during his re-election campaign, full attention was paid to the four *former* Presidents who *were* in attendance this day at Nationals Park. It marked the beginning of a season-long story line that would play out in the national media unlike any other race of its kind.

In the middle of the fourth inning, the Racing Presidents—larger-than-life caricatures of George Washington, Thomas Jefferson, Abraham Lincoln, and Theodore Roosevelt (George, Tom, Abe, and Teddy)—emerged from an opening in the center-field wall as they had done during every Nationals home game since their debut midway through the 2006 season.

Just as the fans hoped today might mark the beginning of the first-ever winning season for their Washington Nationals, so too were they hoping for a first-ever win for their favorite former President.

With chants of "Teddy, Teddy!" ringing throughout Nationals Park, the 26th President began the race this day, rumbling across the warning track toward the left-field foul pole. The other three had tripped at the starting line, victims of Teddy's pre-race chicanery. He had exploited the trio's afternoon nap time and tied their shoelaces together. Unfortunately for Teddy, a resourceful and determined Tom was able to slip off his shoes, catch up with his rival, and sprint barefoot across the finish line to eke out the win.

The victory was the 135th of Tom's career. Teddy's record dropped to 0–453.

While more than a dozen ballparks around the major leagues stage some sort of character race during games, Washington's Presidents Race tops the list in terms of creative story lines, sponsor integration, and national media acclaim. Although the races started in 2006, fans were able to track Teddy's progress (or lack of it!) starting in 2008 via Nationals season ticket holder Scott Ableman's cleverly crafted blog, *Let Teddy Win*. Ableman has chronicled almost every race (well over 1,000) and roster expansion since 2006, and his blog is a treasure trove of videos, masterfully written summaries, media coverage, standings, and records. Three times between 2013 and 2016 the original four competitors welcomed another past occupant of the Oval Office to join the fun: William Howard Taft (the first President to throw out the first pitch on Opening Day) in

2013, Calvin Coolidge (2015), and Herbert Hoover (2016). But Bill, Cal, and Herb have since retired to Florida where they enjoy spring training games. "The Rushmores" continue on in Washington.

However, 2012 was a year like no other for the Racing Presidents, especially Teddy (and Ableman). As Teddy's losing streak neared 500, the national media was whipped into a frenzy. The baseball world had not been this excited about a losing streak since the Baltimore Orioles opened the 1988 season by dropping 21 straight! By August, stoked in part by Ableman's entertaining blog posts, some of the most famous and powerful voices in sports and government took notice of Teddy's circumstance. As Washington was closing in on its first-ever NL East Division title, the "Let Teddy Win" movement was generating unprecedented support and media attention. Ableman fielded dozens of calls from virtually every major media outlet in the country. His expertise and insights on the topic were unparalleled.

In an ESPN special E:60 finale "Teddy Roosevelt's Rough Ride," producers compiled seven of the most hilarious minutes of deadpan humor you will ever see. Narrated in dramatic fashion by acclaimed documentarian Ken Burns, the piece featured a compelling conspiracy theory from Ableman and impassioned insights from people devoted to the legacy of the former President including his great-great-grandson, Winthrop Roosevelt, and Senator John McCain. The Arizona Republican even called for a congressional investigation, which prompted a response from the Obama Administration.

White House Press Secretary Jay Carney, who generally struggled finding things on which the President and his opponent in the 2008 election could agree, was quick to acknowledge, "Senator McCain gave an important interview the other day, and I think it's an indication that there's still a possibility of bipartisanship, bipartisan cooperation, and agreement." He reaffirmed McCain's assertion that Teddy's losing streak was an "outrage."

"I agree with Senator McCain," Carney continued. "I'm comfortable saying my boss agrees with Senator McCain."

On October 3, 2012, history was made. On the season's final day both the Nationals and Teddy celebrated historic wins. For Washington, their 5–3 win over the Philadelphia Phillies was their 98th of the season, a franchise record, and tops in the major leagues. For Teddy, with an assist from a Phake Phillie Phanatic who took out Teddy's rivals near the right-field foul pole, it was his elusive first victory.

The longest losing streak in sports history was finally over.

For box scores, play-by-play and more, visit www.OpeningDay5050.com
or use this QR code

2013

D.C.'s Greatest Sports Fan

The Game

Who:	Washington Nationals 2, Miami Marlins 0
Where:	Nationals Park, Washington, DC
Attendance:	45,274
When:	Monday, April 1, 2013
Weather:	60s, sunny and wind blowing out to right. Bryce Harper's kind of day!

Hall of Famers: None (as of March 2022)
Future HoFers?: Nationals OF Bryce Harper and Marlins OF Giancarlo Stanton (eligible five years after retirement)

Game Highlights: After collecting his 2012 NL Rookie of the Year Award during pregame ceremonies, Bryce Harper picked up on Opening Day 2013 where he'd left off in 2012. He delivered a pair of solo homers to provide the Nationals's only runs. The 20-year-old became the youngest player ever to hit two home runs on Opening Day, the only runs starter Stephen Strasburg needed as he made short order of the formerly-Florida-now-Miami Marlins. The 24-year-old Strasburg looked well rested and fully recovered from his 2010 Tommy John surgery that limited him to only five appearances in 2011 and a team-imposed shutdown with a month left in the Nationals's 2012 playoff push. Straz gave up only three hits in seven innings, retiring 19 in a row after Juan Pierre's first-inning single.

Harper was not the only Nationals player picking up hardware before the game. Teammates Adam LaRoche, Ian Desmond. and Strasburg all earned 2012 National League Silver Slugger Awards for being the best hitter in the league at their respective positions. LaRoche also accepted his 2012 Gold Glove and skipper Davey Johnson took home the second Manager of the Year Award of his 17-year, five-team managerial career. Davey was a winning skipper wherever he managed, winning a World Series with the Mets in 1986, guiding the Los Angeles Dodgers back to respectability (1999–2000), and turning around losing teams in Cincinnati (1993–95), Baltimore (1996–97), and now Washington (2011–13), leading each to the postseason.

The Story

By Opening Day 2013 sports in the nation's capital had entered a new era. For the first time in nearly 80 years, the city was celebrating a championship, of sorts, for its baseball team. Not since the Washington Senators won the American League pennant in 1933 had DC's baseball team won anything. Only five times between 1934 and 2011 had Washington posted a winning record! The last winning season was 1969, manager Ted Williams's rookie year at the helm of the Senators, two years prior to baseball's 33-year hiatus. The city's exuberance on Opening Day 2013 was understandable. The largest regular-season crowd since the night of baseball's historic return in 2005 celebrated the modern-day equivalent of a banner-raising as the cover was removed from atop the center-field scoreboard at Nationals Park to reveal the official signage: 2012 NATIONAL LEAGUE EAST CHAMPIONS.

After just eight seasons, these Washington Nationals had earned a spot near the top of the ladder for DC sports fans. Local interest in the NFL was in a slow but steady decline after winning three Super Bowls between 1982 and 1991. In the 21 years since Washington's last football title, the team made only five postseason appearances and no trips to the conference championship. The Washington Bullets (now Wizards) won the NBA title in 1978 and returned to the Finals in 1979, but in the 33 years since, won only two postseason series. The Capitals hockey team had never won a Stanley Cup up to that point in the 38-year history of the franchise. And Major League Soccer's DC United, the latest iteration in a dizzying array of pro soccer teams to call the nation's capital home, never garnered the volume of fan support to match their four MLS Cups in the eight years before the Nationals joined them at RFK in 2005.

By Opening Day 2013, cheering for the Nationals was easy. Clinging to all five pro teams was only for the very best Washington sports fans. I was *officially* one of them.

Really.

Seriously.

This is legit!

In October 2011 *The Washington Post* announced a search for "D.C.'s Greatest Sports Fan," a comprehensive, four-round, month-long competition seeking "the best combination of spirit, local sports knowledge, and loyalty."

I finished second. In the broader context of the city's sports teams, that felt about right—strong regular season, but came up short in the end.

Round one required contestants to ace a trivia quiz and provide concise answers to a trio of essay questions including:

> 1. Your defining moment as a DC sports fan (see RFK sod story, Chapter 2007)
>
> 2. Who is Washington's all-time most unheralded athlete (Super Bowl VII QB Billy Kilmer)
>
> 3. "Why me?"

Responses were limited to 750 characters. "Many are fans of certain DC teams," I answered. "Few are fanatics of all. This passion has lasted a lifetime. My dad instilled it in me, and I passed it on to his grandchildren. I've found a way to attend so many memorable events: the NFC championship games at RFK, Pele's first-ever appearance there, the Wizards debut at MCI, and more. I celebrated my acceptance into college by attending a Caps game that night. Even got thrown off the Cap Center court by security after the Bullets beat San Antonio in '79. Much to the amazement of my fair-weather friends in Philly, I've stuck with some miserable teams (e.g., Caps in the '70s, the current Nats), but have cherished the bright light of winning when the sports gods have allowed it to shine on us!"

The answers were enough to make it to round two with nine other fans. To narrow the field to six, the next assignment was to describe what you would do to fix one of Washington's pro teams. Since the football team was in the greatest state of disarray, I took the easy route, suggesting the need to focus on building a strong offensive line to protect the quarterback, open holes for the running backs, and keep the defense off the field. According to *The Washington Post*, "Commenter 'PhillyPhan' agreed, writing 'Wow, very insightful. It's easy to gawk at the flashier play-makers but he's dead on in his contention that strong teams are always built on strong bases.'"

The third round required a 90-second video describing your most cherished piece of DC sports memorabilia. With 30 years in or near the television business, I had an unfair advantage. But as we often told our kids, "Life isn't fair." While other contestants showed a special item and ad-libbed a heartfelt speech while staring into a phone or computer for a minute and a half, I visited the production studio of a generous friend. The crew was ready. Makeup person? Check. Lighting? Perfect. Teleprompter? "The script you wrote is already loaded, Mr. Ortman." Relying on that box of RFK dirt described in Chapter 2007 and other video props, Renegade Productions cranked out one impressive piece.

News of the round three victory spread like wildfire across the Internet. The Facebook post garnered 22 comments and 55 Likes! LOL!

Only two more rivals to vanquish and my social media profiles would forever change to "Michael Ortman, D.C.'s Greatest Sports Fan, *The Washington Post*."

The three of us were summoned to the newspaper's downtown office for a timed 30-question, 54-point quiz with no Internet access. I was nervous but confident. The other two competitors weren't even born yet when the Washington Senators left for Texas in 1971, but they knew their baseball. Fellow finalist John Mann described his great-grandfather's ticket stub from the 1924 World Series, won by the Senators. The other, John Pence, was a Nationals season ticket holder during the team's RFK years (2005–07).

The test was extremely challenging but very fair. Considering the city lacked Major League Baseball for 33 years, the fourth and final round had a healthy serving of baseball questions:

+ Score of the last Senators game? 9–0, of course (forfeit).

+ Why are three seats painted white in RFK Stadium's upper deck? Frank "Hondo" Howard home runs. Piece of cake!

+ Which Nationals player hit for the cycle in the second game of the inaugural season (at Philadelphia)? Brad Wilkerson. On a roll.

+ Name the Nats relievers selected to the NL All-Star team during the team's first seven seasons: Chad Cordero, Matt Capps, and Tyler Clippard. Three pointer!

+ Which Senators player appeared in every inning of every one of the team's three World Series appearances (1924, 1925, and 1933)? No clue. [Correct answer: "Goose" Goslin]

When the judges tallied the points, Pence had 29, I had 30, and Mann had 32.

Missed points haunt me to this day. It's one thing to not know the three DC United goal-scorers in the 1996 MLS Cup. But to suffer a brain cramp when asked to name the only two Nationals players on the 2011 roster who were also on the inaugural team in 2005? Inexcusable!

Correct answer: Ryan Zimmerman and Liván Hernández.

My answer: Zim and John Lannan.

How could I forget Livo, the Opening Night starter in 2005?
I choked under pressure.

For box scores, play-by-play and more, visit www.OpeningDay5050.com
or use this QR code

2014

Wheel Me In, Coach!

The Game

Who:	Atlanta Braves 2, Washington Nationals 1
Where:	Nationals Park, Washington, DC
Attendance:	42,834
When:	Friday, April 4, 2014
Weather:	50s and overcast

Hall of Famers: None (as of March 2022)
Future HoFers?: Washington OF Bryce Harper and Atlanta 1B Freddie Freeman (both eligible five years after retirement)

Game Highlights: The Washington Nationals's reign atop the National League East Division lasted exactly one season (2012) due in large part to their head-to-head performance against the 2013 Division champion Atlanta Braves. Washington lost 13 of 19 games between the two clubs, and the Braves ran away with the division. It seemed to make 2014's first homestand that much more important for first-year manager Matt Williams. After winning the season's first three games at New York, the Nationals came home flat. Washington squandered multiple scoring opportunities against six Atlanta pitchers, going 0-for-7 with runners in scoring position. Jordan Zimmerman and three Washington relievers pitched well enough to win, giving up only six hits and two runs. By season's end, this loss did not matter in the 2014 standings. The Nationals would return to the top of the NL East, outdistancing the Braves and Mets by 17 games with a league-leading 96 wins.

The Story

Today was a day to reflect on the six venues I visited on past Opening Days and appreciate how far we have come regarding improving access for people with disabilities. As a volunteer leader for the Arthritis Foundation for 20 years, I advocated for continued improvements in access to care and facilities. My son Daniel needed significant assistance getting around. He was diagnosed at age 11 with severe Juvenile Rheumatoid Arthritis (see Chapter 1993 and Daniel's interaction with Cal Ripken Jr.). But today wasn't about talking the talk, or even walking the walk. It was about "rolling the roll." I had pushed Daniel's chair for years, but today, for the first time, I attended a sporting event in a wheelchair.

My Opening Days in the 1970s and '80s were at Memorial Stadium, RFK, Comiskey Park, and Wrigley Field, stadiums built in the 1960s and earlier, with little thought given to the game day experience of a person in a wheelchair. These were relics of a time when some venues had a quarantined "handicapped section" where a dozen or more wheelchairs were clustered, perhaps with a folding chair nearby for a companion. The lines of sight were varied, especially if able-bodied fans in front stood to cheer. Concessions and hard-to-use restrooms might be half a stadium away.

In 1990 the Americans with Disabilities Act (ADA) changed all that.

When baseball unveiled the new Comiskey Park (now Guaranteed Rate Field) in 1991 and Oriole Park the following year, it ushered in a new era in stadium design that expanded game access for people with disabilities, especially those in wheelchairs. Every baseball venue built or renovated since has followed suit. President Ronald Reagan's Press Secretary Jim Brady, wounded in the 1981 assassination attempt on the President, visited Oriole Park in his wheelchair just prior to Opening Day 1992. "This is a place that's friendly to me and to so many of my friends who are fans with disabilities," Brady said, as he observed some of the 448 specially designed "swing to the side" seats in the wheelchair locations spread throughout Camden Yards. Each such pairing included one permanent seat and a second that could easily be flipped out of the way to accommodate a wheelchair when necessary. "This ballpark welcomes us."

Brady's appreciation for the impact of the ADA was profound. He described the accommodation over and over to reporters. "Remarkable, remarkable. Everything I've seen is first class."

What was new in '92 was the new normal 20-plus years later.

By 2014 we all were taking these features for granted. In addition to bathroom accommodations and improved parking and curb cuts we now see at all public facilities, the ADA spelled out specific requirements intended to standardize stadium access and improve the experiences of fans with disabilities. On this Opening Day I was able to experience those improvements firsthand.

Let's turn the clock back a couple of weeks. My brother-in-law Ed and I returned late Monday night from our first annual trip to Nationals spring training. On that frigid Tuesday morning at 5:30 a.m. with a computer bag in one hand and coffee mug in the other, I walked out the front door to begin the daily commute. Clearly, my feet were still in Florida. When they encountered a patch of black ice, the coffee went flying and so did I. The resulting torn quad tendon above the right knee required significant reconstructive surgery and no weight bearing for four weeks.

I had only one concern: How will I get to Opening Day?

Two themes came to mind, one from the US Postal Service and the other from some high school literature class.

1. "Neither snow nor rain nor heat nor gloom of night stays these couriers from . . . their appointed rounds."

2. "Necessity is the mother of invention."

In other words, nothing was keeping me from Opening Day, and we had to figure something out.

When game day arrived, we had a companion plan. Steve Ebner, a lifelong friend, accepted the assignment. He had the perfect résumé for the job: a Nationals fan with Opening Day experience who knew how to navigate a wheelchair through large crowds. In May 1982 he traveled from Washington to Notre Dame for graduation weekend so he could wheel my mom around campus. She was battling cancer at the time. On Opening Day 2011 my sons Pat and Greg sat with Steve and his three kids at Nationals Park.

On Opening Day 2014 Steve made the hour-long drive from his Virginia home to my place in Maryland. He helped position my braced right leg across the back seat of the car and collapsed the wheelchair into the trunk. We were off.

An hour later, with temporary permit in hand, Steve parked in a specially marked blue handicapped space close to the ballpark. We were welcomed at the center-field entrance by a delightful attendant who scanned the tickets and escorted us through the extra-wide swing gate. Once inside, we were greeted by the newest addition to the cast of Racing Presidents, William Howard Taft, affectionately "Bill." Our 27th President succeeded Teddy Roosevelt in the White House in 1909, and in 1910 he began the Presidential tradition of throwing out the ceremonial first pitch on Opening Day. Bill knew in an instant that I was *his* kind of fan, an Opening Day kind of guy! Bill insisted on a photo. Tap, tap.

We had arranged for special seating. As required by the ADA, stadiums now designate at least one percent of all seating for handicapped fans, spread throughout the ballpark, each with a space for a wheelchair and a seat for an able-bodied companion. Our setup atop the third-base box seats was perfect— high enough to see over the fans in front of us who would soon be standing for player introductions. Just as important, we were close to concessions and accessible bathrooms.

After the game we decided to roll down to The Bullpen at the Half Street Fairgrounds, a popular pregame and postgame hangout adjacent to Nationals Park. The Fairgrounds was an ingenious entrepreneurial undertaking by local developers to make good use of a large city block while waiting for economic conditions to improve enough to support more profitable development. Beginning its seventh season, The Fairgrounds was a bare-bones tailgate party without the parked cars, complete with live music, food trucks, cold beer, and a long row of more than a dozen port-a-johns including an extra-large one with that now-iconic blue wheelchair access symbol.

After a postgame beverage, I left Steve and propelled the chair over to the end of the line of patrons awaiting use of said facilities. Gracious fans offered assistance and encouraged me to go to the front of the long line. I parked the chair, locked the wheels, and used my crutches to navigate the next few minutes.

When I emerged, the wheelchair was occupied by someone's empty beer cans and other trash.

Lovely!

The trash cans must have been full. Realizing I could not hold the crutches *and* clear the debris, two helpful bystanders quickly disposed of the garbage.

While the ADA addressed so many concerns about facilities access, it couldn't fix the behavior of an isolated drunk.

For box scores, play-by-play and more, visit www.OpeningDay5050.com or use this QR code

2015

Baseball Superstitions: Same Seats!

The Game

Who:	New York Mets 3, Washington Nationals 1
Where:	Nationals Park, Washington, DC
Attendance:	42,295
When:	Monday, April 6, 2015
Weather:	Spectacular! Sunny and 70s

Hall of Famers: None (as of March 2022)

Future HoFers?: Mets P Jacob deGrom, Nationals P Max Scherzer, and OF Bryce Harper (all eligible five years after retirement)

Game Highlights: Bartolo Colón? Isn't he the same pitcher who started for the Cleveland Indians in Baltimore on Opening Day 15 years ago? Indeed, the Mets's 41-year-old starter proved this day he still had plenty left in the tank, striking out eight and allowing only three hits and one run in six innings. Two of those three hits came off the bat of 22-year-old Bryce Harper including a home run to lead off the fourth. On the other side, the Mets were only able to scratch out four hits off Nationals newcomer and 2013 American League Cy Young Award winner Max Scherzer during his seven and a third innings. A pair of errors by Washington shortstop Ian Desmond led to three unearned runs for New York.

The Story

During the summer of 2014, Kate and I took our two oldest grandchildren—four-year-old Johnny and two-year-old Charlotte—to a Sunday afternoon Nationals game. They were less interested in baseball and more interested in the ice cream, the Kids Fun Zone near the right-field gate, and the splash park a few blocks away. But by Opening Day 2015, I decided Johnny was ready to focus on the game and join his grandfather for this annual rite of spring. After all, he was now five! What could possibly go wrong?

We found our way to our seats above the right-field wall. I hoisted Johnny onto my shoulders for what turned out to be a lengthy pregame ceremony. On top of the customary player introductions, outfield-sized American flag, national anthem, and military flyover, we also had presentations of 2014 honors: National League Manager of the Year to Matt Williams and Silver Slugger Awards to shortstop Ian Desmond and third baseman Anthony Rendon, plus the historic announcement that Major League Baseball's All-Star Game would be played at Nationals Park in 2018, Washington's first since 1969. I hung on every word from special Opening Day pregame announcer James Brown of CBS Sports, a Washington native and an investor in the franchise.

Johnny was bored out of his mind.

He politely tolerated my childlike enthusiasm. Besides, I was his supplier of pizza, french fries, soda, and ice cream. The junk food kept him happy for nearly an hour until Bryce Harper led off the fourth inning with a home run that landed a couple of sections away. Johnny wondered aloud if the game was over since the players no longer had a ball to play with.

Maybe because the Nationals were winning, or because his grandfather was so happy, or because the baseball had left the yard, Johnny asked, "Can we go now, Grandaddy?"

I tried to explain that the Nationals's new pitcher Max Scherzer had not yet given up a hit, and that if we left, it would bring him bad luck. The explanation bought some time from this generous little soul, but not much. Fifteen minutes later we were heading for the exits. As we passed through the right-field gate with two outs in the top of the sixth inning, we could practically feel Scherzer's bubble burst. A walk, an error by Desmond, and the Mets's first hit of the game and poof! Just like that, the no-hitter was gone, and so was Washington's lead. New York went on to win 3–1.

And it was all my fault.

When things are going well, silly tradition holds that baseball fans are supposed to stay in the same seats. Because I left my seat, Scherzer walked a guy, Desmond interfered with teammate Dan Uggla's catch of a simple popup, and the distracted Max then gave up a two-run single.

You would think I would have learned by now!

Less than three years earlier, the heavily favored Nationals trailed the St. Louis Cardinals two games to one in the best-of-five 2012 National League Division Series. Jayson Werth's walk-off home run in the bottom of the ninth inning of Game Four pulled the Series even. I returned the next night for the decisive fifth game in, of course, the same seats. The Nats picked right up where they left off the night before and led 6–0 after three innings. The Cardinals chipped away, but Washington scored an insurance run in the bottom of the eighth, making it 7–5. I then had a brilliant idea driven more by sentimentality than common baseball sense. If Washington was about to lock up the city's first postseason series win since the 1924 World Series, wouldn't it be special to celebrate in real time with my brother-in-law Ed, seated up a level with his son Bob?

Between innings my friend Steve and I left Section 127, sprinted upstairs, positioned ourselves right behind Section 225 and made eye contact with Ed and Bob! Seven Cardinal batters later, the score was St. Louis 9, Washington 7. Steve and I just slipped away. If only we had stayed in our same seats!

It took seven years and three more postseason disappointments to shake, but at some point in October 2019 during the Nationals's magical run to the World Series championship (perhaps after sweeping these same Cardinals in the NLCS?), all was forgiven. It's not clear if actual forgiveness was required or if it was simply time to retire the lighthearted story line. Good times have a way of extinguishing bad memories.

There are as many baseball superstitions as there are baseball people. The game day rituals of players are quirky, yet sacred. Many players deliberately step over the foul lines fearing that disrupting that chalk brings bad luck. If a no-hitter is in progress, no one dares speak of it to the pitcher. In fact, most won't talk to him at all.

Some of these superstitions have spilled over to the fans, encouraged by players-turned-broadcasters. The taboo on "no-hitter" talk includes phrases like "something special is going on here tonight" or "we may have history in the making" but never that two-word combination. Other fan favorites are just silly fun, like turning your hat inside out in order to exhort the baseball gods to bring about a desperately needed run late in a close game—the "rally cap"—or the ritual that nothing changes when things are going well.

Especially your seat.

For box scores, play-by-play and more, visit www.OpeningDay5050.com
or use this QR code

2016

No Ticket? No Problem.

The Game

Who:	Miami Marlins 6, Washington Nationals 4
Where:	Nationals Park, Washington, DC
Attendance:	41,650
When:	Thursday, April 7, 2016
Weather:	Started out beautifully (60s, sunny) but went downhill from there

Hall of Famers: None (as of March 2022)

Future HoFers?: Marlins OF Ichiro Suzuki (eligible 2025) and Giancarlo Stanton, Nationals OF Bryce Harper and P Max Scherzer (all three eligible five years after retirement)

Game Highlights: Washington's new manager Dusty Baker got lost trying to find his way to Nationals Park for the first time. His hitters got lost trying to find an RBI after a 90-minute rain delay in the middle of the second inning. After Daniel Murphy's three-run double in the first, the Nationals went 0-for-11 with runners in scoring position. Baker let his starter Tanner Roark resume his outing after the weather break, but he never found a rhythm. The Marlins pounded out 13 hits off five Washington pitchers, 10 of them singles. Bryce Harper hit a solo home run in the seventh to make it closer. Before the game Harper collected his 2015 MVP Award. The 22-year-old outfielder was the youngest unanimous selection for MVP in baseball history.

The Story

Over the course of my Opening Day streak, the approach to securing tickets ran the gamut. While I have no idea how my dad got tickets in 1970 at a sold-out RFK, I know hundreds of fans camped out overnight at the stadium box office for the chance to buy a pair of printed tickets. Lower box seats sold for $4.50 each. By 2017 an all-digital experience for those same seats could be purchased instantly online from the team or an authorized reseller for $100 each or more (sometimes much more!).

On Opening Day 2017, with my usual companions either unavailable or already paired up with family, I tested a ticket approach I had been refining the past few years outside Citizens Bank Park in Philadelphia: show up with no ticket and limited cash. The guiding principle I adopted was: You don't need a good seat, just get into the ballpark and upgrade from there.

During the Phillies's post-dynasty lean years, weeknight tickets were easy to come by. If I was in town overnight on business, I'd hop the Broad Street Line to Pattison Avenue, arriving just after game time. No sooner would I extend my index finger skyward than a swarm of aggressive ticket brokers (formerly known as "scalpers") would approach, all touting the high quality of the tickets they had to sell. I would then reach into my pocket and extract the only cash I had: a $5 bill. A few would walk away on principle.

Hoping I had a $10 or $20 bill in my pocket, one hungry entrepreneur would bark something like, "Lower box . . . face is 75 bucks . . . look . . ."

He would point to the price on the printout. "I'll give it to you for $25." Indeed, there might have been a higher retail price on that piece of paper, but tonight, to me, any one of the tickets in his wad was worth exactly $5. And with the game inside heading toward the second inning, the worth of that piece of paper to him was nearing $0. When the gentleman realized that $5 was all the cash I had, and that $5 was better than $0, he shuffled his ticket printouts, found an upper deck single, and we had a deal.

Once inside I would head straight to the concession stand to load up, not just to satisfy my hunger and thirst, but to ensure both hands were occupied when attempting to enter a section of lower box seats. I learned a carefully balanced beverage box with a hot dog, fries, and two beers virtually guaranteed the usher would not ask to see your ticket. Works every time!

Attempting this approach on Opening Day was riskier. A weeknight crowd in Philly was typically less than 20,000. Opening Day in Washington was

40,000-plus. Prices would be higher, I assumed, and few brokers would have singles. I arrived very early and took my chances at the top of the Metro escalator on Half Street, just a long block from the ballpark. Instead of holding up a finger, I held up a $20 bill.

Brokers were nowhere in sight.

But within five minutes, three fans emerged from the subway. One spotted my cash. Without a moment of hesitation, the man approached, said something about their fourth who couldn't make it, handed me a ticket, and gladly accepted the $20 to pay for his first two beers of the day.

[Author's note: The only other time I did this on Opening Day was 2017. Same result. This system really works!]

In and around Nationals Park, the festive atmosphere that defines Opening Day was in full swing on this sunny afternoon. Once inside, navigating past an usher wasn't on my mind. Instead, I wandered around, visited friends, and enjoyed some of the standing room locations specifically designed for socializing. My brother-in-law and his wife came out from their club level accommodations for a pregame visit. I connected with another college friend who was huddled with colleagues at a bar in the right-center-field concourse. As game time approached, the staff, coaches, and players were introduced, the customary field-sized American flag covered the outfield during the anthem, and the jets flew overhead. Must be Opening Day!

The Marlins and Nationals scored a combined six runs during a marathon first inning before storm clouds rolled in. During an hour and a half rain delay, I found dry refuge in the concourse with another old friend and his daughter. What a wonderful visit! By the time I actually made it to the seat I had paid for, it was the third inning and pushing 7:00 p.m. Few fans remained. With Miami leading 5–3 in the fifth, the trio from whom I had purchased the ticket headed out. I am reasonably sure they consumed more than the two beers I had paid for four hours earlier. Many more.

Seat upgrades were plentiful. But with the temperature falling almost as steadily as the rain and drizzle, staying warm and dry became the preferred option.

I had gotten my money's worth!

For box scores, play-by-play and more, visit www.OpeningDay5050.com or use this QR code

2017

Mr. Opening Day, Bryce Harper

The Game

Who:	Washington Nationals 4, Miami Marlins 2
Where:	Nationals Park, Washington, DC
Attendance:	42,744
When:	Monday, April 3, 2017
Weather:	Sunny and 60s

Hall of Famers: None (as of March 2022)
Future HoFers?: Marlins OF Ichiro Suzuki (eligible 2025) and Giancarlo Stanton, Nationals OF Bryce Harper and P Max Scherzer (all three eligible five years after retirement)

Game Highlights: A masterful performance by Nationals starter Stephen Strasburg was almost not enough to earn him the win. After seven innings of work and only 85 pitches, manager Dusty Baker sent newcomer Adam Lind to the plate to pinch hit for Strasburg with Miami leading 2–1. Lind delivered a two-run homer, putting Washington ahead and Strasburg in position to get the "Curly W." He allowed only six hits, struck out three, and walked none.

During pregame ceremonies, there were plenty of trophies handed out to Nationals players for 2016 achievements: the National League Silver Slugger Award for a second baseman to Daniel Murphy; NL Comeback Player of the Year to third baseman Anthony Rendon; and Max Scherzer's first NL Cy Young Award. He won it in the American League while with the Detroit Tigers in 2013 and would win it again in Washington for 2017. He is one of only six pitchers to earn the honor in both leagues. Four of the other five are in the Hall of Fame (Gaylord Perry won it while with Cleveland and San Diego, Randy Johnson with Seattle and Arizona (four times), Pedro Martinez with Montreal and Boston (twice), and Roy Halladay with Toronto and Philadelphia). The other, Roger Clemens, won it a record seven times (three times in Boston, twice in Toronto, and once each with the New York Yankees and Astros (in 2004 when Houston was still in the NL), but was shunned by Hall voters for steroid allegations.

The Story

If Ryan Zimmerman was Mr. Walk-Off (See Chapter 2008), then Bryce Harper was the team's Mr. Opening Day.

As Harper walked up to the plate in the bottom of the sixth inning with Washington not yet on the scoreboard, it was clear something was missing from the Nationals's 2017 home opener. We had seen player intros, the huge flag, a spectacular anthem, military flyover, and pregame awards, but not the other Opening Day ritual we'd seen four times in four years: a Bryce Harper solo home run.

Minutes later the day was complete. Harper parked a 2-2 pitch in the right-field seats, making him the first player in major-league history to hit five Opening Day home runs before age 25.

Throughout his seven seasons in Washington, Harper was perhaps baseball's brightest young star. After being selected by Washington with the No. 1 overall pick in the June 2010 amateur draft, Harper made his major-league debut early in the 2012 season, earned Rookie of the Year honors, and helped propel the Nationals to their first of four NL East Division titles in a six-year span.

His first Opening Day in Washington was in 2013. He provided all of the Nationals's offense that day with two solo home runs in the 2–0 win over Miami. After his second bomb of the afternoon, the delirious crowd insisted on a curtain call from their 20-year-old superstar.

After only managing a single in Washington's home opener against Atlanta in 2014, Harper again provided the team's only offense on Opening Day 2015, a solo homer against the Mets.

His Opening Day exploits were not confined to Nationals Park. In 2016 the team opened in Atlanta where Harper kicked off Turner Field's final season with a solo homer in Washington's 4–3 win. Three days later he did it again in the Nats's home opener, a 6–4 loss to the Marlins.

During his time with the Nationals, one topic of conversation was constant: where would Harper sign once he became an unrestricted free agent after the 2018 season? The New York Yankees were the most common answer with their seemingly unlimited payroll. Perhaps the LA Dodgers (closer to his Las Vegas roots)? Meanwhile, the Lerner family insisted the Nationals would make a serious effort to keep the six-time All-Star in Washington. It all led to an awkward offseason as Harper tested the open market.

The Nationals reportedly made a 10-year, $300 million offer late in the

2018 regular season with much of the money deferred. According to multiple published reports, Harper was hoping for a record deal, well north of the 13-year, $325 million contract Giancarlo Stanton had signed four years earlier. Arguably, the $30 million-per-year offer from Washington exceeded the $25 million per year Stanton was getting. No matter. When the process came to a close early in spring training, Harper said he got what he wanted: 13 years and $330 million. For a few days (until Mike Trout re-signed with the Los Angeles Angels for $426 million), Harper's was the richest contract in baseball history.

Seven seasons of adulation in the nation's capital evaporated with a single swipe of his pen. Harper had signed with the arch-rival Phillies.

Three years earlier on Opening Day 2016, following Harper's MVP season, DC Mayor Muriel Bowser presented Bryce with a key to the city. By Opening Day 2019, the city had changed the lock.

When the Phillies came to Washington for the second series of 2019, more than 35,000 fans braved a cold, miserable night to express their disdain. The visible venom for Harper was more than some expected. Hundreds wore their aggressively defaced No. 34 Nationals jerseys. When the team attempted to honor their former star with a tribute video on the center-field scoreboard, "BOOOOOOs" cascaded from every section of the ballpark.

In the top of the first, the crowd rose to its feet and resumed the thunderous chorus as Harper came to bat. When Max Scherzer struck out his former teammate on a 2-2 change up, the ballpark erupted.

"Well, the Nats have never won a world championship," Phillies broadcaster Tom McCarthy told fans watching on NBC Sports Philadelphia, perhaps gloating about his team's 1980 and 2008 World Series titles. "but they're celebrating as if they've won something."

Scherzer fooled Harper again in the third. Another eruption. The celebration continued.

With Washington trailing 2–0, Scherzer was lifted for a pinch hitter after five innings. The Phillies feasted on the Nationals's bullpen for four more runs in the sixth. The combination of the weather and the score soon had many heading for the exits.

They had gotten what they came for.

By the top of the eighth, the overwhelming majority of spectators remaining were Phillies fans, many clustered above the right-field wall where they could see their new hero up close when Harper was in the field. They'd come by train, bus, and automobile to taunt, "We've got Harper!" When he blasted an eighth-inning two-run homer over their heads into the upper deck, it was their turn to erupt.

They, too, had gotten what they came for.

After the game an understated Ryan Zimmerman shared a diplomatic perspective on the return of his teammate of seven seasons. "That was unique," he told Tom Boswell of *The Washington Post*. "A fun atmosphere. I would have cheered Bryce. He did a lot here. But I understand that he's a polarizing figure. I don't mean that in a bad way. That's the way it's been since he was 12. It's been like that his whole life."

One thing wasn't unique. It might not have been Opening Day, but for the sixth time, Harper homered during his first game of the season at Nationals Park.

For box scores, play-by-play and more, visit www.OpeningDay5050.com or use this QR code

2018

#ALLCAPS

The Game

Who:	New York Mets 8, Washington Nationals 2
Where:	Nationals Park, Washington, DC
Attendance:	42,477
When:	Thursday, April 5, 2018
Weather:	Cold! 40s, partly sunny and breezy

Hall of Famers: None (as of March 2022)

Future HoFers?: Mets P Jacob deGrom, Nationals OF Bryce Harper, and P Max Scherzer (all eligible five years after retirement)

Game Highlights: The Nationals's bats were as cold as the April air and starter Stephen Strasburg was not as sharp as he had been in the season opener a week earlier at Cincinnati. The Mets tagged Straz for four runs in six innings including a solo homer by Yoenis Céspedes and a two-run shot by Michael Conforto. Jay Bruce blew the game open with a grand slam off reliever Brandon Kintzler. For the seventh time in the last 13 Opening Days, the Nationals had a new leader. Unlike Dusty Baker two years earlier, rookie manager Dave Martinez had no trouble finding Nationals Park on Opening Day. He had been in the visitors' clubhouse quite often over the past few seasons as a coach for the Chicago Cubs, the team that eliminated the Nationals from the 2017 postseason just six months earlier.

The Story

Steve Ebner and I had experienced Opening Day together before, and we both were well prepared on this chilly afternoon, wearing multiple layers under our Nationals jerseys. Normally we might have headed home early, once the Mets went up 8–2 in the seventh inning, but we had serious postgame plans: a DC sports doubleheader. After Wilmer Difo grounded out to end the game, we put that loss behind us and turned our focus to the next game. We had three hours to kill before puck drop at the Capital One Arena, just four Metro stops away, where our Washington Capitals would play their second-to-last game of the National Hockey League's regular season.

As the players left the field, we reached under our seats and pulled from our backpacks the uniforms for our next game. I shed the Ryan Zimmerman No. 11 jersey and transitioned to the "Great 8," Alex Ovechkin. Steve replaced No. 7 Trea Turner with No. 19 Nicklas Bäckström, Ovi's teammate of 11 seasons.

As it turned out, our little jersey swap was but a footnote in the dramatic nine-week (some would say 19-month) story line that firmly cemented the "*team*-mance" (group equivalent of a "*bro*-mance") between these two teams and forever changed the attitudes of DC sports fans. It would culminate with a first-ever Stanley Cup championship for the Capitals exactly nine weeks later (and a first-ever World Series championship for the Nationals in October 2019).

The Capitals lost that night to Nashville. No matter. They had already clinched the Metropolitan Division title and were heading to the playoffs for the 28th time in the last 36 seasons. Capitals fans, much like Nationals fans more recently, had come to expect great regular seasons followed by bitter endings come playoff time. The Caps had been doing it longer than the Nationals, but the cruel and unusual punishment was the same: 44 seasons and no championships.

The feeling did not skip generations. My son Patrick had learned to expect it, too. After the 2016 Chicago Cubs won their first World Series since 1908, my hockey- and baseball-loving son tagged me in a social media post that included a piece about a North Carolina man who traveled more than 600 miles to an Indiana cemetery so he could listen to the final game with his dad, something he'd promised more than 50 years earlier. "I'll do this for you," my son wrote sarcastically, "when the Caps finally win a Stanley Cup Finals in 2062!"

The Nationals had won four National League East titles since 2012, each followed by an early playoff exit, an NL Division Series loss to a lower-seeded foe. The Capitals had helped prepare Nationals fans for this ritual disappointment. Over the previous 10 years, the Caps made the playoffs nine times, including seven division titles. Almost every year, they then lost to a lower-seeded team. The abuse included *five* heart-crushing Game Seven losses *at home*! We were well schooled when the Nats did the same thing year after year, losing the decisive, final game at home against the Cardinals (2012), Dodgers (2016), and Cubs (2017). Heck, in 2014 against the Giants, after failing in two one-run games at home (one in 18 innings, the longest postseason game in baseball history), then losing Game Four of the best-of-five series on the road, the team never came back to Nationals Park. They broke our hearts in San Francisco!

Our depression each time lasted only a few days, not weeks. We'd had multiple doses of the postseason vaccine administered by the Washington Capitals.

After the Caps lost this night to Nashville, Steve and I pondered postseason ticket plans and came to the same conclusion: the price of tickets for up to 16 games was too high and our immune systems were too fragile. For the first couple of rounds, we planned to practice social distancing, watch on TV, hold our breath, and cover our eyes when necessary.

Call us in a month.

In the first round the Columbus Blue Jackets, a wild-card team, won the first two games of the Series in overtime *in Washington*. It felt a lot like that Nationals-Giants series in 2014. But unlike the Nats four years earlier, the Capitals rallied to win the next four games to advance.

Might this year be different?

Next up: The rival, two-time defending Stanley Cup champion Pittsburgh Penguins, a playoff matchup that had meant bad things for more than 25 years. These two teams had met in the postseason 10 times between 1991 and 2017. Pittsburgh had won nine.

DC's almost unshakable postseason pessimism extended beyond hockey and baseball. Over the previous 19 years—71 NHL, NBA, MLB, and NFL seasons—the city's teams had made the playoffs 29 times, and *not one* advanced to their sport's equivalent of the final four. A win over the Penguins would get that 800-pound gorilla off the back of every sports fan in town.

The Capitals played well in the first five games and took a 3–2 series lead to Pittsburgh. In Game Six, the teams skated to a 1–1 tie through three periods, forcing the eighth sudden death overtime playoff game in the past 25 between these bitter rivals.

Less than six minutes into overtime, Capitals center Evgeny Kuznetsov scored the biggest goal in franchise history. I sprang from my seat in stunned disbelief, arms overhead, screaming! As the celebration unfolded on Pittsburgh's home ice, the voice in my head was that of Al Michaels as the US Olympic hockey team did the impossible, defeating the Soviet Union at the 1980 Winter Games.

"Do you believe in miracles? YES!!!"

DC sports had entered a new phase. The playoff cloud which had hung over the city for a generation disappeared in an instant. Suddenly, everyone, it seemed, was pulling for the Caps. Sports fans suddenly had permission to think differently.

#ItsOKToBelieve

In the next round the Capitals rallied from a 3–2 deficit to win the Series, 4–3, shutting down favored Tampa Bay in the final two games by a combined score of 7–0 to advance to the Stanley Cup Finals.

I was ready to take out a second mortgage, if necessary, to attend the games in Washington. The tickets I wound up with on the 200 level for Games 3 and 4 against visiting Vegas were just 25 feet from where Hall of Famer and three-time Super Bowl champion head coach Joe Gibbs whipped the Capital One Arena into a frenzy before Game 3. Two nights later, the Nationals Ryan Zimmerman and Max Scherzer had the same assignment.

Same spot. Same seats.

Ryan and Max were serious fans, completely into the electricity and delirium of the night. They wore Caps jerseys and traded in their batting helmets for hockey helmets and baseball bats for hockey sticks! "LET'S GO CAPS!" they screamed over and over. The packed house rocked with them. It rocked all night. The Caps won Game 4 and two nights later, Washington held on to finish off the Golden Knights in Las Vegas.

Capital's radio voice John Walton was delirious. "The words that DC fans have been waiting to hear since 1974!" he screamed, as only John could. "The Washington Capitals are the 2018 Stanley Cup champions! It's not a dream! It's not a desert mirage. It's Lord Stanley, and he is coming to Washington!"

Lord Stanley's Cup, accompanied by some very happy, hungover hockey players, arrived in Washington the next afternoon. With the most iconic, one-of-its-kind trophies in all of sports in tow, the players then embarked on a four-day, nonstop party with the fans, stopping first at Nationals Park and culminating along the National Mall with the city's most raucous victory parade ever. It was the first such rally of any kind in more than a quarter century since coach Gibbs last hoisted the Vince Lombardi Trophy in January 1992.

The Capitals arrived at the ballpark around noon on Saturday, less than 36 hours into their reign as champions. They went straight to the Nationals locker room for a "*TEAM*-mantic" rendezvous, complete with high fives, hugs, and selfies. Few pro sports teams in the same city were as close from top to bottom as these Capitals and Nationals. The owners got along. The players did, too. They genuinely liked each other. Throughout the two-month playoff run, Nationals players routinely wore Capitals t-shirts on game days under their jerseys and ALLCAPS hats during pregame warm-ups.

Nationals manager Dave Martinez seized the moment. He wanted his players to savor this experience as much as their hockey-playing pals. The combined group photo made it hard to tell which ones were which, happy athletes all wearing white and red.

Minutes later Caps owner Ted Leonsis and Ovechkin led their team out of the dugout and onto the field. Ovi clutched that three-foot-high, 35-pound trophy with both hands. He hadn't parted with it for more than a minute since taking possession Thursday night. He placed the Stanley Cup on the back of the pitcher's mound for a team photo. His teammates were wearing Stanley Cup champion hats and Nationals shirts.

Superfan Scherzer had to fight off teammates for the honor of catching Ovechkin's ceremonial first pitch. Ovechkin's initial toss sailed well over Scherzer's head, but the Russian did not miss his second shot.

Just nine days earlier during his start at Baltimore, Max was sneaking away from the dugout while his teammates were at bat so he could watch the Caps in Game 2 at Vegas. Max tweeted that night, "Best part of having a DH tonight is that I can stay in the clubhouse and watch the Caps game while we hit!" Max pitched eight efficient innings that night in a 2–0 Washington win, wrapping things up early so he could watch the third period of the Capitals win in peace.

The Capitals were expected to leave Nationals Park after the pregame festivities. Instead, they held the party bus and delayed their fan-filled pub crawl through Georgetown by three hours, camping out in a suite at the ballpark all afternoon. Players posed for pictures and did entertaining interviews. They lifted the Stanley Cup to the delight of the 37,000-plus fans in the ballpark. More often though, they lifted bright blue cans of Bud Light.

Nationals fans could not keep their eyes off that shiny trophy. Each had the same thought.

"I want one, too!"

For box scores, play-by-play and more, visit www.OpeningDay5050.com or use this QR code

2019

Made It! 50-for-50

The Game

Who:	New York Mets 2, Washington Nationals 0
Where:	Nationals Park, Washington, DC
Attendance:	42,263
When:	Thursday, March 28, 2019
Weather:	Fantastic! Sunny and upper 50s

Hall of Famers: None (as of March 2022)

Future HoFers?: Mets P Jacob deGrom and Nationals P Max Scherzer (both eligible five years after retirement)

Game Highlights: As Opening Day pitching matchups go, they don't get any better than this: the National League's reigning Cy Young Award winner Jacob deGrom of the Mets against the guy who finished second to deGrom in 2018 and had won the award himself in 2016 and 2017, Washington's Max Scherzer. The duo did not disappoint. DeGrom struck out 10 in six scoreless innings while Scherzer fanned a dozen, giving up two runs before leaving with two outs in the eighth without any run support. "Life after Bryce" in Washington was off to a dubious start. The Nationals could have used one or more of Harper's customary Opening Day home runs. They managed only five hits off deGrom and three relievers. During the offseason, New York acquired two superstars in a trade with the Seattle Mariners: second baseman Robinson Canó (who had served an 80-game suspension the previous summer after testing positive for a banned substance) and closer Edwin Díaz. Both made their marks on Opening Day. Canó accounted for all of the Mets offense with a first-inning homer and an eighth-inning RBI single. Díaz retired the side in the ninth to earn the save. Fielders had a tough time staying alert this afternoon. Nearly half the outs—26 of 54—came by way of the strikeout, 22 from the two starters!

The Story

I told Steve I planned to spare no expense. This was Opening Day number 50 in a row. I wanted really good seats, down where we could see the face of the franchise, Ryan Zimmerman. After all, I'd spent Opening Day with Frank Howard, Cal Ripken Jr., or Zim 36 of the past 50 years. I wanted to be up close for my 14th straight home opener with the Z-Man. Steve and I spent $200 per ticket on StubHub to sit six rows from the field near first base.

For a milestone like this, a pregame meal at an actual restaurant was in order, not a food cart or concession stand. After lunch at Gordon Biersch, we enjoyed a celebratory cigar and beverage at what was left of The Half Street Fairgrounds and Bullpen. A construction boom had cut the once massive "tailgate party without the cars" into a shadow of its former self. We entered the ballpark early, made the rounds, and visited other Opening Day regulars: TJ, Ed, Garland, and others.

Not long after the obligatory Opening Day selfies, we had our first sighting of a DC notable. Kellyanne Conway, Senior Counselor to President Donald Trump, settled into her seat two rows in front of us and proceeded to carry on a conversation with a gentleman in the row *behind* her. Tap tap. Photo taken. Social media post: "Watch the game, Kellyanne!"

Wish we'd had that in 1981 when Craig and I sat behind David Israel!

Admittedly, this was a milestone that meant nothing to anyone but me: 50 straight. It was a conversation piece that usually generated a respectful smile from slightly impressed strangers. It also afforded an opportunity to ponder all that had changed since Opening Day 1970.

President Nixon, who had thrown out the ceremonial first pitch on Opening Day 1969, showed up late in 1970, leaving first pitch duties to his son-in-law David Eisenhower. Like each of his 10 predecessors and the next seven who followed him to the Oval Office, Nixon respected the game with this time-honored tradition. Kellyanne's boss did what baseball's 33 years in exile from DC could not. President Trump became the first US President to *not* throw out a first pitch at a Major League Baseball game during his presidency since Teddy Roosevelt.

Most Nationals fans were okay with that.

The Opening Day starting pitchers in 1970, Dick Bosman of the Washington Senators and Mickey Lolich of the Detroit Tigers, two of the best in the game at the time, earned less than $100,000 that season . . .

. . . *combined!*

For the 2019 season, today's starters, Max Scherzer and Jacob deGrom, together would earn $54 *million.*

Bosman, Lolich, and their teammates were the property of their team owners in 1970 with no freedom to ever play where they wanted or to offer their services to the highest bidder. That would change dramatically in the decades that followed. By Opening Day 2019, both deGrom and Scherzer had been through the full free agency cycle and earned their mega contracts. It was a road paved for them by the selfless decisions made by players in the early 1970s like Curt Flood and Dave McNally. When major-league players last went out on strike in 1994–95 to protect the free agency system, Scherzer was 10 and deGrom was 6.

Lolich pitched all nine innings that day in 1970, the 63rd complete game of the 29-year-old's career. Both Scherzer and deGrom had stellar outings this day, each leaving the game at around 100 pitches. The "pitch count" wasn't a "thing" in 1970 and wouldn't become an official statistic until 18 years later. Bosman and Lolich would finish their careers with a combined 224 complete games. Scherzer and deGrom will finish about 200 shy of that number.

MLB had grown from 24 teams in 1970 to 30 in 2019. Only five were still playing in ballparks built before 1970: the Red Sox, Cubs, Dodgers, Angels, and Athletics.

On Opening Day 1970 utility infielder Ken Szotkiewicz braved the elements at RFK on the Tigers's bench. His warm-up jacket covered his jersey No. 42. The same number was more visible on the back of Senators first-base coach Nellie Fox. They were two of several big-league players and coaches wearing the number that day, just 14 years since Jackie Robinson retired. By Opening Day 2019, no one wore it. The number had been retired throughout all of baseball in perpetuity.

Outside RFK in the days leading up to Opening Day 1970, thousands of fans waited in line in miserable conditions to pay about $4 each for a paper ticket for the biggest game of the year. Fifty years later virtually all of us bought them electronically and many didn't think twice about spending hundreds. And if you didn't buy a ticket, you just watched the game on satellite or cable TV like every other game. In 1970 we were lucky to have a handful of regular-season road games to watch at home on a TV with rabbit ears. Maybe it was a color TV.

Still, so many things remained the same. It was the first game of the season. We all had high hopes this might be the year our team would win it all. Someone sang the national anthem. An umpire yelled, "Play ball!" There were nine players in the field and one in the batter's box. Nine innings later there was usually a winner and a loser and 161 games left to play.

Because it was Opening Day.
And I was there.

For box scores, play-by-play and more, visit www.OpeningDay5050.com
or use this QR code

EPILOGUE

Three Life Lessons from Davey

After watching the Nationals lose on Opening Day for the fifth time in six years, I returned for game two of the 2019 season with my son Patrick and his son Johnny who was celebrating his ninth birthday with his friends. I couldn't help but recollect my ninth birthday with the Washington Senators, watching Frank Howard hit a gigantic home run. It was probably the day I fell in love with baseball. Meanwhile, Johnny was still processing the departure of his favorite player, Bryce Harper, now in Philadelphia.

Unlike that Saturday afternoon in 1969, my assignment this afternoon was to shuttle back and forth from the crowded concession stand, keeping these boys well stocked with hot dogs, french fries, and ice cream.

Much to Johnny's disappointment, the Nationals's bullpen imploded in the final two innings, and the Mets won, 11–8. The hit parade of battered relief pitchers included newcomers Tony Sipp, Trevor Rosenthal, and Kyle Barraclough, none of whom would be with the team by season's end. A lot changed between Opening Day and October, as the Nationals would go on to become one of the more improbable champions in sports history. Overcoming an abysmal 19–31 start, the team fought its way back to earn a wild-card playoff spot. A string of historic late-game, postseason comebacks brought Washington, DC, its first World Series championship in 95 years.

Over the course of an incredibly rocky season during which countless fans and supposed experts called for his ouster, second-year manager Davey Martinez remained calm and consistent, supporting his underperforming players without hesitation. Although he was disrespected in the NL Manager of the Year voting, in the playoffs he toppled three of the four managers who finished ahead of him, becoming a World Series champion and oft-cited philosopher.

His three mantras that would become the battle cries and signature of a most memorable season are concise lessons for baseball and life, as they certainly were for me.

"Go 1–0."

It should be the official tag line of Opening Day: Go 1–0! If your team wins on Opening Day, you want to start printing World Series tickets. Lose, and local talk radio is overwhelmed with negativity.

About a third of the way through the 2019 season, after losing four straight games in New York to these same Mets (three blown by the aforementioned bullpen), the fourth-place Nationals fell 12 games below .500 and 10 games behind the division-leading Phillies. No team in any major professional sport had ever overcome such a deficit to win a championship. Only a handful of Major League Baseball teams had ever overcome such a bad 50-game start and even made the playoffs. The oddsmakers gave these Nationals a 0.1% chance of winning the World Series.

Davey asked his players to try to do only one thing: go 1–0. Don't worry about trying to win 12 straight to get back to even. Don't worry about the other teams in the division. Just worry about what each individual, and we as a team, can do today.

Martinez certainly wasn't the first to embrace such a focused approach, but his corny philosophy became contagious. It applied to players recovering from an injury. It applied to specific at bats when his team was trailing. It applied to situations beyond his team and into everyday life challenges. It applied to kids struggling in school, families struggling with life during the pandemic, and cancer patients enduring treatment.

I was volunteering one Saturday morning at Baltimore's Bus Stop Breakfast, a service for recovering addicts dedicated, in part, to our daughter Theresa who we lost to an overdose in 2018 at the age of 23. I met a man named Greg, a recovering addict who'd just done his weekly methadone check-in at the clinic across the street. He was grateful for the breakfast sandwich, hot coffee, and conversation and provided a powerful insight on what it means to go 1–0.

"I bet you take things one day at a time," I offered.

"Nope," he responded. "A lot can happen in a day. I take things one *step* at a time."

Greg had been going 1–0 for 12 years.

In May 2020, just a few weeks into the COVID-19 lockdown and only seven months after that World Series championship, Steve, my lifelong friend and Opening Day companion in recent years, began his second fight with cancer. In a pep talk through the online celebrity service Cameo, a Nationals broadcaster told him, "I know you're 19–31, so to speak, but you can turn this around. I want you to go 1–0 every day. Don't look at the big picture. Just win the day. That's all you can do right now. That's all any of us can do right now."

"Stay in the Fight."

Baseball is one of the few sports that operates without a clock. As a result, as the great baseball philosopher Yogi Berra would say, "It ain't over 'til it's over." No matter the score, a baseball game is not over until the final out is secured or the final run scored. No matter how lopsided the score or insurmountable the odds, there's always a chance, however slim, for a team to come back.

The 2019 Nationals proved this again and again in September and October. It seemed to be in response to Davey's other directive: "Stay in the Fight." It was as simple as his first. Keep trying. Every at bat. Every pitch. Every game. Every series.

As the Nationals won two-thirds of their games from June through August, fans celebrated the likely return to the postseason for the fifth time in eight years. But perhaps they realized something magical was happening one Tuesday night in early September. The players showed their fans, and themselves, what it meant to "Stay in the Fight."

Ironically, the opponent was the New York Mets once again, the same team we'd seen to open the season, and the same team that drove four straight nails into the Nationals's ill-fitted coffin back in May. The pitching matchup was a re-peat of Opening Day, Max Scherzer and Jacob deGrom, although both were long gone when things got interesting. The Nationals's sloppy late-game defense and unreliable relief pitching combined to give the Mets a seemingly insurmountable 10–4 lead. When up by six runs or more in the ninth inning, major-league teams in 2019 were a perfect 274–0.

But this is baseball. "It ain't over 'til it's over."

The Nationals stayed in the fight. Washington's first six batters delivered five base hits and two runs. Ryan Zimmerman doubled home two more and cut the Mets's lead to 10–8. With two men on, catcher Kurt Suzuki stepped to the plate with a chance to win the game against Mets closer Edwin Díaz. Díaz, who had earned the save for deGrom on Opening Day, was hoping for one more.

Suzuki stayed in the fight. With the count full, he deflected the next two bullets, then parked a third straight 100 mph fastball in the left-field seats.

Make that 274–1.

"Stay in the Fight" t-shirts were everywhere.

In the postseason, the Nationals faced elimination five times: once in the wild-card game against the visiting Milwaukee Brewers, twice in the National League Division Series against the 106-win LA Dodgers, and twice more in the World Series against the 107-win Houston Astros. In each elimination game the

Nationals trailed. Each time they came back to win.

Unprecedented.

Just as with his "Go 1–0" edict, Davey's directive to "Stay in the Fight" resonated beyond baseball.

On the final day of the 2019 regular season, Nationals team chaplain Monsignor Stephen Rossetti celebrated Sunday Mass with the team, as he usually did. "In my homily I told them that they would never be in the playoffs if they had given up in May," he wrote for the website Aleteia.org. "They never gave up hope, even when so many others had given up on them. I told them that all of us have dark times in our lives. But we, too, need to 'Stay in the Fight,' a good motto for life. If we do, we too will be winners regardless of what may come."

"Bumpy roads can lead to beautiful places."

Like his other two catchphrases, Davey's signature proclamation on the 2019 season wasn't new. It was just perfectly timed and repeated often. After his team vanquished the St. Louis Cardinals in four games in the National League Championship Series to earn the city its first World Series appearance in 86 years, Martinez took his turn on stage at the postgame celebration in front of more than 40,000 delirious fans and a national television audience.

"I can't put this moment into words," he said as he reflected on the journey. "I can say this. Often bumpy roads lead to beautiful places, and *this* is a beautiful place."

Ten days later we were back at Nationals Park. Our World Series Game Three crew included some regulars, like my annual spring training companions Steve and Ed. We were also able to get tickets for Patrick and Johnny. One each of Roundy's children, grandchildren, and great grandchildren couldn't miss it!

I thought a lot about Roundy that night. The last time a World Series game was played in the nation's capital was 1933, the same year he graduated from our mutual alma mater, St. John's College High School. It was the middle of the Great Depression, an economic downturn that devastated the country for a decade. He lived with his parents just a few blocks from old Griffith Stadium where Games Three, Four, and Five were played. With a staggering 25 percent of Americans unemployed and his parents clinging to government jobs, it's unlikely any of the Ortmans took time off from work or school to attend or listen to any of the games. The New York Giants won that Series, 4–1.

While Davey's reference to a "bumpy road" was clearly about the ups and downs of his team's 2019 season, I reflected on the longer ride. Washington's journey back to baseball's highest peak had been a bumpy road for 86 years. For the first 77 years of that ride, the city experienced only five winning seasons, which included 33 years when Washington had no team. Baseball fans in Boston and Chicago celebrated the end of the painful title-less streaks of their Red Sox and Cubs in 2004 and 2016, respectively, but neither city watched baseball from the outside for a single season.

For all those Opening Days before baseball returned to Washington, I had to experience the greatest day of the year in another city while mine was teased by broken promises (like the San Diego Padres relocating in 1974 or the Houston Astros in 1995) or runner-up status during each of three expansions (six cities got teams while we waited).

Sometimes the bumpier the road, the more beautiful the destination. Perhaps the bumps in this road made this place even more beautiful than Davey understood. The long and winding bumpy road through all those seasons, and 50 Opening Days, made this place atop the baseball world the most beautiful of places.

###

For some special photos, visit www.OpeningDay5050.com or use this QR code

INDEX

Note: page numbers in **bold** indicate entry is subject of a chapter

C

X